W9-DII-438

Ain't Misbehavin'

Ain't Misbehavin'

The Story of Fats Waller

ED KIRKEBY

in collaboration with

DUNCAN P. SCHIEDT AND SINCLAIR TRAILL

Illustrated with photographs

DA CAPO PRESS • NEW YORK • 1975

Library of Congress Cataloging in Publication Data

Kirkeby, W T Ed.
  Ain't misbehavin'.

  Reprint of the ed. published by Dodd, Mead, New York.
  Discography: p.
  1. Waller, Fats, 1904-1943. I. Schiedt, Duncan P.,
joint author. II. Traill, Sinclair, joint author.
III. Title.
[ML417.W15K6 1975] 780'.92'4 [B]   75-14124
ISBN 0-306-70683-0

This Da Capo Press edition of *Ain't Misbehavin'* is an unabridged
republication of the first edition published in New York in
1966. It is reprinted with the permission of Dodd, Mead & Company.

Published by Da Capo Press, Inc.
A Subsidiary of Plenum Publishing Corporation
227 West 17th Street, New York, N.Y. 10011

Ain't Misbehavin'

Ain't Misbehavin'

The Story of Fats Waller

ED KIRKEBY

in collaboration with

DUNCAN P. SCHIEDT AND SINCLAIR TRAILL

Illustrated with photographs

DODD, MEAD & COMPANY
New York

Illustrations

Acknowledgments

In the preparation of this story the valuable assistance and time of the following persons is gratefully acknowledged. One of the pleasures in writing about Thomas Waller was the genuine enthusiasm and kindness of his friends and people, without whom the true story of the great pianist couldn't have been told.

Louis Armstrong, Gene Austin, Count Basie, Russell Brooks, Una Mae Carlisle, Al Casey, Eddie Condon, J. Lawrence Cook, Joe Davis, 'Doctor Rhythm', Don Donaldson, Duke Ellington, Charlie Gaines, W. C. Handy, Reuben Harris, Fletcher Henderson, Earl Hines, Connie Immerman, J. C. Johnson, James P. Johnson, Myra Johnson, 'Slick' Jones, Billy Kyle, Harry Link, Ken Macomber, Capt. George Maines, Flournoy Miller, Clarence Page, Ralph Peer, Andy Razaf, Don Redman, Edgar Sampson, Frank Schiffman, Buster Shepherd, Irving Siders, Zutty Singleton, Reuben Smith, Russell Smith, Willie 'The Lion' Smith, Beryl Steiner, Paul Stewart, Art Tatum, Jack Teagarden, Chas Turner, Cedric Wallace, Anita Waller, Edith Waller, Naomi Waller Washington, Doc Wildeson, Clarence Williams, Corky Williams, Spencer Williams, Edith Wilson, and many others.

It will be noted that Chapter 1 to 13 of this book are written in the third person, but that from then on the narrative continues as told by the author, drawing from his personal diary — an exclusive document dealing with the period when he first became Fats Waller's manager, up to the time of his death.

The nearest place is a town called Hopkinsville, the time, a year in the late Thirties. It is a steaming night, humid as only a summer night in the Mississippi River country can be.

Across a clearing in the forest is a large, dark, barn-shaped building, the only light from which shines from an open door. Half-lit figures pass now and then, some bound for the great shed, others, in pairs, coming out to rest awhile in the hot night outside that is only slightly cooler than the inferno within.

The music that could be heard in the building has stopped. 'Fifty cents to get in,' says the small dark-skinned man standing in his shirt-sleeves at the door.

It is a backwoods dance, and it looks as if every Negro within ten miles is there. The men are stripped to their shirt-sleeves or less, but the girls have on their prettiest frocks, gay and colourful against the dark hue of their skins: some of them have fixed flowers in their hair.

The humidity is overpowering, and in the hall there is no relief from the reek of perspiration and the cheap perfume of the women. The walls have no windows, and the effort of a fan to relieve the awful heat is pathetically feeble.

At the far end, a small knot of men are peeling off pastel-coloured dinner jackets, as they mount a small platform, on which is an old upright piano with a few music stands. Five pairs of hands grasp instruments slippery with sweat, while a sixth pair rests lightly on the yellow-stained keys of the piano. These are large hands, but well-formed, to match their owner. He must be nearly three hundred pounds in weight, and of considerable height. His huge face is dominated by a pair of black eyebrows that rise and fall over luminous brown eyes; his nose wrinkles as he enjoys a huge laugh with a man standing nearby. He winks slyly at a pretty girl across the room. His big head goes up, and down again as his hands begin to move across the keys. Simultaneously the rest of the band move with him, blowing and strumming their instruments as one man.

Herman Autrey, Gene Sedric, Al Casey, Cedric Wallace, Slick Jones, and the big man at the piano – this is Fats Waller and His Rhythm.

The Waller band is in the midst of one of its nerve-and-muscle-straining national tours of one-nighters. This is a lesser stop but it is a memorable one. The band arrived just before the appointed time, after a gruelling bus ride which left them tired and in low spirits. They are further depressed by the total absence of ventilation, and after the first twenty-minute set they are dripping with per-spiration. Off come their jackets and they play the next set dressed very much as are some of the dancers on the floor. The hot night bears in on them, and the sweat runs down their faces until they have to wipe their eyes to see the music before them. But the screaming, stamping din in the hall continues until, with a mighty crash on the keys, Fats gets to his feet and hollers, 'Okay boys – take 'em off!' He unbuttons his shirt, strips it off and in a few minutes one of the top little bands in the nation is playing to a packed house in their undershirts.

A large fan is hauled through the crowd, and set in position directly in front of the musicians. Trained straight at them, it dis-regards its proper function and, with scant courtesy, sweeps the music sheets from the stands, and sends them flying all over the hall in utter disorder. The band looks at Fats. He looks back at them, and then at the crowd. He raises those eyebrows.

'Well, all right then!' he booms, and hits the introduction. For the rest of the night the band improvises. But this is typical Waller – clamorous, uninhibited, inspiring. Like many things of its kind, it springs from peace and tranquillity. It is hard to believe, while listening to one of Fats' records, that this man began life as the son of a churchman, and as a youth spent countless Sundays playing a harmonium on the sidewalk for his father's services.

*   *   *

Edward Martin Waller, Fats' father, was born about 1870 in a district in Virginia known as Bermuda Hundred. A tall slender youth, he was extremely reserved, and gained much of the solemn dignity of his mature years from a slow measured speech, a left-over from a boyhood affliction. He was plagued by a severe stammer, and sometimes, caught midway through a sentence, he would stamp his foot in rage and frustration at not being able to get out the words he wanted. But gradually he cured himself, and this same self-discipline seems to have remained with him for the rest of his life.

The woman he chose for his wife was, by contrast, a large, warm-hearted girl. Adeline Lockett's vivacity matched her big body and she became the perfect partner for Edward. Becoming engaged in 1878, they talked long about marriage and their future. The plans that Edward laid before her were few, but definite. Seeing the poverty about him, he determined that no child of his would be brought up in the South, when there was the big metropolis of the North, where it was said that every child could have the same education, and, what was more, was *obliged* to attend school up to a certain age.

Edward proposed that he should go to New York first and find work. Then, having made himself secure, he would return for Adeline. He felt that his background in handling horses might prove an asset in the big city where there were in those days many horse-drawn carriages and trucks.

And so it happened: he secured work at a stable almost immediately and within a couple of short months he was able to come south to fetch Adeline. They married, and set out by train for New York. Foremost among their wedding presents was a large Bible with space inside its cover for the family history: births, marriages and deaths. This was to be their bulwark against the sins of the big city – the book on which the lives of the Wallers, big and little, forever after was to be founded.

Their first home was in Waverly Place, in Greenwich Village. Here before the turn of the century dwelt much of the city's Negro population, not very large at that time, but showing a noticeable increase as the years went by. Southern poverty had got worse since the Civil War, and Negro emigration to the large cities of the North had grown accordingly. Their Churches travelled with them, and among these was the prominent Abyssinian Baptist Church, which soon established itself in Waverly Place. Adeline, always a religious girl, found herself at 17 a stranger in the great

3

city, and, true to her teaching, quickly gravitated to the Church. Edward also joined, and together they rapidly became active in the religious and social affairs of the growing congregation.

Adeline quickly took command of the little home. With her winning personality and warm-heartedness, she soon won for herself a place in the affections of her neighbours, often looking after their sick children, and caring for those who were well, when their mothers were ill. She was a mother through and through, and yearned for the large family which she felt she was meant to have.

Edward's sober mien, coupled with his deep, well-modulated voice, was soon noticed by the Church officials, who prevailed on him to undertake some street corner sermons – a practice which he continued for many years.

The first entry in the fly-leaf of the family Bible was made on the day they married. The second reads, 'Charles A. Waller', born in September 1890. This child, their first-born, died as an infant, a loss which foreshadowed many heartbreaking years to come, when eleven more children would have their names inscribed on the page, of whom six would pass away in infancy. Of the five destined to live, two followed quickly – Edward Lawrence and William Robert, both always called by their middle, rather than their first, names. Lawrence, born in 1892, resembled his father, whereas Robert, born the following year, was of stockier build, and took after his mother. By this time the family had moved uptown to 63rd Street, where another large Negro colony had settled.

The roll-call of the children who came and passed away would have discouraged lesser people, but Adeline never lost heart or faith that hers would be a large and closely knit family. The church they frequented had also moved uptown to West 40th Street, by Eighth Avenue, and Edward, who by now had his own trucking business, was a familiar figure on the street corner, leading passers-by in hymns and exhorting them in his deep, earnest voice to accompany him into the nearby house of worship.

Harlem, at this time, was a town all on its own, not uptown as it is today, but actually a sedate white neighbourhood, with its own shopping centres and large homes. Seventh and Lenox Avenues were wide, free streets, picturesque carriage runs, for by the turn of the century the automobile had scarcely sullied the atmosphere with its fumes. In the last decade of the old century a startling change was taking place. The pleasant life of Harlem had not been overlooked by the real estate interests, and a terrific building boom had begun, filling the open spaces north and south of 125th Street with block after block of brownstone apartment and rooming houses. As like to one another as so many rows of dominoes, the new houses opened up vast new areas for suburban living to the people downtown, and did nothing to enhance the appeal of the area.

But the very remoteness of Harlem from the city proper worked against the immediate success of this development. The Eighth Avenue elevated trains provided the only means of rapid transit to the business districts, and those residing by Lenox Avenue and eastward had to rely on the slow electric trolley. Consequently the landlords found property difficult to sell and for a while things went hard for them. Philip Payton, a Negro real estate man, whose sense of timing proved him a pretty smart operator, seized the opportunity to make an offer for a few of the properties; he promised to fill the houses and keep them filled, and immediately moved in several families of Negroes from downtown. The new arrivals settled first on East 134th Street, and even though houses had to be shared, they certainly made more desirable homes than the old buildings that they had occupied downtown; all told, it was such a popular move that more and more coloured families looked to Harlem for a fresh start. Among these early settlers were the Wallers. They took lodgings in a house at 28 West 134th Street, just between Fifth and Lenox Avenues. Here in 1902 their first daughter, Ruth Adeline, was born, only to die before her third birthday. May Naomi, the next in line, survived, to become the oldest daughter of the family; she was the first to be born at the next family home on 107 West 134th Street. The two boys, Lawrence and Robert, were by this time going through the throes of learning at Public School 89, situated conveniently but perhaps oppressively, according to the point of view, next door to the house where they lived.

One morning in May 1904, a venerable man carrying a black bag was going westward across Lenox Avenue. He stepped on to the sidewalk, turned and made his way through the crowds of children who were pouring out of the school gates on the corner. Most of the little coloured kids passed him on their way eastward, going home for lunch. A little group pranced ahead of him down the pavement, and two broke off at the first house past the school yard. At the step, the younger one, about 10 years old, looked back at the man as he came closer. The black bag caught his eye.

The man turned into the house, and looking down at the boy, he asked, 'Son, aren't you one of the Waller boys?'

'Yessir, my name's Robert. You're the doctor, aren't you?'

'Yes. I'm going up to your place right now.'

The boy's eyes widened. He called to Lawrence, but his brother had already gone upstairs. Robert hesitated, and then ran inside ahead of the man, sounding the alarm as he climbed the stairs. As he reached the top, a door opened, and his father stepped out on to the landing.

'Robert! Hush your mouth, and stop racing up the stairs like a hooligan! You'll have the whole house down on us.'

Robert was packed off with Lawrence to eat lunch with a neighbour, and the doctor was warmly greeted by their father and taken into the house.

Some time later that afternoon, a new voice made its presence known. A lusty-lunged baby, to be known as Thomas Wright Waller, had arrived and it seemed sure he was going to stay awhile.

A thoughtful father gazed down on the sleeping mother and child and wondered if he and Adeline would be able to bring little Thomas through the perils of the big city, and see him on to a full and useful life. Maybe this one will go into the Church, he thought . . .

2

In 1904, counting the new baby, Thomas, there were five children in the Waller household. Adeline was happier now than ever, but her joy was to be short-lived. Alfred Winslow, the third son, died in August 1905, shortly after his tenth birthday; and then in 1906 and 1907, two more infants, Esther and Samuel, were born and died. Yet another, who was never named, died at birth. Adeline bore these heart-breaking losses without bitterness, but was weakened bodily when the final child, Edith Salome, was born on 25 July 1910. The birth confined her to bed for some time, and the infant was sent south to Virginia as soon as possible, to live with an aunt. The child, indeed, spent her early childhood there and returned to her parents only intermittently, until war broke out in Europe.

The streets of Harlem in those days swarmed with children, but Thomas and Naomi, always inseparable playmates, were not to be found among the hordes that laughed, fought and chased each other up and down in front of the Waller house. The Waller kids were kept indoors most of the time, for their mother was afraid that the other kids would have a bad influence on her carefully nurtured little brood. It was not until, in her later years, she began to fail in health, that her children were let out to play with the others. Fats' father always backed her up; what she said went. But after Edith's birth, the strain of keeping the kids indoors and having to watch them all the time, proved too much, and now and again they began to get out on the streets. Naomi was a big child for her years and could take on any boy her own age in straight combat if necessary. If ever her younger brother Tom became involved in an altercation that he couldn't handle, and the going became too rough, he would take to his heels and lead his pursuers straight into the arms of his tough young sister Naomi, who usually made short work of them. It wasn't for nothing that Naomi earned for herself in the neighbourhood the nickname 'Jack Johnson'!

Corporal punishment was almost never administered to Tom.

His sister absorbed enough for both of them, and with a discerning eye, he early in life analysed his mother's strength and weaknesses. He soon found that religion was the chink in her armour, and if punishment loomed ahead he could call on the Bible at will for reasons why it should be put off – it nearly always worked.

His mother, besides being actually active in church affairs, carried religion into her home, and with her husband's help, did her best to instil in the children the principles by which she lived and which she felt were fundamental to a good life. The example set by their parents penetrated even Tom's mischievous personality, and all the Waller children showed in later life that spark of goodness and kindness that sprang from these early teachings. From their mother they obtained their vivacity and warmth, their irresistible personality and capacity for love; from their father came seriousness and depth of feeling. There were Bible readings every day, and Edward Waller put the same care and intensity into these home affairs that he would into preaching to a group of lost souls on the corner of Lenox Avenue and 135th Street. Each Waller child, from its earliest years, knew by heart passages from the great Bible that formed the bulwark of their existence. Then there was singing. The kids would wake in the morning to the deep, full voice of their mother singing in the kitchen, and would sit proudly in church as she stood as leading soloist with the choir, singing 'Abide With Me,' her favourite hymn. Singing was, indeed, so highly regarded by the Waller family that they longed for a piano in the home, both to accompany the voice and as a stimulus to religion. Pianos were an expensive luxury in Harlem, and though Fats' mother played organ and piano, the raising and feeding of a family swallowed up all their money. But eventually something came about which got Mrs Waller to thinking very deeply about acquiring a piano.

One day the family were all at home. Six-year-old Tom was in the parlour, playing alone; his elder brother Bob stopped in the doorway returning from the kitchen, and his eyes fell on a strange sight. Tom had two straight-backed chairs placed side by side and was kneeling in front of them, his hands gliding back and forth across the front edges of the seats. His fingers, slightly curled, rose and fell in rhythm – the kid was imitating a pianist. Crossing over to Tom, Bob said, 'How would you like to play the piano?' Startled, Tom looked up at his big brother and said, 'I sure would. I played one upstairs – the lady let me.'

A series of conferences convinced Bob that the Waller finances could not take on the cost of a piano and he racked his brain to find some way it could be arranged. Finally he consulted an uncle – Patrick Bolling, his mother's half-brother – and it was planned they would all go in on it together. One day soon after, Tom was sent out on an errand which kept him from home until the middle of the afternoon. On his return he entered the living-room and stopped, wide-eyed: a new Waters upright! He stared; he couldn't believe his eyes. Then he made for the piano and stayed at it the whole afternoon. He didn't know just what to do with it– he just sat there in his glory. At first he didn't get any lessons; they couldn't be afforded, for there was yet another baby on the way, the twelfth child for Edward and Adeline – and their last.

Although the piano kept the kids interested for a while, they were getting restless and wanted to see more of the world. The only outings they got were either visits to relatives, Sunday church, an occasional walk with their parents, or picnics in Central Park; a visit to Coney Island was an outstanding event. Tom and Naomi fretted around the house, and even the piano didn't hold them for long. So when they were asked out by brother Lawrence's new girl friend, Mabel Brown, who was trying to make a good impression on the parents, they were eager to go. Their mother, with her mind torn between having an afternoon free from the strain of watching them and the duty she felt about protecting them, said it was all right for them to go if they took good care and behaved themselves. Mabel Brown was of the younger generation and her idea of taking care of the kids was considerably different from their mother's. She didn't know how little they knew of Harlem and things in general, so she thought the best thing to do was to take them to the cinema a couple of blocks from their home. The two were thrilled beyond description and trooped eagerly into the little Crescent Theatre – their first ever visit to a forbidden 'place of sin'. They were enthralled by the spectacle of violence and Indian warfare shown on the screen and absolutely entranced by the dramatic piano which accompanied the film. Directly they got

9

home they burst into the kitchen and told their mother all the exciting things they had seen on the screen.

'For land's sake,' said their mother who had never seen the inside of a nickelodeon, 'where you children been?' But although the cinema was quite near by, they couldn't tell her where they'd been because they didn't know. When brother Lawrence came home, however, and listened to them he knew well enough where they had been but he didn't give them away. Instead he roundly bawled Mabel out for taking them to such a place. 'If you want Momma and Poppa to like you, *never* take the kids there again.' Mabel promised to straighten things out with Mrs Waller, whose horror on learning the source of the kids' blood-and-thunder tales was matched only by Mabel's repentance. After that, however, they were allowed out a little more. The hot summer greatly increased the strain on Mrs Waller and after the baby had arrived she was ill for quite a time. She never recovered her old energy, but now, with the children at school all day, things were easier.

One rainy afternoon when the baby was sleeping peacefully and Tom and Naomi were playing with the piano stool – Naomi sat while Tom spun her round – they got the idea of giving the baby a ride as well. So Naomi and baby Edith were passengers and Tom turned them round on the revolving stool: slowly at first and then, as Tom worked harder, the speed increased; higher and higher until suddenly the top came off, cascading Naomi and the baby on to the floor. Fortunately, baby Edith, although frightened and shaken up, was still safely in Naomi's arms. Hearing the commotion, Mother rushed in from the kitchen. All she saw was the top of the piano stool on the floor, with Naomi and the crying baby beside it. Seizing the baby, she put it back into its crib, and then turned her attention with a strap to Naomi's bottom. But Thomas sat in the corner, meek as a lamb, softly singing, 'Everything That's Not Of Jesus Shall Go Down', – and with a sad expression on his big round face, he said, 'Momma, I don't know what got into me, I really don't – that naughty ol' devil he told me to do it. Don't you think we ought to pray?' So, with Naomi still smarting, Tom and his mother knelt and prayed for forgiveness.

Tom's method of escaping punishment came naturally to him.

He knew his mother's weakness for a penitent approach, and on countless occasions exploited it unscrupulously. Once, he and his sister were in the pantry where there always stood a can of Magnolia condensed milk. Spread on bread, it was one of the children's favourite snacks, but, going at it hot and heavy, Tom and Naomi this time practically drained the can and finished off the greater part of a fresh loaf of bread. Realizing they were in for trouble, the children started singing to put their mother in a good frame of mind.

Fats, seeing his mother heading for the pantry, suddenly piped up, 'Momma, when are we going to church again? I love to go to church. I feel so much like it. I had a dream about the Lord last night. He was so kind to me.'

His mother smiled and looked radiant, but continued on her way to the pantry. Presently, the inevitable, 'Naomi! Have you been at the Magnolia milk again?' Tom, of course, got off with a mild scolding: his unfortunate sister once again taking the blame.

In Harlem, the Wallers were very active in the Abyssinian Church. Edward was now Chairman of the Board of Deacons, and Superintendent of the Sunday School. But things were to change abruptly. A Reverend Morris, visiting minister of the Pentecostal faith, preached the doctrine of sanctification, and the Wallers, after hearing his address, were so impressed that they talked it over and transferred their membership to the new Church. They had all been baptized at the 40th Street Abyssinian Church and were now re-baptized at the Refuge Temple, 56 West 133rd Street. Edward went at the new work with a will and quickly became a mainstay of the organization.

A typical morning street service would present the Waller family *en masse*: an inspiring and persuasive address from Edward Waller with the voices of the rest of the family rising above the little congregation, and on the sidewalk, below his father, Thomas, whose fingers would hesitantly work out the simple chords of the hymns on a small portable harmonium. It was on such occasions as these that the boy got his first real feeling of making his contribution. The inspiration of his mother's voice, sweet and clear in the Sunday morning air, and the quiet authority of his father, lent impetus to his desire to play the instrument more competently.

The chords began to come more easily, and in time his fingers grew less awkward. He felt good. Life was sweet, and he was with his family.

The services, which lasted from an hour to an hour and a half, including hymns, Bible reading, and testifying, were held mostly on Lenox Avenue, between 130th and 134th Streets, just a couple of blocks from home at most. Sometimes Edward Waller saw fit to go over to Fifth Avenue, where the population contained a much higher proportion of Negroes. His listeners numbered whites and Negroes alike, and the memory of his sermons lingered long after he had passed from the Harlem scene.

Their youngest son's enthusiasm for music impressed the Waller parents sufficiently for them to invest in piano lessons for him, although Naomi was the main pupil. She was the one whom her mother thought to be destined for musical achievement; Tom was sent along as well, partly to keep him out of mischief. They were to be taught by a Miss Perry. Thomas was excited, and chafed until the magic day arrived. Mrs Waller took them both over, and Miss Perry made them welcome. The first lesson was chiefly explanatory and dealt with the charm and ease of playing the piano. Thomas already knew about the charm; as for the ease, he was particularly glad about that – there was no use in doing things the hard way. Naomi was only mildly interested, and secretly wished she was back home.

The next week they had their second session. Thomas and Naomi sat at the piano, and Miss Perry started to explain the positions of the notes on the scale, and the value of a quarter-note, a half-note and a full note. Thomas looked over at Naomi; Naomi looked back at him. He raised his eyebrows, and Miss Perry's voice cut in with a question, 'Thomas, how many beats do we give to this kind of note?' She pointed at the music before them. Off guard, Thomas guessed 'Two'. Nodding her head, Miss Perry smiled and turned the page. Thomas sighed with relief, and Naomi stifled a giggle. The weeks passed by, and the lessons were turning a little sour. Naomi just wasn't interested, and with each succeeding lesson Thomas became more and more restive. Miss Perry was losing heart. 'Thomas,' she said, 'I don't think you're interested in these scales and exercises. But you know you must go through these stages before you can play anything else. Just what is it you want to play?'

'Music, ma'am, and that's all!' Thomas looked on top of the piano where some sheets of popular music were stacked. 'Would you play this for me, Miss Perry?' She smiled and played it through for him, twice. Intently Fats watched her fingers – listening to the popular melody, he seemed lost in absorption.

Later, when they reached home, Fats sat at the piano, and without hesitation played the piece through by ear. 'When ever did you learn that?' his mother asked incredulously.

'Oh, I just remembered it,' he replied.

Soon the piano lessons petered out altogether, and from then on Tom went along the hard way, learning by ear – sight-reading wasn't to come his way for some time.

*   *   *

By now, Adeline was beginning to feel the strain of many years of child-bearing, and her health began to fail perceptibly. The growing children were now able to go out and play a lot more, and baby Edith was again sent to Virginia. But she still felt bound to the duty of keeping her brood protected from the influences of the neighbourhood in which they lived. The streets were more and more crowded, and the sounds of fights, cat-calls, and noisy games rang through the canyons formed by the tall apartment houses.

One afternoon, a knock came at the door, and Mrs Waller opened it, to see a small boy looking at her. 'Is Fats home?' he said.

'Who?' she asked.

The boy repeated his question.

Puzzled, Adeline said, 'No, son, nobody called Fats lives here.'

The little boy shrugged, and turned away, and Mrs Waller closed the door. Naomi called out from the next room, 'Who was that, Momma?'

'Just some little boy wanting someone named Fats. I guess he mistook the house.'

'Momma, I think he wanted Thomas.' Naomi stole a quick glance round the door at her mother's face.

Adeline frowned. 'You mean—?' She ran to the window and

threw it open. Leaning out, she called to the little boy three storeys below, 'His name is Thomas, not Fats!'

But from then on his name *was* Fats. Indelibly and irrevocably, Fats. The youngest of the Waller boys was putting on weight fast and, in the mercilessly frank manner of schoolboys, he had been appropriately named. His sister says that at that time he was a 'big bunch of somep'n' comin' along'.

But his mother rebelled at the nickname, just as she couldn't reconcile herself to Robert being called 'Zip'. 'Robert,' she would say, 'tell them your name's not "Zip" – tell them it's Robert.' Robert would squirm uncomfortably and plead, 'I know, Momma, but they *know* my name's Robert. They just want to call me Zip.'

But childhood was mainly a happy time for the Waller children. At Christmas time in 1912, The King's Chapel Assembly presented a play and the Waller children were included in the cast: it was a little playlet entitled 'No Room At The Inn'. Naomi, wrapped in voluminous robes, played the part of the Virgin Mary, while Fats had the role of the hard-hearted innkeeper. A hush fell over the audience of proud parents as the curtains jerkily parted. In the first scene, Joseph and Mary approached the inn, seeking shelter for the coming night. Fats, looking out over the inn half-door, and seeing them and the donkey in the background, made no mistake with his first line. 'There is no room here,' he said firmly, and closed the door in their faces.

But Fats' big moment was to come. Later in the play, the action shifted back to the inn, following the miracle of the birth of the Christ child. Standing by his door, he had been given the news that the Messiah had been born, and to the very folk that he had turned away – the innkeeper was dumbfounded! Fats took a deep breath, turned a darker hue under his dusky skin, and in an attitude of remorse, delivered himself of these lines: 'Gosh! If I had only known!'

The audience was transfixed, and for several years afterwards, whenever the name of Thomas Waller came up, people recalled this *tour de force*: Fats' first stage appearance.

Such public appearances began to appeal to the performer in Fats, and he felt that life at home lacked the excitement that abounded all around him in Harlem. Music offered an outlet, but it looked as though he would have to learn to read it properly. Public School 89, which they all attended, had a school orchestra, and the music teacher, a sweet-natured woman named Miss Corlias, encouraged Fats to try for it. Accordingly, he began to branch out, and started violin and string bass lessons. These were, however, of a desultory nature, and the piano soon resumed first place in his affections. With time, his reading of music improved a little, and he was able to approach the instrument with more assurance. It fell to him to play during morning assemblies, and the large body of schoolchildren, by now predominantly coloured, knew Fats better by his piano accomplishments than for any other reason. Friendly and easy-going, he soon won himself a niche in the hearts of the other kids in his grade. Among his early friends at school were Edgar Sampson, later a prominent musician and arranger, and composer of *Stompin' At The Savoy*, and Canada Lee, later to become a famed actor on Broadway. Sampson well remembers those days when the school would assemble, the kids shuffling down the aisles to the piano played by Fats, inspired by a newly found off-beat. The school looked on him as a clown, and he would often raise a laugh by rolling his eyes, or making a face over his shoulder as he played. At assemblies he would cause a sensation by bringing his large hands together in a thunderous clap, and his solos during these gatherings would set the kids clapping their hands, tapping their feet, and rocking to his music. In spite of the teachers' frowns, wild applause always followed one of these performances.

As soon as his music-reading ability had made enough progress, Fats joined the school orchestra. It consisted of eighteen to twenty members, led by Edgar Sampson on the violin. This popular following at school was to bear fruit later in his life in unexpected fashion.

Edward Waller was now quite proud of his son's accomplishments on the piano, and, anxious to steer him into the proper channels, took him to hear Paderewski give a piano recital at Carnegie Hall. He thought that the sight and sound of that great pianist might inspire Fats to love the classical side of music. It was evident by this time that Thomas wasn't going into the ministry, as he had hoped, but if he could persuade his son to follow good music, he would have been delighted. Fats was impressed with the great pianist's performance and talked about it for weeks; indeed, he never forgot the experience, although he didn't live up to his father's hopeful expectations. It became discouragingly clear to both parents that their son was attracted to what they considered the shady side of music. It was the lively ragtime which made the strongest appeal to him. Edward Waller always declaimed against what he called 'music from the devil's workshop', and would never allow it to be played in his own house. Mrs Waller saw no good either in 'this abomination, this jazz', and blamed it on Fats' un-savoury associations in Harlem.

One Saturday, when doing the family shopping, Naomi and Fats went over to a nearby grocery, where Naomi was deeply impressed by the sight of a tall, dark beauty, heavily made up, and beautifully clothed. She stood gazing raptly at the woman, who represented to her the ultimate in glamour and attainment. As she watched her, a well-dressed man entered and, flashing a toothy smile, duplicated in brilliance by a diamond on his finger, came over to the woman.

'Hello, pimp!' was her greeting.

As they walked off together, Naomi followed them with her eyes, and directly she and Fats got home, she told her mother all about the beautiful woman she had seen. Her mother didn't take much notice of her daughter's story, until Naomi ran to meet her father at the door as was her custom, and in her most charming manner greeted him with, 'Hello, pimp!'

Her father took off his hat, walked past her, and without turning around, said, 'What did you say, Naomi?'

'I said, "Hello, pimp!" '

'Where did you hear that?' he asked very quietly.

When he heard her story of the well-dressed man and woman, he gently put his arm around her, and said, 'Now listen, Naomi! I appreciate your thinking that I too am well-dressed and someone that you are proud of, but you'll find some day that that man and I are a world apart – and "pimp" is a word you must never use; one day you'll know why.'

By this time Fats and Naomi had become known to a lot of the shopkeepers in the neighbourhood, and soon Fats began a round of home deliveries for Eckert's Delicatessen. He also delivered for two cousins, of whom one ran a grocery, and the other a pig-foot stand. They paid him the munificent sum of seventy-five cents a week – one week the grocer paying him forty cents and the other coughing up thirty-five cents, and the next week the other way round.

In a mixed neighbourhood there was bound to be racial rivalry, and gangs of kids often joined in fights, or attacked lone representatives of the opposite colour, spurred on, no doubt, by remarks made by their parents. Feeling ran particularly high among property owners, and the children bore their share of the feuding. While making a delivery for Eckert's one day, Fats was set on by a gang of whites, and stabbed before he was able to get away. His distressed mother rushed him over to Dr Porter on West 139th Street, and his wound was happily pronounced to be superficial. To the credit of his parents, this affair didn't alter their feelings towards the white race, for the Wallers lived by faith in God, and pointed out the way of God to their offspring. Fats was by no means the least devout of the Waller family and he was never guilty of short-sightedness in his relations with white people at any period in his life – though at times, later in his career, he had more than ample justification.

At this period he was always a step ahead of his sister in the family circle, as was amusingly shown one year at the family baptism at Tottenville, Staten Island. Mr and Mrs Waller and the older children went in first and were duly baptized. Fats followed in the next group and, although spluttering, came through with decorum. Naomi, further back in line, was preceded by an enormous woman who went into the water with her mouth open. Choking and gasping alarmingly, she was assisted back to the bank but Naomi, horrified at the sight, lost her courage and refused to go into the water, much to the embarrassment of the family. Fats, however, made great capital out of the occasion, crying out for all to hear, 'I went in,' and to the rest of his family, 'She has no faith at all. She needs to pray, doesn't she, Momma?' That was one of the longest days in Naomi's young life.

Shortly after this a move was scheduled for the family. The piano, which had been pretty heavily handled during its short stay with the Waller family, was presented to the Pentecostal Church, for luckily there was already a piano in the house to which they were moving. On arrival at the new house on East 134th Street, Fats took a can of paint and painstakingly inscribed WALLER on the stoop. It remained there until the building was demolished many years later.

Life was a magic thing for the youngsters. Home, to all the Wallers, was a warm nest, feathered by their mother's tender ministrations and Edward Waller's serene protectiveness. Even baby Edith, scarcely able to walk before she went away to live with her aunt, and only back in New York at intervals, regarded the house where she was born and their subsequent apartment east of Lenox Avenue as home. Dinner-time especially enthralled them. It never varied much, but each time they sat down hungry young eyes searched the platters of food, impatient to get past the prayer and on to the business of eating. But prayer took precedence over all else. Their father led off with grace, and then each child was called upon in turn to quote a short passage from the Scriptures. With bowed heads and closed eyes, they awaited the call – each hoping to be first, so as to be able to blurt out the shortest of all the passages they knew: 'Jesus wept.' As soon as prayers were over and their father started to serve the meat, the aroma assailed their nostrils until they could almost taste it before it had reached their plates. Luckey Roberts, who knew the family well, says the Wallers were the 'eatin'est family in Harlem' – 'they sure pushed a mean crumb,' he says with a smile. Many years later, when Fats was asked in an interview if he had ever run away from home as a lad, he answered abruptly, 'What? No sir, the food was too good around that table.' But his memory wasn't quite infallible, apparently, for he did make one abortive attempt.

When war broke out in 1917, Harlem was filled with excitement as men went off to join the forces and huge parades filled the main thoroughfare almost every day. The schools were let out and Fats and Naomi would stand on the kerb and watch the lines of soldiers file past – the women weeping and the men stealing glances as they marched by, trying to find their families and friends on the side-walk.

There came a day when Lawrence Waller was sent overseas. When weeks later a message was delivered reporting him missing in action, Adeline Waller was sick at heart. But her prayers were answered; Lawrence was found and posted back to his unit and subsequently returned safely home.

At this time Mrs Waller had undertaken to help the son of a neighbour, a little boy who suffered from rickets. She spent many weeks with him and treated him so successfully that he recovered completely. The older boys weren't home so much these days: Lawrence was overseas and Robert, in addition to his job which kept him occupied all day, was always out with his girl friend. Naomi too had her girl friends and was beginning to show interest in the boys, so Fats was more or less at a loose end when night fell. He had a certain amount of liberty and he found there was a lot going on in Harlem that he didn't know about – particularly at night. The place was familiar to him in the daytime, but when the street lights went on it seemed to undergo a magic transformation. It was difficult to get out at night, so he schemed to get away, be on his own and enjoy some of this unknown night life. So one Tuesday afternoon, after school, he didn't return home. Missing him at dinner, his parents searched all his familiar haunts, the delicatessen, his friends' houses, and the school yard. It was to no avail. The worried family waited through the whole of the next day. On Thursday morning, Fats turned up at a Mrs Johnson's, one of his mother's friends, with the story that he had left home because his father didn't want him any more. Being a sensible person, the good woman took him in, asked no questions and, thankful that he was off the streets, put him to bed. In the morning he rose and left again. Mrs Johnson hurried over to the Wallers and told Adeline what had happened.

'Send him home,' said his anxious mother; but Fats didn't show up again at Mrs Johnson's. Later in the day his father saw him on 135th Street, between Fifth and Lenox Avenue, and brought him home. He sat down and, addressing himself to Fats, who stood before him, he said, 'Thomas, I know that sometimes boys want to run away from home. They usually have a reason. You didn't. But in case you ever decide to do that again, I'm going to give you a reason. I've only whipped you once before, as you remember. This is the second time, and I expect it to be the last time.' Fats was on his guard, and still fairly rebellious. His father went for him, and Fats made a show of resistance; but Edward Waller was still the better man – Fats got that tanning. His mother was so overwrought by the episode that she fell sick and the doctor had to be called. This hurt Fats more than the whipping, and in addition it cost Edward ten dollars for the doctor's call. As further punishment, Fats was forbidden to see the big parade of the 15th Regiment, arranged for the following Monday. Adeline had been asked over by a Mrs Carter, living on Lenox Avenue, to see the event from her window. As she made preparations to leave, she saw Fats in the corner of the room, moping and looking generally disgusted with life. Her heart melted and she went over to him.

'Now, Thomas, have Momma or Poppa ever done anything to hurt you?'

Fats shook his head. His eyes brimming with tears, he looked so downhearted that they both burst into tears simultaneously. His mother told him to go upstairs and apologize to his father, which he did. Fats saw the big parade.

Although by now a very big boy, Fats was still in short pants. One day, when getting ready to go to a party to which he had been invited by a girl in the neighbourhood, he caught sight of his bare knees in the mirror and decided to do something about it. Rummaging through his brother Lawrence's closet, he found a sharply creased pair of black trousers. He quickly put them on and stood again in front of the mirror. The trousers sagged around his ankles, but it took only a few minutes to shorten each leg by four inches. Scissors in hand, Fats smiled at his reflection.

That night, when the festivities were at their height, the door burst open, and in strode Lawrence. Seeing Fats, he grabbed him by the ear.

'Steal my pants, will you?' he shouted. Then, as he saw the mutilated state of his best pair of dress trousers, his face went red. Tightening his grip on the unfortunate Fats, he dragged him from the scene.

After the school session of spring 1918, Fats decided to leave and take a job. During the summer, he and Naomi worked together in a jewel-box factory in Lower Manhattan. Their father was still employed as a trucker, and as he did a certain amount of work for the company, he managed to secure jobs for them. This was Fats' first real work, apart from his deliveries in Harlem. His job was to buff the outside of the boxes on a flywheel polisher, while Naomi assembled the padded linings for the insides.

Just three blocks away from their factory stood Trinity Church, one of New York's oldest places of worship. During lunch hour, they used to go over to the church, and while the bells rang out the noon carol, Naomi sat in the gloom and listened, while Fats played the church piano, having made a friend of the sexton who let him play until just before afternoon service. One day Naomi and Fats, so enraptured by the atmosphere and the music, completely lost track of time, and arrived back at work late. The boss gave them a stern telling off in no uncertain terms.

But Fats soon tired of this job, saying it was 'too dirty'. In truth, it wasn't music, and music was all he wanted. So back to Harlem he went, his brief career on the assembly line over and done with.

3

During the years the Wallers lived in Harlem, the place had undergone a radical change. From being a quiet residential white section in the early 1900s, it had grown to metropolitan status and, under the steady impetus of an ever-growing Negro population, enriched by war money, it had become an area of magnetic quality and fascination to the outsider. Negroes from all the Southern States flocked there in their hundreds, bringing with them their local customs, until it became a melting pot inside the greater melting pot that was New York itself. Seventh and Lenox Avenues were no longer speedways for the carriages of the wealthy, but social and business centres of new vitality.

The attraction of Harlem to outsiders was not limited to Negroes. Indeed, a large part of Harlem's active business involved entertaining the white sightseer from downtown, or the out-of-towner. Alert business men from other parts of the city saw their opportunity and quickly converted cellars and stores into small, intimate and lively clubs, which provided employment for thousands of Harlem's citizens as waiters, singers, dancers, and musicians. The response was immediate, for the town was loaded with talent. Local entrepreneurs also joined in the game and furthered the cause of the small clubs. The larger, white-owned clubs were frankly geared to rake in the ever-growing stream of dollars from downtown.

Culturally, too, Harlem began to change. Lenox Avenue was the first centre of theatrical activity, and the Lincoln Theatre, on 135th Street, formerly a nickelodeon, hard by the 'Crescent', scene of 'Mabel's Folly' with the young Waller kids, was now the hub of vaudeville, housing the greatest of American Negro talent, Bill Robinson, Bert Williams, Miller and Lyle. The Lafayette Theatre on Seventh had a background of legitimate plays and productions of large-scale musicals, that established it as the mecca of legitimate theatre in Harlem. This theatre in 1913 produced a musical, 'Dark-town Follies', the routines and first act finale from which so impressed Florenz Ziegfeld that he bought the rights for use in the forthcoming edition of his 'Follies'. Another 1913 attraction was a presentation of 'Othello'.

Fats Waller found himself in the midst of this thrilling atmosphere. From every other cellar on 133rd and 134th Streets, west of Lenox Avenue, could be heard the beat of drums and the tinkling of pianos against a background of clinking glasses and the high-pitched laughter of girls. Often the sobbing plaints of a blues singer, calling down her mythical lover, came up into the night. Fats stood and listened and absorbed all he heard.

He quit his old job and, not knowing what to do, he went over to Immerman's delicatessen which was run by two brothers, Connie and George, who were known locally for their fine 'chitlin's and hogmaws'. They gave him some delivering to do for them, but warned him to be careful. More often than not, there were a couple of bottles of liquor aboard when he left the store on his trips, so, with a weather eye open for the law, he would complete his deliveries as fast as he was able. The Volstead Act, newly passed, was proving a bonanza for the many shopkeepers serving as outlets for contraband spirits. Immerman's delicatessen, long established in Harlem, was no exception. It was a favourite haunt for the young men of the neighbourhood, but one day the law descended on the store, and held all the occupants while a routine investigation was made. Fats recalled many years later how, after giving his name and address, he walked out of the store, the wide-eyed innocent, right under the noses of the officers, loaded down with bottles carefully concealed in his baggy pants and loose jacket; a little bulk on that fatness didn't show.

For some time past, Fats had been attracted to the Lincoln Theatre, partly because it represented the sort of life he sought, but mainly for another reason. A small pipe-organ was situated down front, next to the ever-present piano, on which was played the dramatic music which enlivened the silent films of the day. Fats visited the theatre as often as possible, and sat enraptured as Mazie Mullins, the pianist, went through dozens of selections, borrowing freely from the classics and popular tunes of the day to fill out her repertoire for the picture. He would emerge from the theatre, never remembering what had transpired on the screen, but with fingers itching to get home and try out on his own piano what he could remember of the music which Mazie had played. His presence and keen attention to what she did soon attracted Mazie's attention. She was flattered by his concentration and soon, having spoken to him a few times, she invited him to join her in the pit where he could watch and learn more readily. It quickly became a custom and presently Fats began to wheedle in his most persuasive manner, 'Why don't you go out and take a break, Mazie? I'll take over for you on the piano.' Miss Mullins, glad to get a breather, was soon confident enough of his playing to allow him to carry on for a few minutes. Once on his own in the pit, Fats soon started to work his wiles on the regular organist, using much the same approach and finally achieving the same results. His joy knew no bounds the day he first sat in front of the organ and played the interval music before the stage show went on.

The Lincoln was owned by a white lady, Mrs Marie C. Downes, who soon began to notice the chubby youngster haunting the pit. Listening to him, she made a mental note, for later reference, that the kid wasn't at all bad, that in fact there was something so spontaneous about his playing that at times it evoked more than the usual desultory applause from the audience. It was not long after this that the regular organist fell ill and Mrs Downes was at her wits' end, luckily for Fats. Mazie passed him the word and Fats immediately offered to step into the breach. The proprietress, with very little hesitation, agreed to try him out. For the next ten days' Fats filled in as relief organist, feeling his way cautiously his chords were often not quite correct but, although he made mistakes, his musical knowledge developed until, in a remarkably short space of time, he had achieved quite a well-rounded programme. Suddenly, one Saturday afternoon, just as he was coming to the end of his interval playing, he was surprised to hear from behind him, far back in the theatre, a youthful cry, 'Hey, Fats, make it rock – like you did in school!' A couple more young voices joined in: 'Yeah, Fats; swing it, man!' With a grin, he turned on his stool and bowed his acknowledgment to his old school friends. The boys who had clapped and shuffled at innumerable school assemblies were right behind him here. The knowledge acted as an incentive to his playing for that show and the results were quite astonishing. The audience stood to applaud him, and Mrs Downes, at the back of the theatre, nodded her approval. From then on Fats had free access to the theatre and could visit Mazie in the pit whenever he wished. When, shortly afterwards, the regular organist left, Fats obtained his very first musical job: organist at the Lincoln at $23 a week. With their musical schoolmate at the console, the boys of the district soon began to flock to the Lincoln in droves. At each performance the theatre would resound with encouraging shouts and the floor would throb to the thump of dozens of feet beating in rhythm.

This happy audience participation had a good effect on Fats' playing and in consequence the quality of his performances steadily mounted. His appetite for music was insatiable. Even when he had finished the interval music he would, when allowed, take over the piano from Mazie for long periods. He played the film music as she had done, but incorporated his own style into what he played, so that his music developed along the same lines as hers.

It was about this time that Fats first began to meet other musicians from the Harlem theatres around him. Hitherto restricted as he had been in his friendships – he had only had a few intimates outside family acquaintances – these new contacts served to sharpen his zest for music. Still unable to play jazz, he talked, listened and hobnobbed with the older men as much as he could. He drank and laughed with them backstage, and observed keenly the contributions each musician made to the orchestra as a whole. For the first time in his life he began to appreciate the value of the other instruments in the orchestra. In school it had been too much of a struggle to read music for him to appreciate the value of the other instruments. His fingers, hesitant and stumbling, had obstructed the broader vision he was now getting.

At home it was no longer a secret that Fats was working at the Lincoln Theatre. When the subject was first mentioned, Edward Waller had been appalled at the idea of his son's working in a 'house of Satan', but parental pride in his son's prowess had in the end overcome his feeling of horror. Eventually both the Waller parents encouraged their youngest son in his chosen career. Jazz, however, remained beyond the pale and they were never to be reconciled to it as long as they lived. Both the word and the sound of it remained, as far as they were concerned, degenerate and demoralizing.

As time went by, the young organist at the Lincoln was fast becoming a local celebrity. His fresh approach to the way an organ could be played was the talk of the town and soon people from all over Harlem began coming to the little theatre. Canada Lee, one of Fats' schoolmates, recalls days when he would sneak in a side door of the theatre just to sit and watch the show and cheer Fats on. But important as were those youthful supporters who spread Fats' renown and whose spontaneous calls made the audiences sit up and take notice, equally so were the show people, the musicians and the publishers' representatives who came so regularly to the theatre. The Lincoln's shows, boasting top-flight acts, always attracted their share of the downtown trade. Invariably on a Saturday night there would be a prominent composer in the audience, up from Tin Pan Alley for a weekly dose of inspiration; an orchestra leader; an actor's agent on the look-out for new talent; or a club owner on the same errand. After the show at the Lincoln they would go round town to visit the night spots in further quest of ideas and talent.

One day Fats met a drummer named Reuben Harris, who was sufficiently impressed by Fats' playing to invite him to join a small band which was going to perform at an open-air block-party in the Bronx. Fats, always eager to get with it, grabbed at the opportunity and went. This band, Fats' first of this kind, included, besides Fats on piano and Harris on drums, Banjo Ike, Joe Williams and Herb Grivey on brass. It was an unimportant local affair but the neighbourhood around 165th Street and Brook Avenue whooped it up for several hours while people hung out of their windows to watch the merrymaking below. It was important, however, in one sense, for Fats caught sight of a young girl dancing around the bandstand who took his fancy. He was told her name was Edith Hatchett – they got into conversation and by the end of the evening they were firm friends. With this new interest, Fats played more dazzlingly than usual and Edith was enchanted. Soon Fats was seeing more of Miss Hatchett and he even went as far as asking her to his home for dinner – much to the surprise of his family.

Fats had had only very limited relations with girls for the shelter of the family circle had kept him from meeting many elsewhere than at school. There he was regarded with a certain amount of adulation, but he was scarcely considered a chaser even though he rolled his eyes provocatively at the girls as they passed the piano. Edith was the first girl in whom he had shown any real interest. His mother scrutinized her carefully as she passed round the plates of food and decided she liked her. In fact everyone did. Edith had a sensible head on her shoulders as well as a soft voice and a modest nature, and she had been brought up in the way the Wallers approved of. Religion had played a large part in her young life – a fact which endeared her to the household. Thomas's first girl friend had won approval and Adeline Waller asked her to come often. Edith did.

Christmas was on its way, and the whole family was busy preparing for the great day. Fats, by this time, was feeling his oats in the family. After all, he was a successful business man now – a musician of some little note, or so he thought. But to the rest of the family he was still just Thomas Waller, the youngest son. Rebellion against this ignoring of his importance broke out on Christmas Eve. His little sister Edith and her girl friend Marie were playing in the kitchen, having been for mysterious reasons forbidden by the older Wallers to enter the parlour that evening. Fats walked in, laden down with boxes of biscuits and ice cream which he had been sent to collect.

'I know a secret!' he announced.

The two young girls looked up at him and chorused, 'Tell us, Tom, please!'

He shook his head. But Edith persisted. 'I'll give you my ice cream if you will tell us.'

He hesitated and again shook his head.

Marie offered her ice cream too. Fats looked from one to the other and said, 'All right. Here's the secret. There ain't no Santa Claus!'

The two girls protested that they knew different and that they'd prove it next morning when the presents were there under the Christmas tree. 'Follow me,' said Fats, 'and I'll show you the real Santa.'

Opening the parlour door a little way, he peered in, and then stood aside. He beckoned to Edith and Marie, who looked through the crack and then looked again. The sight of Momma and Poppa Waller trimming the tree and laying out the parcels under its branches met their eyes, and their wails of disillusionment soon brought the Waller parents in from the parlour with a rush. That Christmas Fats only received his usual money for music lessons – there were no presents for him under that tree.

And so came New Year, 1920. It was to be a year of years for Thomas Fats Waller.

4

The year started calmly enough. Fats played the organ at the Lincoln as usual and after the last show, from which he would get out at about ten o'clock, he would spend his nights running around town in search of the jazz pianists who played the all-night clubs. Because of his obvious youth, Fats often couldn't get past the front door, but here and there he was able to get in and he would sit as near the piano as possible, listening and absorbing all he heard. He often wondered if he would ever be able to hold his own with these masters of the keyboard.

One night he walked to the corner of 140th Street and Lenox Avenue where, on a vacant lot, there was a dance place just off the street. It was only a large tent, the admission was ten cents a head, and the crowd on the floor was usually fairly sparse. But it was practically the only place in Harlem where one could dance publicly, except for a spot called the Dolphin. Hearing some solid piano playing coming from inside, Fats pulled aside the canvas flap and looked in. A grin spread over his face as he saw Russell Brooks, one of the party-piano men whose local fame was considerable. Fats knew Russell's younger brother Wilson, an erstwhile schoolmate, and he had a speaking acquaintance with Russell himself. There were very few people on the floor and it seemed a good chance to get to talk to the musician, so he slipped inside and approached the bandstand. Russell saw the fat youngster coming across the floor, and he nodded his head and smiled.

'Hey, Fats! How are ya?'

Glowing with anticipation, Fats said, 'Hello, Russell. Mind if I sit and watch you?'

'No, kid. Have a seat.' He motioned to a chair. 'How do you like this rag I just wrote?' He began to change the tempo, picking up the beat, and the choppy rhythm floated out over the floor. The few dancers began to bounce up and down, and Fats' foot tapped out the beat. His eyes were glued to the keyboard and Russell's flying fingers which moved faster and faster, until with a final chord the number finished. 'How about that, Fats! Think it's okay?'

'Gee, Russell – that was great!'

'Fats, why don't you get with this music? I heard you at the Lincoln, and you're doing all right, but you gotta swing out more, boy, if you're going to make it.'

'Yeah,' murmured Fats. 'I want to play like that, but I just can't seem to get it somehow – my fingers get all tangled up when I play fast. I've been tryin' to play some rags, but they're hard to learn, man. I need someone to help me, I guess – a real jazz pianist, like you or Jimmy Johnson. You know him, Russell? He's real great!'

'Yeah, I know James P., Fats, like a brother. Tell you what, kid, one of these days I'll take you along to Jimmy and we'll see if he can help you out on them chords and changes. He'll straighten out your tangled fingers, but you'll have to work, boy!'

Fats got to his feet. 'I gotta go,' he said. 'Good-bye, and thanks, Russell. I'll see you again about takin' me to James P. Johnson.' He ran towards the exit.

Skirting the dance floor, he dodged between a set of ropes, but as he passed, he caught his foot in one of them. Thrown off balance, he fell against the other guy-ropes, which promptly pulled free, collapsing the whole tent around Fats, Russell and the few remaining dancers. As he fought his way out from under the immense load of canvas, Fats heard Russell's smothered voice call out, 'Why don't you get someone to untangle your feet while you are about it, too!'

The opportunity for a change that Fats was looking for came soon, but in a tragic manner. His mother's health was steadily failing, and she finally succumbed to the ravages of diabetes. Her death came as a profound shock to everyone, perhaps hardest of all to Fats. In his young life, his mother had always been a shining light, his protector, and the rock on which his whole existence was built. To Edward Waller, too, it was a light extinguished, but his grief was a little mitigated by the fact that his family was now grown and fairly self-sufficient. The older boys were married, and Edith was again sent off to her aunt's home in Virginia, so Edward continued to live on with the married ones. Naomi and Fats felt suddenly alone, for the thing that had held their home together was gone, forever. The house seemed empty and cold. The piano, which had reverberated through the rooms as it accompanied their mother's hymns, was silent – no one would touch it.

One summer night soon after Adeline Waller's death, Wilson Brooks was walking along 133rd Street on his way home for the night, when he saw a familiar figure sitting on the stoop. It was Fats.

'What're you doing, Fats?'

'Oh, I just left home, Wilson. I don't wanna go back either.'

'Gee, Fats, where'll you stay?' Then a thought came to him. 'C'mon upstairs with me. They'll be all in bed, I 'spect, so you can sleep on the davenport.'

It was early next morning when Wilson's father came into the parlour from the bathroom. His eyes mistook the figure huddled on the couch for his son, but, turning him over, he was confronted with a strange face. Fats looked up apprehensively, but Mr Brooks turned away, and crossed the passage to his son's room.

'Wilson! Who is this boy?'

A sleepy voice answered, 'Oh, Father, that's Fats Waller – you know, Reverend Waller's boy.'

'What's he doing here? Why isn't he at his own home?'

'He left home, Pop. I found him in the street and asked him in to spend the night.'

Just then Mrs Brooks entered from the bedroom, wondering what was going on. When they had told her what it was all about, she smiled at Fats to reassure him, and then turned to her husband.

'Now, dear, don't let's get all upset. The boy has just lost his mother, and I think I know how he is feeling.'

'But he must go back to his family – they're probably worried to death about him by this time.'

'Never mind that now, Father. Thomas – that's your name, isn't it? – would you like some pancakes with us? You must be hungry for breakfast.'

Fats nodded, and looked back and forth at the man and woman. 'Come on,' Wilson chimed, 'let's go and get washed up.' – an invitation Fats gladly accepted.

Over breakfast Mrs Brooks decided that it would be best for young Thomas to stay with them as long as he wanted to. Wilson was delighted, and Mr Brooks said he would go over and explain to Tom's father. If the Reverend Waller agreed, it would be all right with him, and at least the boy would be off the streets.

On thinking the matter over, Edward Waller agreed that perhaps it would be better for Fats to live away from home if he wanted to, and so an amicable arrangement was made. Fats' father knew Mrs Brooks as a good woman, who would treat Thomas as a mother would. Naomi stayed on at home and kept house for her father.

At the Brookses', besides finding a home, Fats was more than delighted to find that they had a player-piano in the parlour. It had been one of his disappointments that the piano at home had not been of that type, for he had sadly lamented the fact that of all the wonderful piano rolls available – featuring such artists as James P. Johnson and Luckey Roberts – he had seldom heard a single one, let alone played any. Searching through the cabinet near the piano, Fats discovered some James P. Johnson QRS rolls and could hardly wait to begin to play them. Mrs Brooks was pleased to hear the piano once again, for her older son Russell had married and left home, and the piano had more or less lain idle since his departure. So with a bunch of bananas, a few oranges and apples, all cut up in a salad bowl together with a whole loaf of bread, Fats would spend an entire day at the keyboard.

One morning Russell came home to call on his family and, as he stopped in front of the house, he listened for a moment. He was puzzled to hear an unfamiliar hand playing a piano. He looked up, for it sounded as if it was coming from his home. Running upstairs, he slipped silently into the parlour and there saw a familiar figure seated at the piano. It was Fats – piano roll in place before him and his hands spread out over the keys. Lifting his hands, he gave the pedals a slight pump and a new chord was struck on the piano. Again his hands went to the keyboard and he fitted his hands to the keys, shaking his head as he found he was unable to span the distance with a single hand. Then he disconnected the locking mechanism and played the two chords by himself, or as much as he could reach with his short fingers. For some time Russell watched him until Fats sensed his presence. Turning round, he broke into a grin.

'I was just practising,' he said, a little abashed.

'That's all right, kid,' said Russell. 'Since when have you been coming over here to play the piano?'

Fats told him about the new arrangement and Russell nodded his approval. 'Now what were you playing there?' he asked.

'*Carolina Shout*,' said Fats.

'You sure picked a hard one. I can hardly play that right myself. It's one of Jimmy's numbers.'

'I know. I wanna learn it, just like it's on here.'

Russell shook his head. 'That's goin' to be tough unless you know how to play that kind of stuff. But keep trying anyway, Fats. Don't let me stop you.' Russell went on into the kitchen and Fats resumed his labours.

Some weeks later, Russell and his friend, James P. Johnson, were on the way home from a parlour social when Russell asked, 'Say, James, do you know that kid, Fats Waller?'

'No, I don't think so.'

'Well, he's the kid that plays the organ down at the Lincoln.'

'Oh yeah, man, I saw him. What about him?'

'Well, James, he wants to meet you awful bad. He's trying an' trying to get to play like you, but he just ain't gettin' nowhere. Maybe you'd listen to him some time. How about it?'

James P. looked at his friend. 'Now you know I don't want to teach piano. Let the kid go somewheres else an' get lessons. How about you showin' him some things – you can play my kind of stuff.'

'No, not me. First place I can never explain what I want to show anybody. An' he wouldn't learn from me – it's you he wants. Just you meet him anyway. You can make up your mind later.'

'Okay,' James agreed reluctantly. 'But I tell you, I won't teach him. Maybe I'll talk him into taking lessons somewheres else. You says he wants to play just like me?'

Seeing that James was interested in spite of himself, Russell pushed his advantage. 'You bet he does. Why, he's tackling the *Shout* and he don't even know how to play a rag.'

They walked on in silence for half a block. 'Tell you what,' said James, 'you bring him round to my place Tuesday morning 'bout eleven. I ain't working Monday night and I'll talk with him. He ain't so bad on that organ – maybe he's got somep'n'.'

Tuesday arrived and Russell, with Fats in tow, mounted the steps of 267 West 140th Street where James P. lived. The door was answered by a pert young woman who smiled at Russell.

'Well, hello, Russell. Where you been lately? And who's this with you?'

'This is Fats Waller, Lil. He wants to be a piano player and James said to bring him over this morning.'

'Well, come on in. James is just having a bite to eat.'

Fats' eyes darted around the room, as they crossed the threshold, and came to rest on two pianos, one a baby grand, the other an upright. He edged over to the grand and reverently touched the keys. He looked at the name in front – an Armstrong. The sound of a chair scraping in the next room brought his head up – he took a deep breath and waited.

James P. entered the room, a big man in his late twenties; he looked at Fats a moment and then said, 'Hello, Russell, I see you showed up. Is this Fats?' He looked back at the boy.

Fats nodded. 'I'm Fats,' he said.

James P. looked him up and down and was not very impressed by what he saw. Fats' short pants were bulging out and threadbare, his shoes were scuffed and dulled through lack of care, and his shirt was patched in several places. Johnson looked back to the face again. Large luminous eyes stared at him, eyes that spoke volumes. James P. smiled. 'Sit down, Fats. Glad to meet you.'

Turning to Russell, he said, 'Didn't you have something you wanted to do or somewhere you wanted to go?'

'Yeah . . . sure, James,' came the answer, 'I did want to go over to Lenox Avenue to get something.' Russell said a hasty good-bye to Lil. 'I'll see you later, Fats,' he said.

Lil went back into the kitchen. James turned back to his visitor. 'Now, let's hear you play something for me on that piano . . . no, not that one. Use the upright.'

Lunchtime came and went and Fats played everything he knew. Johnson watched and listened, now and then interrupting with a suggestion. Sometimes he would tell the kid to move over and make room, but most of the time he kept quiet. Now and again he would play the same passage as Fats but with trills, or he would break up the rhythm with a counter-rhythm in the bass, and time

34

and again he went back to the basic principles of the scales, and sharps and flats. Beginning with the major keys of C and F, he explained the various transitions of harmony in a simple piece. His pupil drank in every word and nodded sharply at each step. Then James P. would leave the piano and let Fats play what he had just learned. Fats' fingers still refused to do all he demanded of them but less vehemently now.

'That's it, Fats, you'll get it.' Johnson looked pleased.

Much later Lil put her head round the door. 'James, you know what time it is?' she asked. 'It's five-thirty and you've got to eat your supper before you play tonight.'

'Let's call it a day, Fats. I didn't know we'd been going so long,' said James P. as he got up and stretched. 'This boy's goin' to be all right, Lil. Got enough food for three of us?'

Dinner over, Fats got to his feet, saying, 'Well, guess I better get going if you're going to work.'

'Oh no, you ain't,' said James P. 'You're coming out with me and you're going to spend some time where it'll do you most good.'

'You mean you're going to take me out with you, to where you work, to Leroy's?' asked Fats incredulously.

'Sure, boy. Where do you think I mean – Church?'

Perhaps nothing in the world could have been more inspiring to Fats than that first night on the town with James P. Johnson, and certainly to an aspiring piano player it was a golden opportunity. James was at that time one of the most lionized heroes amongst the pianists of Harlem. His piano rolls had spread his fame throughout the nation and, coupled with his numerous vaudeville appearances, were making the name of James P. Johnson a fabulous one with jazz-lovers everywhere.

Born in New Brunswick, New Jersey, on 1 February 1891, Johnson had taken up the piano at an early age, receiving his initial instruction from his mother, who, unlike Adeline Waller, was fortunately enthusiastic over the music of her race, the stomps and rags that she had heard from early childhood. Accordingly, James as a child was imbued with many of the elements that make up jazz. The music was an integral part of the life he knew, and it was only natural that he should take the straight path to outstanding musical achievement.

As a child he had been taken to the country square dances, which the early Negro emigrants had brought to town in their original form from the South. A set of square dances was called a cotillon, and a prize was offered at these events both to the fanciest-dressed woman and to the man who could step the funniest. The juba dance ('juba this – juba that – juba all 'roun' the cotton patch') would be sung, accompanied by the harmonica, a pair of bone clappers, and a jew's-harp, and the music would fill the air as the ladies danced towards the centre, lifting their skirts a little as they met, revealing petticoats and pantaloons gaily decorated with colourful little bows, whilst the sideliners would call out, 'C'mon Sara, show your laundry!' and such-like remarks.

So it was in this atmosphere, truly Southern and truly Negro, although far removed from the scene of its origin, that young James P. learned the fundamentals that were to pervade his creative writing and performances throughout his life. And despite constant engagements in the more commercial world of musical comedy, vaudeville and band work, he never lost his strong jazz connections. Among his compositions in later years, both *Carolina Shout* and *Carolina Balmoral* were directly the result of his early recollections of the square dances he attended in his youth.

At the age of 9, he was given formal lessons by an Italian teacher with a will of iron, who laid down the law stringently on the correct performance of passages, no matter whether they were classical or ragtime. Under this tuition he developed his technique steadily until his early teens, when his family moved to New York and settled in the West Sixties. San Juan Hill in those days offered plenty in the way of encouragement for a kid pianist, and he was soon working at clubs in the district. Learning as he went along, he was able to acquire valuable tips on his playing from such notables as Luckey Roberts, Charley Cherry, and the strangely named Abba Labba. His reputation grew steadily, and by the time he married and settled down in Harlem, he had built for himself an enviable following.

In 1911 he recalled meeting Jelly Roll Morton, even then a character of the first water, whose arrival in Harlem created something of a furore, even in that district of gaudy characters. Word of Jelly's pianistics had preceded him, but people were hardly prepared for the flashily-dressed musician who strolled down 134th Street, or along Seventh Avenue, a 'queen' on either arm, and grasping a heavy leash, at the other end of which padded a bulldog. In later years in Chicago, while on tour with 'Plantation Days', James P. entered a club one night. As usual, he was greeted with enthusiasm by everyone present. He played a couple of numbers and then joined some friends at their table for a drink. Presently, in walked Jelly Roll, as large as life, and twice as natural. Acknowledging the applause, he sat down at a table, until someone came over and pleaded with him to play. He consented and had just got to his feet when, across the room, he spotted James P. Suddenly he changed his mind. No, he wouldn't play – he wasn't feeling too good. However, after much persuasion, during which it was pointed out to him that it might look as if he was scared, Jelly's pride got the better of him and he rose, ceremoniously folded his coat and laid it on the piano top. Then he sat down, rolled off a terrific *Pearls* and immediately afterwards grabbed his coat and dashed out of the club, saying he had another appointment. This was one battle of music lost by default before it had begun.

In New York, the piano-roll business soon began to capitalize on the commercial value of the pianists of the day and all the popular heroes of the keyboard were recorded profusely. All the better-known men were tried out, QRS issuing Luckey Roberts' *Pork And Beans*, *Junk Man's Rag* and *Molasses* in quick succession. James P.'s roll of *Carolina Shout* was a best-seller immediately it was issued and quickly became the popular hit of the day in the race market. His *Harlem Strut* and *Keep Off The Grass* were other original compositions which helped swell the coffers of the QRS company, and he quickly became their leading race artist. Other companies were also active in the field, and Jelly Roll himself made many recordings during the flourishing years of the piano-roll market.

From the outset of his first regular cabaret job, at Barron's, James P. Johnson was a hit with everyone who heard him. That thriving Harlem custom known as the parlour social (of which more later) provided him with a chance to play with other pianists and do battle with them on his own terms. He thus, very soon, became the reigning king among pianists in town. James P. had only to be booked at any event to ensure its success.

So, although there was actually only a ten-year gap between their ages, it was with pride and awe that Fats Waller tagged along that night with James P. and his wife Lil, who was appearing at Leroy's as a dancer. As they pulled up outside the place, she straightened up Fats' clothes a little and then took him inside. James P. introduced him to the cast and the rest of the musicians, who made him welcome. He was given a chair by the piano and at once just settled down to listen. Every now and then James would lean over and say, 'Now get this, Fats,' as he ran off an intricate phrase during a solo. Later on that evening, as a blues singer was being introduced, he turned to Fats with, 'Now, here's where *her* turn comes. When playing for singers, just you stay in the background. She'll let you know when to come on.' True to his word, James P.'s piano accompaniment never interfered with the singer, and only when she paused did he fill in the break with a few choice blues chords. He then receded into the background again for the singer to take up the melody once more. This was new stuff to Fats, who hadn't even heard the blues, let alone played them. He thought of that organ at the Lincoln where he'd be playing tomorrow, and resolved from then on that the audience would hear something very different. The evening finally came to an end, and Fats, tired and happy, made his way back to his new home.

The next afternoon at the Lincoln, as the movie started, new sounds began to issue from the organ. Some of the patrons started whispering, and Mrs Downes looked hard at the pit to see if someone else had taken over from Fats. Some of the music was, to say the least, dissonant, but Fats got things swinging more easily and the music flowed more smoothly. Mrs Downes relaxed and sighed – and returned to her office.

Through the days and weeks which followed, the gradual transition began to evolve. Fats was learning fast. James P. and Lil got him a pair of long pants, which he wore whenever he visited Leroy's, but James P. always sent him home after a few hours, for Lil thought it wasn't good for a young boy to be out late. James himself would finish up at the club and then on to a tour of parlour socials until the morning. Usually accompanied by sundry other pianists including Willie 'The Lion' Smith and his friend Russell, they wouldn't arrive home until after daybreak. After a while James P., noticing the great progress Fats had made, decided that it was time for him to see a little more of what was going on in Harlem. He had been pressed by Fats for some time to take him out to a parlour social and he finally consented. He thought it was time that Fats was introduced to some of the other pianists about town – and there were plenty to meet!

From the very early days in New York, the Negro race had boasted a plentiful supply of piano players. Before the war particularly, there had come into prominence a group of now almost legendary characters, roughly equivalent to the 'professors' of the South. They were the rage of the town and their particular stamping-grounds were the parlour socials which have been identified in the main with Harlem, although undoubtedly there were counterparts in most of the large cities where there was a substantial Negro population. The parlour social probably harks back to the original church social where, in the church basement or annexe, festive meetings were held with good food and games. The proceeds of these functions often provided the pastor with a sizeable bonus to his usually meagre stipend. The paying-party principle was eventually carried over to private houses and apartments of hard-pressed families, often financially under the thumb of greedy landlords. In the early days high rents were charged to discourage coloured families from settling in Harlem. Later on, a reluctance to lower the high rents proved too much for many average Harlem families. Thus one of the ways of avoiding eviction was to double and triple up. Houses became crammed, four or five people in a single bedroom being the rule rather than the exception, and even worse crowding was quite common.

Another and popular way to meet expenses was the parlour social, or, as it later became familiarly known, the 'rent-party'. Sometimes it was alluded to as a 'Saturday night funk-shun' but, by whatever name it was known in the early days, it amounted to the same thing.

A family would decide to throw open the house for a night and would invite one and all, but usually by invitation only, so as to keep numbers to a practical limit. The admission charged at the door, usually a dime, covered the music, dancing and entertainment, which was usually contributed to by the guests themselves. The kitchen would be converted into a snack bar where one could gets pigs' feet, chitlin's or fried chicken at a reasonable price. Drinks ranged from beer to whisky and gin, and, needless to say, the word 'prohibition' was unknown. Prices were fairly stable – whiskey at a dollar for a half-pint and a gallon of bathtub gin for a finn. In the parlour the main festivities took place, and the centre of attraction was the inevitable piano. A person who didn't have a piano or couldn't borrow one from somewhere in the building could never throw a party. So from these rent-parties grew the Harlem 'professors'. Almost a race unto themselves, they would battle with one another at the keyboard all night and on into the daylight hours. It was as if they lived entirely for the event, and so indeed some of them did.

These were the professional party pianists whose style, gaudy and exhibitionist, set the pattern for a whole school of piano playing that persists even to this day. Rags, stomps, blues, even *risqué* songs were featured at these performances, and a real party pianist would think nothing of playing for seven hours at a stretch with only a short pause between numbers. They were usually relieved at intervals by a lesser pianist who made up in novel effects what he lacked in stamina and virtuosity. It was rare for any number played to be completed in the usual four or five choruses; anything from sixteen to twenty would be the usual length for a tune at a rent-party. When two of these piano giants confronted one another, it was nothing for upwards of thirty choruses to be played before the rival would push in on the piano stool and take his turn at laying it on them. This method of entertainment, with its demand for the constant improvising of new variations and finding of new tunes, was the reason for the emergence of so many superlative pianists in the Eastern States; in contrast to the relative dearth of piano players in the South, where instruments more suitable for playing parades, funerals and street dances made greater headway.

Naturally, with the tremendous competition in those days, a man had to keep bang up to snuff. He was pretty well forced to meet all comers, lest he be accused of faint-heartedness, and, in addition, he had to master a repertoire which would make an impression on the crowd and force the best from his rivals. Thus, in order to continually present new material, a player had not only to compose his own show pieces but also work out his own arrangements of them. The first thing he did when he met a rival pianist would be to play his latest composition and 'throw it on him' to impress him. The other, if he could, would come right back with his own set.

James P. Johnson was perhaps the most prolific of these. His *Carolina Shout* was composed in 1914 in Jim Allen's Cabaret in the San Juan Hill section. It was a show piece and his great stand-by at parties for years, and it was lifted and borrowed by countless others in their time. But although others played this piece, the buoyant stride which James P. applied to its performance and his great technique made him absolutely invincible. Moreover, he made a point of having a 'cutter' in every key – sharps and flats notwithstanding.

Luckey Roberts, Johnson's forerunner as king of the Harlem pianists, also had his own specialities, notable amongst which were *Spanish Venus* and *Pork And Beans*. Roberts' trade-mark was a left hand of dazzling speed and a unique method of playing tremolo in the treble, repeatedly and with phenomenal rapidity. It was easy to see how he cut his rivals and rated the plaudits of all who heard him.

Strangely enough, in the early days of the rent-party, the blues were but rarely heard. Apparently they slowed the pace of the show too much, and even with the arrival on the musical scene of the female blues singer, the only concession was a fast pseudo-blues form, usually made up of endless suggestive verses. Specializing in these *risqué* vocals was a singer named Corky Williams, a wiry light-weight who pioneered the song-and-piano combination at the parties and who continued his trade until his death in 1950. One of the most frequently heard songs in the rent-party repertoire was *The Boy In The Boat*, a broadly sexual song with many verses composed over the years by many singers. It was to have an important place in the career of Tom Waller, who came to use its melody as a speciality.

The names of some of these knights of the keyboard were as

picturesque as their clothing. For some, their very names suggest their own place in the jealously guarded hierarchy – Jack the Bear, Willie 'The Lion', Lippy, Seminole, Jersey, the Beetle, and One Leg Shadow.

Reigning around Harlem in the early days when James P. Johnson was just coming up were such stalwarts as Charley Cherry, Sam Gordon, Willie Gant, and Dickie Robinson. Eubie Blake and Luckey Roberts were contemporaries: Blake deserted the field for the more lucrative one of musical comedy and vaudeville, and later composed such unforgettable hits as *I'm Just Wild About Harry* and the musical score of the historic trail-blazing show 'Shuffle Along'.

These in turn were joined by up-and-coming youngsters: James P. Johnson, who assumed the mantle from Roberts; Willie 'The Lion' Smith, who would terrorize a timid young pianist by putting the eye on him, and who was celebrated for his exploits in France during the Great War; Stephen Henderson, known as the Beetle; and Donald Lambert, who remained until his recent death a tough man to beat on the piano. Donald was one of James P.'s favourites, and could cut anybody on a good night. Also in this select circle were the aforementioned Russell Brooks, no mean performer himself, and Lippy, whose pianistic ability was less celebrated than his talkativeness. Several others, lost in memory now save for an occasional nostalgic reference when pianists get together, rounded out their numbers and inhabited the night of Harlem, gravitating from party to party wearing ivory from the keys of every piano from 125th Street up to 149th Street and beyond.

Though most major rent-parties were held on Saturday night, there were some taking place every night of the week; so it was possible for the more prominent professors to work seven days a week if they chose. Some of them did. As the parties gained favour, reservations became more and more necessary, and soon tickets were for sale in advance on the streets. They were sold either by the promoters or certain of their selected friends, and cost anything from twenty-five cents to a dollar each. Always listed on the back of the ticket were the date and place of the function, and a list of the stars who would be performing – 'James P. Johnson and Willie

"The Lion" will be there', or 'Come and see the Beetle and Jersey battle it out', and other similar captions.

But, as with so many successful innovations, commercialization soon followed. In next to no time an enterprising group of men started up a series of similar parties, but as added attractions introduced gambling and a few well-endowed and willing women in the back rooms. These new and, to some, irresistible attractions ensured success, and the better-known pianists were certain to make a good-time party of this sort at least once in a night's tour. One of the more prominent of these party-promoters was a man named Dad Brooks (no relation to Russell) who, with his partner Kid Morris and a gentleman of the name of Broadway Jones, operated the Greenleaf Social Club. They raised the price – worked up the calibre of their parties from the ten-cent to the twenty-five-cent class. Their good-time houses were always well stocked with queens, and a really good piano was provided. The result was that all the best pianists flocked to them, and some of the more memorable battles took place at Brooks' on 101 West 135th Street, over Leroy's cabaret.

So, although the rent largely went out of the rent-party, actual rent-raising affairs continued into the Thirties and are even occasionally put on today. Eventually, of course, as was inevitable, racketeers, seeing a profit in this party business, ran them as a cover for exploiting prostitution and dope-peddling.

But the rent-parties were for Fats nights of magic. Introduced by his mentor, James P. Johnson, to the other pianists who showed up from time to time, he would sit alongside James and nearly burst with pride every time his idol carved the opposition with his own version of the *Shout*. Fats ached to sit in Johnson's seat, but knew that he had a long, long way to go before that could happen. He looked at his thick fingers, and wished they were longer, but at least he could now stretch his fingers across ten white notes – a tenth, the basis of a lot of James' style of playing.

On their way home one night, James said, 'How'd you like to see Willie "The Lion"? He's playing at Leroy's tonight.'

5

Apart from his friend James P. Johnson, there was no one that Fats wanted to meet more than Willie 'The Lion' Smith. Fearsome in reputation as the beast whose name he bore, Willie was, and still is, one of those rare persons who can talk about himself, his art, and his achievements, and who also has the ability to back up his statements with a more than adequate performance. Unique among jazz pianists, 'The Lion' has always been noted for his immediately identifiable and unorthodox approach to the piano. His jazz is delicate, at times almost dainty, but when the occasion arises, his attack can be as vigorous and swingy as anybody's.

A solidly built man, of good height, 'The Lion' always made a deep visual as well as aural impression on his listeners, and he was consequently in great demand at all the Harlem clubs. This fierce independence of his, however, had led him to walk off jobs at the slightest provocation, and more than a few times he left behind him a grateful pianist who had taken on a job that Willie had left in a huff.

The general picture that he presented to the public and to the visiting musician, however, was challenging. A favourite habit, a trade-mark of his in fact, was his way of immediately putting everyone he met on their mettle from the very first word – and throughout the years this had gained him the reputation amongst employers of being a hard man to deal with. The man who couldn't face up to the challenge of 'The Lion' would squirm uncomfortably and often left feeling himself vaguely defeated in some invisible combat. But to all those who proved themselves by word or deed, he was a loyal and lifelong friend.

Born William Bertholoff of a Mohawk Indian mother, Willie early in life moved with his family from Goshen, New York, to Newark, New Jersey. Here the youngster lived in a neighbourhood predominantly Jewish. To keep him out of trouble Willie was sent along to some nearby Yiddish classes, and he thus soon gained a knowledge of the tongue, which he speaks fluently to this day. At an early age he was taught to play the organ, but soon graduated to the piano. Jazz was at that time sweeping up so many young musicians in its wake, and 'The Lion' soon became very active in the parlour-social Harlem parties. In 1917 he volunteered for army service, and in France served with the 350th Field Artillery. He earned his nickname whilst up in the front line, where for many weeks he was part of a team firing a French 75 mm. cannon. He had volunteered for this dangerous mission, and so justly deserved his leonine nickname. He later attended Howard University, and took a post-graduate study in Newark.

From his earliest days in Greenwich Village, Willie lived the life of a young sport. He realized the appeal and impressiveness of fastidious clothes, and, along with others of his set, bought his suits from Braunburgers. A $40 suit from this establishment would invariably fetch $20 in pawn whilst a $150.00 overcoat from Wilkovitch, an uptown tailor, could likewise be pawned for half its original cost. His fifty-dollar hats were another of his trade-marks and he claimed to be the first pianist to affect a derby at the keyboard. 'The Lion' was a good friend and companion of James P.'s, and at this time he was taking over the job of resident pianist at Leroy's whilst James P. went off on a short trip with a touring vaudeville show. Leroy's was a club run by Leroy Wilkins, whose brother Barron was the better-known operator of Barron's, a white trade night-spot in Harlem which had moved there from downtown. James P. often played there and Lil performed there in many a floor show – in fact, she was there now. The show starred Mamie Smith and Her Jazz Hounds with Willie Smith on piano; Tommy Benford on drums; Leroy Parker, violin; Dope Andrews on trombone; Ernest Elliott, clarinet; and Bubber Miley or Addington Major on cornet.

Entering Leroy's, James P. made straight for the grandstand. The floor manager regarded the shabby youth at Johnson's heels with obvious distaste but Fats looked straight ahead at the figure at the keyboard. Willie sat in his customary, distinctive attitude. Leaning far back on the piano stool, his legs crossed and his derby tilted rakishly over his forehead, he blew out clouds of smoke from a long black cigar. As Fats drew nearer, he could hear the man grunting – it was 'The Lion' roaring.

'Hello, Lion,' said James, easing himself on to the bandstand.

Chewing on his cigar, Willie greeted his friend warmly. His hands moved around the piano like lightning as he started a frenzied chorus of the number he had been playing. Willie looked out of the corner of his eye and James P., his big face creased in a smile, nodded approvingly. The number finished, 'The Lion', beaded with perspiration, took a large handkerchief out of his pocket and used it ceremoniously and thoroughly. Then he picked up his glass from its resting place on the piano and finished off his drink in a gulp.

'Good brandy,' he said, smacking his lips. 'Nothing better! Those French really have got the right idea.' His speech, like his clothes, was precise and clean cut.

'Who the hell's this?' he asked, seeing Fats for the first time.

'Oh, this is Fats Waller,' said James. 'I'm just takin' him around town a little. Like to help him along?'

Willie scrutinized the baggy pants and the old patched shabby shirt. 'You can't bring a kid looking like that in here. Go and get his pants pressed and throw away that shirt. This is a high-class joint!'

'Take it easy, Lion,' said James P. 'This kid's got more on the ball than you think. You let him play something. He knows some of my numbers good.' But 'The Lion' merely turned his back on them, muttering, 'Don't you bother me none.'

'As you say, Lion,' said James. He moved to a nearby chair, winked at Fats and motioned him towards the piano player. Fats nodded dubiously. Another set came to an end and 'The Lion' got up from the piano. He excused himself and went over to join some friends at a table near the wall.

'Now's your chance,' Johnson said. 'Go ahead, get in there an' play.'

With some trepidation Fats looked at 'The Lion' but he was still talking and was facing the other way. The piano was just ahead and Fats sat down on the stool. His chubby hands went out over the keys and he went softly into the first theme of a classic rag which James P. had taught him. James P. looked over at 'The Lion', who didn't indicate that he heard anything unusual. Fats' playing was stronger now and if once or twice a passage was slightly slurred, the rhythm never wavered. Fats was sweating but he carried on and on the last chorus he played like a demon. When he finished he turned to James P. who, still looking at 'The Lion', said, 'Nice goin', boy, you really got it that time.'

Willie left his friends and walked back towards the stand. At first he didn't say anything but finally it came. 'That was pretty good, kid,' as he glanced at Fats. Fats' heart leapt and he stumbled out a word of thanks.

'You better look out, Lion,' said Johnson as he got up. 'Some day I'm gonna make this kid play better than you. Let's go, Fats.'

'Why'd ya say that to him, James?' asked Fats as they reached the street.

'Oh, The Lion would like that, Fats. He's a funny guy in many ways but he liked what he heard – I know! You keep at it, you'll play as good as him if not better.'

*   *   *

Ever since his mother's death Fats had felt alone. The Brooks family, wonderful as their hospitality was, weren't really his own folk. Some day, he knew, he was going to have to break away and go out on his own. There were nights when, lying awake on the davenport bed, he thought of his father. Now a strange, brooding man, he still in a manner kept the old Waller home going. As Fats' thoughts wandered, he suddenly remembered the girl from Brook Avenue, Edith Hatchett. She was a sweet kid – it was time he looked her up again. Do it tomorrow, he thought, as he dropped off to sleep. A few weeks later Fats and Edith stood before the Justice of the Peace in city hall and a marriage was made. Fats and his bride went immediately to live with Edith's folks on Brook Avenue.

It was a surprised James P. Johnson who congratulated Fats some nights later. 'Don't suppose we'll be seeing you on the town so much now, Fats?' he queried.

Fats shook his head. 'Don't let it worry you, I'll be around.'

It was not long after the wedding that a vaudeville show left the Lincoln for a tour of the nearby New England theatres and included as accompanist for an act called 'Liza and her Shufflin' Six'

47

was Fats Waller. After some weeks the show reached Boston. Fats made his way to the theatrical boarding house, and after a clean up, prepared to go on the town. As he descended the stairs he looked down to the hall and there saw a welcome face. None other than Bill Basie, a pianist from Red Bank, New Jersey, whom Fats had met a few times when going the rounds with James P. Johnson.

Basie pumped his hand. 'I saw you guys were in town – you playing Keith's Theatre?'

'Yeah, packin' 'em in too,' Fats replied. 'What you doin' up here?'

'Mutual Burlesque,' said Basie, ruefully. 'You know how much jive comes out of there.'

Fats winced. 'Yeah, man, I know. How about comin' backstage this afternoon? There's a solid piano and I got a brand new tune. Wrote it myself.'

Later that afternoon they wrapped themselves around a pint of gin, whilst Fats played his new number for Basie.

'That's sharp, man, real sharp,' said Basie as Fats finished.

'Now you listen to the words,' said Fats. His raspy voice began to chant a familiar verse, bawdy and crude.

Basie's eyes lit up. 'That's the words for *The Boy In The Boat*,' he said, grinning.

'Sure it is,' said Fats. 'I made a tune for it. Wanna get it published but those words just won't do. I think I'll call it *Boston Blues* and leave it as a plain instrumental. What you think?'

'It's sure a good tune,' said Basie. 'Would sound good on that old organ at the Lincoln. When you get time, Fats, I'd like a lesson on that organ.'

'Lessons from me?' Fats started to laugh. 'Okay,' he said, 'we'll be back in two weeks. See you.'

Back in New York again, Fats lost no time in playing his new tune to James P. Johnson. The older man listened carefully, said he liked it very much and that he was proud of Fats. He really did like it, inasmuch as it was unmistakably inspired by the second theme of his own composition *Fascination*. This was the tune which perhaps influenced and inspired Fats Waller more than James P.'s better-known *Carolina Shout*. It served as a springboard for several of the young pianist's compositions, his first published composition, *Wildcat Blues*, being its first cousin and itself a forecast of *Handful Of Keys*, a number to become famous later.

Now that she had him home again it wasn't long before his wife, Edith, began to wonder if she hadn't got a tiger by the tail. She had never had much contact with show business and she was dismayed at the fantastic hours her husband kept. Valiantly attempting to adjust her ways to the demands of his profession, she found herself awakening to his homecoming in the early hours, and then sitting with him and his friends in the kitchen as they ate breakfast, yarned and finished up the gin. By the time she was properly awake, her husband was off to bed, to sleep until past noon. At two o'clock he was up again and on his way to the Lincoln. His day off would be spent at the piano with one or another of his friends, either composing new numbers or trying to fit music to the words of a lyric writer. Soon she had news for him – she was going to have a baby.

Fats took this announcement with deep appreciation of its seriousness. He felt a sudden strong pride and lost no time in spreading the word around. Fats Waller was to be a father.

In the meantime, Bill Basie, whom Fats had run across in Boston, had taken him at his word and had shown up at the Lincoln for his lessons. He would come in from backstage and sneak through the pit to a spot directly beneath Fats' console. With his hands, he manipulated the bass notes, while Fats tapped out the rhythm with his feet and carried on the treble as usual with his hands. Soon Fats, feeling the urge for a nip, slipped out by the side door to a nearby club, leaving Basie alone at the organ.

Basie, always a shy man and lacking confidence in his abilities, would wait until he was sure that Fats was well out of the theatre before he began to play. One night, when Fats had gone and the theatre was in darkness, Basie stayed on alone. He played a few times for his own amusement, and was just lighting a cigarette when he spotted a pair of large shoes protruding from under the curtain. It was Fats, listening quietly. He had never left; curious as to how Bill Basie was progressing, he had stayed quietly in the room. When he told Basie what he thought of his playing, the Kid from Red Bank wasn't shy any more – he'd made it.

Among the characters around town in those days was a musician known as Lippy, whose real name was Raymond Boyette. He acted as an agent for the rent-party pianists. At one time he had been a fair player himself, but he had been on the 'jive' so long he was no longer any good at the keyboard, and contented himself with setting up shindigs and getting jobs for the boys. James P. naturally got his share of these, but at that time there was enough work to keep everybody busy.

One night James P. and Fats were crossing Seventh Avenue, when they ran into Lippy. 'Hey, Lippy there, how about getting my boy here a job at a funk-shun some of these nights?' James raised his eyebrows.

The handsome Lippy turned his eyes on Fats. 'Well now, how does he do?'

'You mean you ain't heard Fats Waller play? Man, he's gonna kill 'em one of these days!'

Lippy said, 'Okay, okay, if you say so. I'll see what I can do.'

James P. gave Fats a nudge in the ribs. 'Now you just wait. I'll see you get on one of these shindigs soon, even if I have to sell you myself.'

'That's good, James, I could use the money. Baby comin', you know.'

Some nights later, James P. called up Fats. 'Well kid, you've got a job. Tomorrow night,' he told him.

'Where's it at?' asked Fats.

'At the Lenox Apartments, on 141st – you, Corky and Russell.'

'Aren't you gonna be there?'

'No, I'm playin' a party uptown – a special one. Might see you later if it breaks up early.'

'How much'll I get?' Fats was eager.

'Mmm . . . maybe three bucks, if they likes you. Otherwise, you get paid off in uppercuts.'

'How's that?'

'That's nothin', son. Just nothin'. But you play it solid, and you'll come out okay.'

Later that evening, after he had finished at the Lincoln, Fats and Johnson were doing the rounds. James nodded here and there to a dozen well-wishers, and as they turned into 134th Street, a man on the corner called, 'Hiya, Fats.'

'Hello,' Fats said in reply; and then to his friend, as soon as they were out of earshot, 'Who's that? I don't know him.'

'Well, he knows you.'

'Who was he?'

'He's one of the guys who's selling tickets for the socials. More'n likely your name's on one of them tickets.'

'Yeah?' Fats was incredulous. 'Excuse me,' he said, and walked back the way they had come.

A few seconds later, he again caught up with James P. 'Gee, you were right, man. That guy did have my name on a card.'

'Well, what's so great about that, Fats? They got your name on the outside of the Lincoln, and you don't pay it no mind.'

'This is different. I don't know . . . it's just different.'

At about eleven o'clock the next night Russell Brooks, Lippy, Corky Williams, and Fats mounted the staircase of the Lenox Apartments.

'Now take it easy, Fats,' Russell was saying. 'Nobody ever made a place rock by tryin' too hard. Just you go easy for a while.'

At the third floor they all stopped and Lippy knocked on the door opposite. His summons brought a quick response, and they all entered. It was a biggish room – the carpet had been rolled back and the chairs placed against the wall to leave space for dancing.

Lippy shouted hello to all the people present and then announced:

'Right, you cats! We got a new man here tonight who is goin' to play your ears off! This is Fats Waller, the baby who plays that mess of organ over at the Lincoln.'

A chorus of hello's followed his words, and a man and a woman came over and said, 'Good to see you, Fats! We're giving this party. Come on over and have a drink before things start.'

Not needing a second invitation, Fats made a bee-line for the bar. Corky by this time was doing the first spell at the piano and the party was on.

'You mind if I go next?' Russell came over to Fats. 'I'm goin' to spell Corky awhile. I gotta work the kinks out of my fingers. I ain't played in a week.'

At a nod from Fats he edged on to the piano bench, and took over from the willing Corky. The strains of a familiar rag filled the room, and Fats grinned. He remembered where he had first heard that number. In that tent. It seemed years ago; before he had met James P., and he felt he had *always* known Johnson! Was it possible it was only eight or nine months ago?

'How ya doin', Fats?' Lippy's voice broke the spell.

'Oh – okay, Lippy. I'm ready to play when you says so.'

'Well, boy, just push that Brooksey off that chair. I wanna hear you, man.'

Fats walked over to the piano. Russell was on a fast last chorus, but on the final bar he felt the pressure he knew so well come in on his left. Without looking up, he said, 'Okay, Fats, it's all yours. Now you remember what I said.'

'Yeah, I got it, baby.' Fats vamped into the same key Russell had been using.

Russell looked round, 'Where'd you get that F sharp?' he shouted.

'Where d'ya think?' Fats retorted, arching his eyebrows.

Russell shook his head and said to Corky, 'Say, that's funny, a few weeks ago he was still messin' around in G.'

'Looks like the kid's catchin' up with you,' replied Corky.

The vamp disappeared and Fats eased into his *Boston Blues*. The metre of the tune immediately caught on and behind him he could hear someone singing *The Boy In The Boat*. Lippy sat in the corner, watching and nodding between sips. The crowded room began to swim a little before his eyes and he took another drink to clear his senses. 'That's my boy, Fats!' he crowed. 'What a left hand!'

Spurred on, Fats switched into a fast stomp, his left hand playing a rapid series of tenths. Feet began to beat and someone started clapping on the off-beat. 'Rock it, Fats!' Fats bounced rhythmically on the piano stool with his face turned up to the ceiling. His left foot slapped the floor, heel and toe alternately, whilst his fingers flew over the keyboard. Sweat rolled down his face but he played on, mopping his brow with his handkerchief and inventing things as he went along. He knew it was time he stopped, but the crowd kept him at it, pushing into reaches of improvisation he didn't know he could command.

Russell and Corky were comparing notes. 'Maybe I'd better take some lessons from James P. myself,' said Russell, shaking his head.

'Don't you worry, kid,' observed Corky sagely. 'Fats is a comer all right, but he don't know 'em all yet.'

It was the custom in those days for all the recognized pianists to be given a nickname. If you hadn't one, you weren't rated one of the gang. Corky Williams, owing to his slight frame, was known as 'Phantom'; Luckey Roberts' squat build had given rise to 'Gorilla'; and the diminutive Donald Lambert was known as 'Muffin' almost from the day he first stepped off the subway in Harlem from Newark. The man who dealt out most of the nicknames was none other than Willie 'The Lion' Smith, and he it was who, on spying Fats in his baggy pants and none too clean shirt, dubbed him 'Filthy'. At first Fats wasn't too pleased with his nickname, but when it caught on amongst the boys, he accepted it with a grin, knowing that it brought with it a sense of 'belonging'.

James P., not to be outdone by 'The Lion', usually called Fats 'Big Filthy' and in return Fats often referred to his friend as 'Jackanapes'.

These names, fitting and picturesque though they might be, were normally used only within the select circle and were not publicly billed to any extent.

Now that Fats was well and truly launched on his career, it naturally followed that he would meet up with some of the more noteworthy luminaries of the period. By 1920 he had met, and knew well, some of the leading lights of Tin Pan Alley. Irving Berlin, Paul Whiteman and George Gershwin – especially the last – were uptown incessantly, making the rounds and drinking in all there was to be seen and heard.

Gershwin wrote down the jazz forms that came at him from the horns, drums and pianos, penetrating even the lowest of the low-down clubs. He invaded the rent-parties and socials and was often to be seen sitting on the floor, agape at the dazzling virtuosity and limitless improvisation that clamoured around him.

Harlem remained for a decade or so a fount of inspiration for the great and the not-so-great songwriters. The careers of such men as Harold Arlen, Vernon Duke, and Jimmy McHugh, to name some of the more prominent, were undoubtedly given great impetus by their frequent haunting of the uptown jazz bistros.

But it was to be expected that eventually the Negro himself

would cash in on his own gifts, in addition to providing the basis of lucrative returns for the downtown writers. One of the early professors who migrated from New Orleans was Clarence Williams. He arrived in Chicago where he set up as a song-writer and publisher of race songs. Located variously at State Street during the World War, Clarence achieved early prominence through his music store and his compositions which rank him among the greatest blues writers of all time. Such hits as *Gulf Coast Blues, Baby, Won't You Please Come Home?* (written with Charles Warfield), *Pretty Doll, I Ain't Gonna Give Nobody None Of This Jelly-Roll,* and *Royal Garden Blues* (the last two in collaboration with Spencer Williams) emanated from the pen of this gifted composer.

Among his other accomplishments, Clarence was a vaudeville performer of some note. He sang and played the piano across the South and East, sometimes with the W. C. Handy shows, and later in New York at the Lincoln Theatre. Here he was deeply impressed by the youthful organist and he often stopped off to talk with him for hours on end. The enthusiastic following that came to the theatre came mainly to see Fats Waller – a fact which left its mark on Williams. When later he returned to Chicago, he carried with him the sharp realization that Fats Waller was a young fellow to watch. Clarence Williams was at heart a promoter. He was also an extremely enterprising man who, sensing the opportunities that lay in the big city, always managed to be a jump ahead of the flow of jazz as it spread northward and eastward. New York was to be his next permanent stop.

In the meantime, Willie Smith had decided that he had had enough of Leroy's and so accordingly he walked out one night. Later he settled at the Capitol Cabaret, 140th Street and Lenox Avenue, but his departure left a hole at Leroy's. James P. was at once sought out by Harry Pyle.

'Sorry, man,' said James P., 'but I'm going out on the road soon. But I got a man for you – just you leave everything to me.'

'Don't jive me now, Jimmy. I gotta have a man fast,' said Harry as he left.

Up on Brook Avenue, Fats was rousted out of bed by a banging on the door. It was 'Jackanapes' Johnson. 'C'mon, Fatness,' he said, 'you get your clothes on, man, you got another job.'

Dressing hurriedly, Fats said, 'I'm due at the Lincoln today. What's up?'

James P. was brief: 'You want to work at Leroy's?'

Fats was even briefer: 'Sure, man!'

On their way down to Harlem, James P. explained the set-up to Fats. 'Now you never did no accompanying before, but Lil and I are gonna show you how this afternoon. Never you mind the Lincoln – call up and say you're sick or somep'n'.'

All that afternoon at the Johnson apartment, the piano played and Lil danced. At first, Jimmy played for her, then he let Fats take over. Fats started well until he got to watching her feet. He thought he was running ahead of her and quickly slowed the tempo. 'No – no – no,' Jimmy hollered above the music, 'keep that beat going – never mind Lil.' Lil danced on and Fats began to get the knack of it. Once the dance routine was mastered, Lil began to sing. Fats felt a little more at home accompanying her singing, and by the time that dinner-time rolled round, things were going smoothly. Lil was enthusiastic. 'He'll do fine,' she said to her husband.

'There's one more thing I gotta do, Fatness,' remarked James P. over dinner. 'I wanna take you over to see the people at QRS. They know I'm goin' out on the road and somebody's goin' to be needed over there to take my place. I thought you might want it. We'll go over before I leave.'

Harry Pyle was well satisfied, Leroy Wilkins was satisfied, and so were the customers. On his first night out, 'The Lion' slipped in by the back door of the club to see how 'Filthy' was making out. As he stood there listening, he saw James P. coming over. He straightened up and made ready.

'Now, how about *that*?' said James P., nodding towards the bandstand.

'Pretty good, James, but why do you keep pushing that boy along? Some of these days you're gonna be sorry you showed him so much. Look at him now – almost sounds as if you were up there noodlin' around yourself.'

'Well, I'll tell you, Lion. There's something about that kid that appeals to me. He just lives this stuff, and when he looks at me with those big eyes of his, I just *have* to show him something else.'

'Well, he's a sweet guy at that, I guess,' answered Willie, 'an' you know, I been listening – not all those things he does come from you either.'

'I thought you'd see that,' said James P.

'Russell told me when Fats played his first social a couple of weeks back, he turned the house inside out the first time he sat down. Russell said he played stuff that nobody ever heard before. But he don't play like that when I'm around.' 'The Lion' set his derby a little farther down on his forehead, flicked his cigar into a nearby cuspidor and walked to the door.

Watching him go, James P. pondered on what he'd said. He went back and sat at his table, ruminating a little as he looked at Fats. Maybe it's just as well I'm going away, he thought. Let the kid alone, he's got what it takes, he'll make out; if not . . . must get him over to QRS to do some piano rolls. That's what'll help a lot – get him known around the country.

* * *

The piano roll business was flourishing, and James P. was riding high on the crest of the boom, having cut rolls for the Aeolian, Ampice and QRS companies. Records hadn't anything to offer the coloured musicians yet, and the best way a pianist could make his talents known was through the older medium. Nearly all well-to-do families owned a player-piano, so a pianist making a vaudeville tour had a certain ready-made audience. The QRS ('Quality Real Service') Company, founded as an auxiliary to the Melville Clark Piano Company of De Kalb, Illinois, before the turn of the century, was a pioneering leader in the field. Its roster of artists included Pete Wendling, Zez Confrey, J. Russell Robinson, and Max Kortlander who now has control of the company. Among the race artists whom it recorded were Luckey Roberts and James P. Johnson. J. Lawrence Cook, who today remains the principal performing artist of the company, is still turning out the hits of the day, and was an original member of the company's golden years. He it was who performed double duty, taking down the pianists' fingering on his mechanical recording attachment and converting it to the familiar perforated roll through various stages of manual processing. So expert was Cook's knowledge of piano players' style and technique that he could make a remarkably faithful interpretation of any of the major artists by himself, aided by his recording piano, mallet and punch.

True to his promise, James P., before he left, took Fats over to East 135th and Walnut and introduced him to Kortlander, Wendling and Cook – the latter was already a Waller fan. He had heard Fats many times at the Lincoln and had been very impressed by the young organist's playing during the movie shows, and by the appropriateness of his selections. Apparently he had never visited the Lincoln on a Saturday afternoon, when the young audience expected and duly received a liberal helping of jazz from the pipes of the little organ. But he was receptive to Fats' music, and the young Waller was accepted – to be called later at some opportune time.

In those days piano rolls paid off well financially. James P. collected fifty dollars a roll. He would knock off at least one in an afternoon session and could count on at least a couple of dates a month.

The procedure in making a roll was as follows. The date would be set, and the performer would be permitted to record either one of his own compositions or a song which was being plugged currently by a music publisher. In the latter case, the artist would be paid from both ends but in the former, of course, he would gain more prestige. A regular Melville piano was used, with special attachments.

When Fats was called to cut a roll he would always show up early and practise for a couple of hours previous to the actual performance. At the beginning of a session the paper roll, referred to as the master, was threaded into the mechanism and moved along to the speed corresponding to the desired tempo of the selection. Steel fingers, actuated by compressed air, were set in motion as the pianist's fingers depressed the keys, and made carbon impressions on the master roll. These impressions were later cut out by punch manually, and the roll was then played on a conventional player-piano. Finally any errors were picked up and erased by covering the punched hole. In addition, the sustaining of notes over several beats was effected by extending a row of holes, since the recording system did not allow for this.

Fats' first piano roll was *Got To Cool My Doggies Now*, written by Clarence Williams and Schafer Thompson. Over the next few years Fats' rolls earned him considerable fame and served to introduce him to a wider public. His rolls were played and heard by such rising young musicians as Duke Ellington, Cliff Jackson and Claude Hopkins, who were all coming on the scene at that time. Out in St Louis, a young musician named Eugene Sedric played the family piano rolls which his father had brought home, and was impressed by the rhythm on those marked 'Played by Fats Waller'. He hoped to meet the pianist some day – as indeed he did later at rent-parties and other functions. Fats took to carrying his latest roll proudly under his arm and playing it whenever possible.

One day Thomas Waller awoke to find he had two shadows: one his natural one, the thick shape that danced on the pavement as his bulky form walked the streets, and the other one, smaller, lively, and talkative. It had a name – Bud Allen. This chipper fellow had taken a liking to Fats and was on his heels incessantly, following him around town, listening to his music, talking him up to anyone who would listen, and generally haunting the spots where Fats might be found. Bud had a little music store on 135th Street near Lenox Avenue and was well-acquainted with the downtown publishers of the middle Twenties, and thus made himself very useful to the musicians he represented. But his first love was Fats' piano; and no matter where the big fellow was playing, you could look around and see Bud Allen somewhere near. Known to all the pianists, Bud had more or less attached himself to the Waller–Johnson–Smith triumvirate, and if anyone asked him who was his favourite, he would unhesitatingly proclaim that no one could touch Fats Waller. Then he liked James P. Johnson, and in the third spot, Willie 'The Lion' Smith. This order never varied, and Bud was faithful till death ended the association. But this constant attendance grew wearisome; and young Fats, who was following James P. around town, found that the same kind of treatment applied to himself didn't sit too well and had gone past the flattering stage. Without making it too apparent, he made constant efforts to duck Bud, who was not always avoided easily.

James P. finally left town and went out on the road with

'Plantation Boys', a touring company that was to take him over the country and eventually to Europe.

For a time, Fats doubled at the Lincoln and Leroy's, and when the job at the nightspot folded up, he kept on at the theatre and continued the rounds with the ever-present Brooksy, Lippy, and Willie 'The Lion', who was getting to be more friendly with Fats as time went on. Parties went on nearly every night and Fats attended as many as he could – he was crazy about them. It seemed to him that just when things got going, the night would be over, and another dawn would spoil the music-making. His heaviness acted as a cushion for an immense amount of drinking. Gin flowed down his eager throat like so much water, and the effect would be worked out in perspiration in a couple of hours, so that he seldom got really high. Men of slighter build were hard put to keep up with the robust Fats, and his reputation in the drinking field almost matched that of his piano playing.

Unlike James P., another avid rent-party enthusiast, Willie Smith was more on the choosy side. Where James would take on anything with keys and strings, and some without, 'The Lion' refused to play a poor piano, and if forced to play one by circumstances beyond his control, he would soon render it useless by either hitting the keys so sharply that a hammer would break, or by the even simpler expedient of pouring liquor between the keys. But when the instrument, the feminine company and the drinks were right, 'The Lion' could not be restrained, and his rumbustious-stride piano would take over the place until something he played would start Fats across the room to answer the challenge. And so the joints kept jumpin'.

Corky Williams had gone back for the summer to Asbury Park, New Jersey, where he and his mother ran the Clef Ice Cream Parlor. When Fats found himself looking for a little more money than the Lincoln offered, Russell supplied the solution. 'Go down to Asbury Park,' he said; 'Corky will take care of things.' Fats took the excursion boat from the Battery and arrived large as life at the seaside resort, right in the middle of the summer crowds. Corky, between stints behind the soda fountain, bade him warm welcome, and after asking how things were up in the city, arranged to put him up, and told him that there was a job waiting for him at a place called Scotty's Bar and Cabaret. That night on the way over, Corky explained the lay-out of the place, and what he might expect from a summer resort crowd. Half-way there, Fats stopped and clapped his hand to his forehead.

'Corky, I clean forgot to tell you, man, I'm a father!'

'Good, Fats! When'd it happen?'

'Just a while back. It's a boy. We named him Tom, Junior.'

Corky said, 'Wonder you could get away from home.'

'Oh, Edith's all right. She's stayin' with her folks up there. Besides I gotta keep workin', man.'

They walked along the street and turned a corner. A brightly-lit sign proclaimed that this was Scotty's, and below, in only slightly less bold letters, another sign read: 'Fats Waller – New York Piano Sensation'. Fats stood there looking at it and smiling. This was his biggest billing yet. 'How in the world did they know I was comin'?' he wanted to know.

'Listen, Filthy, when Russell Brooks says he's sending you down here and to get you a job, Corky Williams takes it from there.' Corky grabbed him by the shoulder and propelled him through the door.

After being introduced to the proprietor, Fats took a look round the hall. He frowned and turned to Corky and said, in guarded tones, 'This place don't look so hot – what's the big attraction? Don't anyone jump around here?'

'You mind your mouth, Fats, you're young yet, man! Else I'd take offence at that,' said Corky. 'Now just because you come from Harlem, don't you go gettin' any ideas that there ain't plenty of cats in little places like these. Why, Jersey is loaded with cats. An' they're good musicians, too. Look at Newark – The Lion, James P., Muffin – Basie from Red Bank; and there's Sonny Greer, and if you wanna see a better drummer, you're gonna have to travel a long way. He's from Long Branch. Those last two boys are over here all the time.'

'Basie come over here?' Fats began to brighten immediately.

'He sure does. We jam together nearly every night. Now you just settle down, boy, and enjoy life by the shore. Who knows, you might even get a little more sunburn!'

This brought Fats down, and he burst out laughing. Maybe

Asbury wasn't so far from Harlem after all, but all the same, he was going to miss those New York parties.

The weeks in Asbury were fun for the happy-go-lucky pianist, and true enough, Basie, Sonny Greer, and other musicians made regular rendezvous at the Clef Ice Cream Parlor. Corky was still out in front as far as piano technique was concerned, so Fats worked on some of the things that Corky threw at him, and came away a better pianist than before.

*   *   *

That fall, back in New York, Fats followed Willie 'The Lion' into the Capitol. It was a large club, run by Johnny Powell, and a definite step upward for him. He played piano in the band and was featured as soloist.

Fats' next job was with a burlesque outfit, which toured the Eastern circuit, and stopped off in Washington, where another nucleus of jazz thrived mightily, though not yet widely known. Its leaders were young bloods named Ellington, Snowden, Hopkins and Sonny Greer, who had now come in from the Jersey shore to tie in with the Washington gang. Already introduced via his brand-new piano rolls, Fats was made welcome and urged these ambitious musicians to get their hides up to New York where things were popping. 'I'm gonna get out of this mess as soon as we hit New York, and get me some more gold,' he swore, as they swapped drinks and stories. The burlesque show finished and Fats made quick time back to Harlem and the Lincoln, his dependable stand-by.

During his absence, however, the Lincoln had been sold. Mrs Downes had accepted a good offer and turned over the reins of the little theatre to Frank Schiffman who, with his partner Leo Brecher, was taking an increasingly active part in theatrical affairs in Harlem. Schiffman had previously taken over the Lafayette and planned to make a change-over, bringing the stage attractions which had for so long been identified with the 135th Street theatre over to Seventh Avenue and the Lafayette, which was now more the centre of community life. As the Negro population had crept ever westward, so had their business and entertainment centres, and Lenox Avenue was assuming a lesser degree of importance.

Moreover, the Lafayette, a straight movie house with only sporadic stage ventures, was a more imposing building, and although it boasted only 1,200 seats, it bordered on an area well endowed with some of the better night spots, Small's Paradise being one of the largest and finest.

Directly next door to the Lafayette was a club called the 'Shuffle Inn' which for various reasons was dying on its feet. The owners of the property appealed to Connie and George Immerman to take over the place and do something with it. The Immermans, who had made their money by selling spirits to the citizenry under cover of a delicatessen, were agreeable and began to work on a new club on this site. It was to be called 'Connie's Inn'.

Schiffman, knowing something of Waller's growing popularity, was quick to see that it would be in the best interests of the Lafayette to get him out of the Lincoln. He therefore made a new deal with Fats, giving him a good increase which brought his pay up to about fifty dollars a week, compared to the twenty-five-odd he had been getting at the Lincoln. The pay eventually rose to over a hundred.

The organ at the Lafayette, a Robert Morton instrument, was a large affair, the first grand organ in Harlem, and Fats' pride and joy. It may be supposed that this alone was sufficient inducement to him to make the change-over, and, indeed, the fact that the organ had been in disuse for some time attests to the Waller reputation even at that early date.

One day, early in 1922, as Fats was practising on the big organ, an usher called into the pit that there was a telephone message for him. He was to call Clarence Williams right back.

An hour later, Fats was on the phone. 'A record date? . . . Okay, Clarence, but I don't need any loot right now . . . who'd you say? Sara Martin? Accompaniment? How about a solo, man?'

Clarence's voice came back over the phone, 'Now, Fats, you get this straight. You get down here at nine o'clock tomorrow morning. No monkey business now. Get to bed early tonight and be ready in the morning. This is an important date and it can do a lot for you. I'll have the music and, as for the solo, maybe if they like you they'll use you on one. But the main thing you've gotta worry about is Sara.'

6

The year 1920 saw a lot of record history get under way. It marked the real beginning of the golden era of recorded jazz which stretched brilliantly through the Twenties and well into the depression years, before the slackening off in favour of the sweet bands that gained popular acclaim. In this year, the first Negro Okeh race record, *per se*, was made. The circumstances surrounding that first recording are interesting, for the accidental flavour of the event.

The Okeh Record Company, one of the foremost in the field, was particularly fortunate in having several able executives at the right moment, which enabled it to get ahead of all competition during this critical time. Foremost, perhaps, among these was Fred Hager, manager of Artists and Repertoire, a former music publisher (Hager and Helf), who, before coming to Okeh, had had a solid background in the recording industry. An astute judge of popular taste, Hager won the gratitude of jazz lovers the world over for his far-sighted appreciation of good jazz and blues. Another was Ralph S. Peer, also experienced in music publishing; as director of Record Production, he had a hand in every stage of the process, from the selection of the artists to the marketing of records throughout the country.

Not the least of these figures was a recording genius, Charles Hibbard, formerly with Edison. He knew his equipment inside and out, and drew magical results from the extremely limited acoustical system. Apart from his excellent equipment, Hibbard's 'personality', as Peer called it, seemed inexplicable at recording sessions. When he was at the controls, the quality he obtained would frequently surpass that of all other competitive labels. Yet if another man took over, difficulty would ensue. He was indeed justifiably termed indispensable.

This first year, for it may be called a legitimate 'First', though Okeh had been in the field for some time previously, Fred Hager approached Peer and said, 'I want to record Sophie Tucker on our label. You know how big an attraction she is, and nothing's being done with her on record.'

Peer immediately raised objections. 'It's impossible, Fred, you know it is. Her voice is too low for this system – you'll never hear it. The records wouldn't do her justice at all. Better wait until the system is improved, if it ever is.'

'I knew you'd say that, Ralph. We've been working on just that thing, and Charley has got it ironed out, he thinks. Let's try it, anyway.'

'Okay, but I tell you it won't work.' Peer shrugged.

In a day or two Sophie was brought in, and they went to work on songs and laid out the date. Right in the middle of everything, however, the door was thrown open and in ran Sophie's manager.

'Hey, you can't record here!' he bawled at Sophie. 'Have you forgotten your contract with Aeolian, it's exclusive!'

Sophie, taken aback, retorted, 'What good is that? They've never used me.'

'No matter, Sophie, a contract's a contract, and violation will put us on the spot. Especially as you accepted a retainer from them.'

So the projected date fell through. But not for long. Okeh had the song, *You Can't Keep A Good Man Down*, almost tailor-made for Miss Tucker, written by Perry Bradford and published by the renowned W. C. Handy. But no singer was available.

Then in stepped Bradford. Still hopeful that his song would be recorded, he caught Fred Hager in his office.

'Mister Hager, your worries are over. I have just the singer for you. You missed out on Sophie Tucker. Okay, never worry, my little girl can do twice as well. She's got the voice for this, like nobody you ever heard. Let me bring her in tomorrow – today!'

'Who are you talking about?' Hager began. 'She'll have to be darn good to out-sing Sophie Tucker.'

'Well, you may not have heard of her, Mr Hager, but she's a big hit in Harlem. Her name is Mamie Smith.'

'Mamie Smith, eh? Mmmmmm . . .' Hager shook his head doubtfully. 'Coloured?'

Perry nodded and said a silent prayer.

Hager deliberated in silence, then lifted the 'phone from the hook.

'Mr Peer, please.' Hager's fingers drummed on the desk, and Perry waited in suspense.

'Hello, Ralph? This is Fred. Look, I have Perry Bradford here. He wants to bring a gal named Mamie Smith to do the cancelled Tucker date. What do you think?'

He listened a few minutes and then hung up.

'He says to go ahead, if I think it's okay. Oh, I forgot to tell him she's coloured. . . . Oh hell, bring her in, Perry. No matter her colour, if she's good they ought to buy it. May as well try her out anyway.' Bradford was gone.

When Mamie arrived, Hager looked hard at her. She wasn't exactly the 'little girl' Perry had talked about; but she seemed to know her way around. They went into the studio at once, where Charley Hibbard had the equipment ready for a test recording. Just as they were starting, Peer walked in. After spotting Mamie at the recording horn, he gave Hager a quick look but didn't say anything. Hager gave the go-ahead to Charley, and in a few seconds Mamie began. A short piano introduction, and a full shouting voice began to pour forth. After a few bars, Hager cut it off and said, 'Now, let's play that much back.' As they heard the first line, everybody winced, and Peer went and sat down at the door. That was it, as far as he was concerned. Hibbard was listening intently, and as the cow-like sounds issued from the speaker he nodded his head. 'I think I can fix that to sound like it should.' 'I hope so,' said Hager. 'They'd run us off the market with that cutting.'

Under Charley's technical direction, the system gradually began to evolve. Various alterations of placement, adjustment of the controls, and the technique of recording Mamie Smith began to shape up. Soon Peer was looking interested, Hager was smiling, and Bradford was hopping around Mamie, saying, 'I told you they'd like you, honey.'

And so, on Saturday 14 February 1920, Mamie Smith finally recorded her version of Perry Bradford's *You Can't Keep A Good Man Down*. It was backed by *That Thing Called Love*, both accompanied by the Rega Orchestra.*

* Although *Blues & Gospel Records 1902–1942* by R. M. W. Dixon and J. Godrich list the personnel for this recording as Ed Cox (cornet); Dope Andrews

The record was a success in every way. When the red-labelled discs went on the market, in limited numbers due to the experimental nature of the record, everyone promptly forgot about them. Everyone, that is, except Mamie and Perry. As Peer had thought, sales were slow the first month, and Okeh was ready to give up Negro singers until, suddenly and quite unheralded, the avalanche began.

From every quarter orders poured in. Pressing upon pressing was ordered from the plant and sold out immediately on reaching the market. Amazed by this unexpected turn of events, Okeh assumed that the tune was responsible for the booming sales. They called Mamie Smith in again, and asked Perry to suggest a song. Without hesitation he recommended his own *Crazy Blues*, recently written, and further urged that the same band be used to back Mamie. Hager and Peer consented, and on 10 August the second session got under way.

The flood was on again – only more so. Where the first had sold some 750,000 copies, *Crazy Blues* backed by *It's Right Here For You* really hit the jackpot for Okeh. It sold the phenomenal total of a million and a half records to a hungry public, and Mamie Smith became a household word. It also made Perry Bradford a virtual tycoon but that, unhappily, didn't last long. The sudden wealth was too much for him to handle and he lost a great deal of money in misguided speculation.

In these post-war years Okeh records retailed at a dollar each – a fair price for a three-minute musical selection. Peer decided that this was the time to do a little exploratory work to find out just who were buying Mamie's records with such enthusiasm. He looked over the orders from outlying districts and saw that an unusual number came from out-of-the-way places – from retailers not normally noted for large orders. Amongst these was a furniture store in Richmond, Virginia. He decided to investigate and headed

---

(trombone); Ernest Elliott (clarinet and tenor saxophone); Leroy Parker (violin); Willie 'The Lion' Smith (piano), it is more likely that the accompaniment was by a white studio band. Perry Bradford himself in his book *Born With the Blues* credits the accompaniment to an 'ofay band' ('The Rega Orchestra') and Wallace Rega was Frederick Wallace Hager's song-writing pseudonym. Frank Banta, the white pianist, who made scores of records during this period, is reported to have claimed that he recorded behind Mamie Smith on this date.

for Richmond. He had hardly shaken hands when the dealer started enthusiastically, 'This is a wonderful Okeh idea, Mr Peer – great. Business is terrific. The coloured folk are buying records and record players like crazy. They don't really have that kind of money to spend. It's these records of Mamie Smith's.'

The light dawned on Ralph Peer. How dense could he have been! It was the Negroes themselves who were the big customers. He returned to New York, where letters from dealers were pouring in with congratulations on the Company's successful venture and asking for more. From then on Okeh was in the race record business.

It wasn't called that at first. The Company, treading warily in a new field, issued the first Smith record as a regular item in their catalogue, assigning it a conventional number and stating on the label 'Popular Blues Song'. They also distinguished it in the catalogue by the term 'Negro Record'. This didn't help sales noticeably so they tried 'Coloured Record' but this title too was soon dropped. It wasn't until some time later that Peer was inspired by a notice he read in the *Chicago Defender*, the prominent Negro newspaper, which made constant reference to 'the race'. He promptly adopted the term for the new line of records and they were given special presentation and a new series number in the catalogue. This got round the problem of the twelve new race discs listed each month.

In addition to Mamie, Okeh wanted more artists immediately for this series. Peer scouted the New York area, the outlying areas of the East and finally the South, in his quest for talent. Having known Clarence Williams through his musical activities in Chicago, he renewed his acquaintance in New York and when Clarence showed up as a pianist, talent promoter and publisher-plugger, it wasn't long before he tied up with this active musician in making some records. Clarence had a very talented wife, Eva Taylor, noted as a singer in her own right, with whom he recorded on early Okeh dates. He had opened a publishing business as soon as he came to New York in 1922, for he owned a few good things, among them *Gulf Coast Blues*, Piron's *Sister Kate*, and his own composition, *Baby, Won't You Please Come Home?* He had contacted Fats Waller soon after setting up business and Fats made many visits to his office to see what was going on in Tin Pan Alley. But it didn't really register on him, for at this time, revelling in the excitement of house parties and jamming with anybody who could play an instrument, he needed little else but longer nights and taller bottles of gin. Clarence found it hard to believe that anyone could be so unconcerned about the business end of music. He smiled and shrugged his shoulders as Fats rattled off tune after tune on the office piano.

'Do you want to stay in Harlem all your life?' he asked Fats one evening.

'Now listen, Cuz,' said Fats, 'don't you go gettin' all steamed up 'bout me. I'm doin' fine where I am. I got more to do than the day got hours. How d'ya like this tune?'

'Fats, one of these days I'm going to make you sit down and we'll write out one of these tunes you make up and I'll publish it. Maybe then you'll wake up.'

'Okay, Cuz, okay.' Fats went into another theme. 'Hey, I gotta get back to Harlem. Got me a solid function tonight.' He winked at Clarence, who shook his head and grinned in spite of himself.

Sara Martin, from Louisville, Kentucky, arrived in town in 1922 and Clarence, who had known her back in Chicago, tried hard to sell her to the record companies. Before leaving Chicago for a tour with a vaudeville company Sara had sought out the composer who, liking her voice, had given her *Sugar Blues* among other numbers to try out on tour. Now, down on her luck and needing work badly, she had followed Clarence to New York. Audition after audition was arranged but the record men weren't buying. None, that is, except Okeh. Aware of what was coming and heartened by the sales of Mamie Smith's records, Fred Hager agreed to an audition. Justin Ring, the musical director, was called in and after a try-out, arrangements were made to record Sara. Clarence rehearsed her carefully, planning to have Fats Waller as accompanist. An accomplished pianist himself, Clarence was so impressed by Fats' touch and feeling on piano that the mere thought of getting him on record surpassed any personal considerations.

Finally the day came, on 17 October 1922. Fats had previously been warned to be prompt and had said he would be. Sara, Clarence and Mr Ring arrived on time but there was no Fats. Fred

Hager walked in and greeted them: 'Hello, Clarence, and how are you, Miss Martin? All set? We have a busy schedule today, we'd better get going.'

Clarence looked out of the window. 'We're waiting for Fats Waller, Mr Hager.'

Neither Sara nor Hager had ever heard the name. They looked at each other and then at Clarence. 'Fats Waller? Who's he?' asked Hager. On hearing who Fats was and how good he was, he shrugged his shoulders and they waited. The minutes passed but no Fats, and finally none of them, except Clarence Williams, could see that there was anything to be gained by waiting further. Eventually Sara walked over to Clarence and said, 'Don't let's wait no more. You can accompany me, Clarence – after all, you done all the rehearsing.'

Clarence said, 'Well, I'd rather wait for Fats Waller.'

Mr Ring applied additional persuasion, saying that after all it was Clarence's own tune they were going to do.

So finally Clarence capitulated, and the recording of *Sugar Blues* was made. It sold a lot of copies and made Sara Martin's name in blues singing. A new stage in the career of the forty-year-old singer had begun. Incidentally, it launched Clarence himself on a long series of accompaniments, this being his first hit backing. His later work behind such artists as Bessie Smith, Sippie Wallace and Ethel Waters is well-known for its excellence. Happy-go-lucky Fats never did show up, nor did he make the second session the following month, when Sara made *Achin' Hearted Blues*, on the backing to her first side. When Clarence called him later and gave him a mild tongue-lashing, Fats merely said, 'Well, Cuz, I just didn't get home this morning. Guess I overslept somewheres.' Clarence sighed and hung up.

In the same month that saw Sara's first recording, the name Waller also appeared on record. A tune named *Muscle Shoals Blues* came up, and Okeh decided to record it. A white band made the first effort but it met with only desultory success on the market. Peer thought the number a good one and he remarked to Hager that perhaps a recording by a Negro would help move the tune along. Hager came back with the suggestion that Fats Waller, a terrific young piano and organ player from Harlem, might be the one to do it. Peer, unaware of the abortive nature of Fats' only previous contact with Okeh, agreed to go along with Hager, although he didn't want to deal with a comparative unknown if there was anyone else available. Hager was fired by the description that Clarence Williams and Perry Bradford had given him of Waller's prowess, and he decided to use him, regardless of his being virtually unknown. There were piano rolls to attest to his ability, and that was enough for Okeh.

This time, when Fats was called to the studio, he appeared on time, and after sizing up the sheet music before him, he made the recording. Peer sat in the control room and listened to the performance. Not bad, but not virtuosity, certainly. He shifted in his seat and, at the end, lsitened to a playback.

'Now, Mr Waller,' he said, as he entered the studio, 'we have to have something for the other side. I leave it up to you.'

'Gotcha, Mr Peer. Make like you're dead!' His fingers began to ripple over the keys. 'This is goin' to be *Birmingham Blues*.'

Peer returned to the control room and took his seat to hear the next selection. It was something easy, gliding, and unrestrained. Waller was not looking at the music now. He looked off to the side, raised his eyebrows to the gentlemen behind the plate-glass, and blissfully smiled to himself as his hands rolled and rocked up and down the expanse of the piano. When it was over, Peer jumped up and said, 'Fred, that's not bad at all. Use that fellow again.'

The master roll was duly processed, and after the successive stages of stamping, labelling, and shipping, the finished disc went out on the market, bearing the name of Thomas Waller, and Okeh number 4757. It enjoyed a fairly good sale. But more important, it marks the point where Tin Pan Alley and 'downtown' began to take on a more serious meaning for the young artist.

His next efforts with Okeh were later that year as accompanist to Sara Martin; the songs were a series of four: first *Tain't Nobody's Bizness If I Do*, and *Last Go-Round Blues*, and then Clarence joined Sara in a vocal duet on the next record, doing *I'm Certainly Gonna See 'Bout That* and *Squabblin' Blues*.

These early efforts of Fats impressed Peer so much that when, later in Waller's career, valuable impetus was needed for his Victor connection, it was gladly given by the shrewd executive.

Back in Harlem in these riotous days, a big event did not go unnoticed. James P. Johnson was back, and there was celebration in the town. A happy Fats bubbled out all the lurid details of his life during the past months, and Jackanapes drank it in. His boy was on the way now – 'Filthy' had grown up.

Lippy paraded his No. 1 pianist through a dizzy whirl of rent-parties, and the gin flowed freely. James P. made his first piano record: his *Harlem Strut* went on the Black Swan label, backed by a solo by Fletcher Henderson. Another side of the big man's career was under way. The rush was on, and nobody asked where it was all going to end. The clubs of Harlem were filled to overflowing, and Saturday night on Seventh Avenue, judging by the toppers and ermine wraps, looked like the lobby of the Waldorf-Astoria. This was the Roaring Twenties – society was doin' the low-down and liking it.

On Broadway in 1921, Eubie Blake had collaborated with Noble Sissle on the score for a tremendous musical, 'Shuffle Along'. This show, the first Negro musical comedy to break into the big time, opened at Daly's 63rd Street Theatre. Of interest is the fact that this show, personally financed by the principals, Miller and Lyles, and by the composer and lyricist, almost didn't make the trip to Washington, where it was due to open at the Howard Theatre, owing to lack of funds. Part of the cast were ready to back out of the affair through fear of being stranded, and the last few dollars needed were somehow scraped together while the cast were assembled on Pennsylvania Station. So they took a chance and travelled to the capital, where they made enough money on the opening night to enable them to give further shake-down performances at the Dunbar Theatre in Philadelphia. After two weeks there, the show went to New York and arrived at Daly's, a theatre out of the regular district, the vestibule of which had been for some time without lights. But right from the opening night it took Gotham by storm. In the cast was a newcomer to the stage, the wonderful soubrette, Florence Mills, and the show was also noteworthy for introducing the hit song, *I'm Just Wild About Harry*.

The principal stars of the show, the Negro team of Flournoy E. Miller and Aubrey Lyles, were to enjoy many years of successful theatrical teamwork. Their type of blackface comedy, much in the nature of 'Amos 'n' Andy' who came along later, formed the nucleus of sketchy plots around which much music and dancing swirled, to electrify the New York audiences. Their dialogue brought into use words in the pseudo-Negro vernacular of comedy sketches, such as 'regusted', etc.

Following this great hit which ran for three years, including its tour on the road, came many other all-Negro musicals and revues in these early years of the Twenties. Notable among them were 'Runnin' Wild', 'Dinah', 'Liza' and 'Chocolate Dandies'. The first-mentioned show, also produced by Miller and Lyles in 1923, featured a dance then for the first time brought from the South to the attention of white audiences: the Charleston. Rhythmically presented to the accompaniment of clapping hands and tapping feet, the number which perpetuated the song and the dance was perhaps James P. Johnson's greatest commercial hit. With James P. hitting the high spots with this composition, Fats decided that maybe Clarence Williams was right after all. One day, after regaling the Williams office staff with a few choice stories and excerpts of his repertoire of party specialities, Fats suddenly grew serious. 'Did you mean what you said about you publishing some tune of mine?' he asked Clarence.

Clarence's eyes widened in surprise. 'Why yes, Fats, if you really think you want to work on it.'

'Well, Cuz, let's get started.'

So they set to writing out some of the things that Fats had dreamed up – the first thing they came up with was *Wildcat Blues*. This number enjoyed a flash popularity for a short time. It was recorded by Clarence's Blue Five for Okeh on 30 July 1923, the Blue Five for this date consisting of Thomas Morris, trumpet, Sidney Bechet, soprano saxophone, John Masefield, trombone, Buddy Christian, banjo, and Clarence on piano. The composition is actually the first published Waller material, preceding *Squeeze Me*, the number popularly supposed to be Fats' first published tune, by some months. James P. Johnson said that *Wildcat Blues* was closely related to Fats' great 1929 piano piece *Handful Of Keys*, thought by many to be his greatest composition. Lyrics were written for this tune by Clarence Williams but they were never published.

The story of *Squeeze Me* is a chequered one. As has been told, the melody is based on the bawdy song *The Boy In The Boat* and it was originally entitled *Boston Blues* by Fats. When he first played it to Clarence and asked him if there was anything in it that could be used, the perceptive publisher assured him that there was. So together they condensed it to sixteen bars of melody with lyrics. The original words were based on a song *Kiss Me Again*, parodying the famous Victor Herbert selections, but the publishers of that beautiful waltz expressed displeasure at this prospect and threatened court proceedings if the lyrics were not altered. Clarence discreetly, and fortunately for posterity, gave up the original idea, and the final version, after three more attempts at a title, emerged as the familiar *Squeeze Me*.

Published in the same year as *Wildcat Blues*, it was not an immediate success, but became a steady, though unspectacular, seller for the Williams Publishing Company. It has never lacked exponents, however, having been recorded time and time again by the giants of jazz, and coming down to us today as an evergreen tune – beloved of musicians for the latitude it provides for improvisation and for the unusual and characteristic chromatic figure that closes each half of the song. Four or five tunes strongly resembling *Squeeze Me* and obviously adapted from its melody line were subsequently released by rival publishers but Clarence took no action against them.

1923

Fats now had a really good friend in Clarence, whose sponsorship in the musical world helped him tremendously. Clarence acted as his unofficial manager for several years and arranged his gig dates, his record sessions, and acted generally as adviser-without-portfolio to the irrepressible pianist. Often, in order to ensure Fats' attendance at a record session, he would journey in the early morning from his home in Jamaica, Long Island, arouse Fats from his slumber and have breakfast with him and Edith before making the subway trip to the studio. Sometimes he would find that Fats had not come home the night before and he would ask of the young wife, 'Don't you worry about that man of yours?' Edith, apparently resigned to her 'keyboard widowhood', would reply, 'I don't worry – he'll come home when he's ready.' But Clarence and other friends could see the disillusionment that lay behind her

73

simple words. The unrestrained world that was Harlem after dark was a grave danger to Fats' marriage but he refused to see what was happening. Edith wouldn't and couldn't join in his party-going and there was no way but for him to leave her behind. Another good friend, W. C. Handy, tried to talk to him about this situation but apparently to no avail.

Clarence was making a lot of money now from his many activities and he invested some of it in a succession of Lincoln cars. In 1922 when he drove the first one up to the office, Fats happened to be there waiting for him to open shop, having finished an active night uptown and still raring to go – although it was morning and he hadn't been to bed. At the sight of the car his eyes goggled and he ran his hands over the shiny body.

'When I get rich, I'm gonna have me one of these,' he said in all seriousness. The impression must have lasted, for in later years, when Waller was riding high, the only car he would have was a Lincoln.

Clarence bought a new home in Jamaica and at the house-warming Fats was an honoured guest and took his full part, drinking so copiously that even his protective bulk protected him no longer. He turned to the spaghetti and, spooning out a dish-panful, he covered it with sauce and ate the lot. Then, full of food and drink, he dropped into an easy chair and promptly fell asleep – his mouth open and arms dangling by his sides. Clarence, Eva Taylor and the rest of the assembled guests decided that such an imposing sight must be duly honoured, so they stuck several cigars in his mouth and decorated the rest of him with so many oddments that he looked like a Christmas tree. He finally awoke, hours later, and nearly choked on a cigar.

Eating was as popular with Fats as drinking. Often he and his friends, notably James P. Johnson, would have eating contests. At Clarence's house one afternoon, they cleaned out the ice-box, the winner consuming ten pork chops. Eggs were eaten as if they were grapes by the voracious contestants. Judging by these adventures in gourmandise, it was fortunate that Clarence always seemed to have a well-stocked larder.

Down at the publishing office and sometimes out at the Jamaica house over a week-end, Clarence and Fats would work on song material into the early morning. Now that he had had some initial success in the commercial sheet music field, Fats was all for this medium, and plunged into it with characteristic abandon. During the five years that he and Clarence were associated, over seventy songs were accepted and paid for by the Clarence Williams Music Company. Although many of them never saw the light of day, their existence excites the imagination. In recent years they were sold, along with the remainder of the Clarence Williams catalogue, to the Decca Company, and the manuscripts, turned out in such profusion by Williams and Waller, remain part of the untold story of Thomas Waller the composer. Probably most of them reflect the formative stage of his musical development, but if they are comparable to his published work of the period there must be a lot of good jazz yet untouched – like the composer, just waiting for a chance to 'strut its stuff'.

The lucky star that shone on Fats during his short life seems to have steered him toward channels in which he would have the greatest success. Arriving on the scene just at the time of the nation-wide flowering of jazz, he was able to reap a harvest of fame, if not immediately of gold – first through piano rolls, then, as the way opened, through gramophone records and lastly through the night clubs. Spending his early years in New York, he was personally popular with many thousands, besides being associated with the greatest names in the field of Negro music, so it followed naturally that in his chosen media he would have an inside track and he only had to follow the straight path to fortune. As is plain to see, however, Fats Waller believed in enjoying life as it came, getting the most out of every day. Making his mark in the world didn't mean so much to him in terms of wealth as it did in having around him his friends and the jolly company he thrived on. He wanted no complications in his life and could no more have filled Clarence Williams' shoes in the business world than he could have played *Nola* wearing boxing gloves. If a true artist is one who cannot survive without proper management, then Fats was certainly a true artist – at every point in his career when he was without able backing or firm advice, the Waller career drifted, mostly through neglect. His credo was simple – what do you need, besides enough money to pay the rent and plenty to eat and drink?

At this time there appeared a chance to get in on the ground floor of yet another new development, radio broadcasting. For a couple of years small radio stations had been sending out experimental programmes but nothing commercial had been done as yet. In the summer of 1922 Clarence had taken his Blue Five, with Vaughn de Leath presiding, to make a broadcast from a little studio over by Tenth Avenue. The place was small, hot and stuffy, and everybody worked in their shirt-sleeves – which was perhaps the only pleasant thing about it. These early pioneering broadcasts were free, for at that time, of course, there were no sponsors. Clarence, however, was happy to be able to plug his songs over the air.

Fats' first broadcast was in 1923 from the stage of the Fox Terminal Theatre over a local Newark station. Eva Taylor and the ever-present Blue Five were also there. Clarence was the pianist with this outfit on all its recording sessions, but on theatre and radio dates, as well as one-nighters, Fats would frequently be at the keyboard. Or sometimes perhaps Clarence would take advantage of a theatre organ and present Waller in this way. When NTG (Nils T. Granlund) started radio station WHN in New York, Clarence and Fats were there, participating in the opening ceremonies. Yet with all this activity outside his beloved Harlem, Fats nevertheless found there were still a lot of hours left in which to enjoy himself. He kept on at the Lafayette and Lincoln theatres, and this steady source of income provided him and his family with the necessities of life.

One of his newer friends this year was a young trumpeter and saxophone player named Don Redman. Just up from Piedmont, West Virginia, Redman was a brilliant student of music, having studied at Storer University and the Boston Conservatory of Music. He was attracted to Waller's organ and piano playing and spent many afternoons at the Lafayette listening to the varied music Fats played. One afternoon Don sat through the show down front near the organ console. The feature film went off the screen and Fats played a short interlude of music while the next show was wound on to the projector. Looking over at Don, Fats said, 'Man, ain't you dry? I could drink a gallon if I had it.' He looked up the aisle and catching the eye of a friendly usher flipped him half a dollar with a 'How 'bout gettin' me a half-pint?' He winked at

Don as the lights dimmed. A newsreel flashed on the screen and immediately Fats began his accompaniment. It floated around the theatre – a blue and vibrant version of *Squeeze Me*. Don settled back in his seat to listen but as his eyes lifted to the screen he saw, to his horror, a solemn procession of a royal funeral in Europe. He peered through the gloom at Fats but that uninhibited musician was just gazing at the tragic scenes without realizing what was going on – while his fingers flexed lightly and gaily through the measures of his jazz hit. The gin arrived at the same time as the management and Fats took an extra swallow in deference to departed royalty.

About this time Fats entered for a piano contest at the Roosevelt Theatre. He was the youngest contestant in a sizeable entry but he won hands down with his playing of *Carolina Shout*. In the audience a young man thrilled to the performance, and as Fats left the theatre, he caught up with him on the sidewalk.

'Say, Mr Waller, I just saw you win that contest. I like the way you play. My name is Andy Razaf.' The young man held out his hand.

'Just call me Fats, Andy'; Fats smiled and grew expansive. 'Can't help winnin' with the *Shout*. It's that kind of a number.'

They walked along some way, chatting, and, stopping off for a cup of coffee, began to talk about music.

'What do you do?' asked Fats of the other.

'I'm a poet and also do lyrics. You won't have heard of me.'

'Can't say I have,' said Fats. 'You live here in Harlem?'

Andy gave his address and Fats cried, 'Well now, ain't that something! That's just on the other side of the block from me. Funny I ain't never seen you before.' The more he talked with this dynamic young fellow, the more Fats liked him and a couple of coffees later they had agreed it would be a good idea to write some songs together. Razaf had a personality and he talked of big things.

Andy Razaf was born Andrea Menentania Razafinkeriefo, which, when translated, means 'noble child of wisdom'. Born in Washington, D.C., his mother was the daughter of the United States consul in Madagascar – then a monarchy ruled over by Queen Rànavàlona III. When the island kingdom was invaded by the French the consul escaped with his daughter and returned to the United States. It is an interesting coincidence that Razaf's mother's maiden name was also Waller but there was no family connection with Tom. Arriving in Washington in 1895, she bore a son in December. Andy had written quite a lot of poetry by the time he met Fats Waller but there had been years of hardship during which he tried to sell his song lyrics and poems. He had even had to fall back on running an elevator for a living but the eagerness with which he tackled his chosen profession paid off in 1917 when he sold a song to a publisher. It found its way into Shubert's 'Passing Show' and became a big hit. It was called *Baltimore*. During the war, he had dedicated a song to the famed Negro 15th Infantry Regiment of the National Guard, later the 369th Infantry Regiment which made so good a name for itself overseas. He composed both music and lyrics and then promoted it personally all over Harlem from the back of a truck, playing and singing the number and selling many copies to the Negro citizenry.

A polished, volatile young man of 28, Razaf aspired to enter the big time as soon as possible; and his new young friend's musical imagination and boundless good nature seemed to be the perfect foil for him. Each was the perfect complement to the other in temperament as well as ability. Waller's aims were confined to the needs of the moment – tomorrow would take care of itself. Andy, on the contrary, even while struggling to sell a song for twenty-five or fifty dollars, always kept one eye on the horizon. Their professional association, over nearly twenty years, besides being tremendously successful, also made them fast personal friends. Perhaps each provided something the other lacked. Certainly Fats needed a serious and careful partner, a check-rein applied lightly to his rollicking didoes. Andy, on the other hand, was immensely inspired by the carefree personality and endless melodic resources of his collaborator.

A fad of the moment in Harlem was the West Indian dialect speech. James P. Johnson found it very funny, and soon cultivated a whole language which he sprang on friends, and by means of which he could pass remarks to his intimates in the midst of a crowd without being understood by the rest. Fats didn't lose any time getting on to this idea, and he too became an expert at this queer off-beat English. The West Indian idea penetrated to the music business, and the first thing that the Waller-Razaf combination tried was to cash in on this new craze.

Sales of sheet music were booming, music publishers were more numerous than ever, and it wasn't long before they were assailed by the new Waller-Razaf combination. So many songs were produced in those early years that it has not been possible to determine the name of the first song they sold. Andy was the singer and Fats the pianist, and the combination of the two was almost irresistible. In the small auditioning room they softened up many a music company executive.

Not so, however, on the occasion about to be described. Having completed a demonstration for a publisher who shall be nameless, Andy turned to him and said, 'Well, how do you like that? Wasn't it terrific?'

Re-lighting his cigar, the publisher paused and said, between puffs, 'Not bad, Razaf. I may buy it. How much do you want?'

'We want five hundred dollars advance,' Andy replied calmly, slightly pressing his luck. He was standing by the window, and Fats, behind the publisher's back, frantically waved his hands in silent protest. The buyer removed the cigar from his mouth and said, 'Don't be crazy – I'll give you fifty.'

Andy went over to the piano, removed the manuscript and tore it to shreds under the startled man's nose, then, with a peremptory 'C'mon, Fats,' he swung out of the door.

In the hall, a flabbergasted Fats caught up with him. 'Andy, what's got into you? You mad? We had a sure sale!'

Andy turned angry eyes on him. 'That cheapskate – fifty dollars for our song!'

Nevertheless, times were not always easy, and songs did go for fifty dollars and sometimes even less. During their first year as partners, sales were few and far between, and Fats began to wonder if it was such a great business after all. One week he was particularly hard up, and he happened to run into J. Lawrence Cook of QRS. They walked together as far as Bud Allen's music shop.

'How about some recording up at your place, Larry?' asked Fats.

'Gee, Fats, things are slowing down lately, and they aren't doin'' much recording of new stuff.'

'Tell you what,' persisted Fats, 'I'll do a roll for five bucks . . .
three bucks. How about that, Larry?'

Cook turned to face his friend. 'Fats, you know I'd record you
all day and every day, but I'm not the one who puts up the money.
I wouldn't record you for five bucks, anyway. If you recorded for
me, it'd be at the regular prices or not at all.'

'Well,' Fats opened his portfolio and displayed a number of
manuscripts. 'I'll let you have all these. How about ten dollars?'

'Now, Fats, what would I do with them? I'm not in the song-
writing business. You keep them and sell them downtown for
what they're really worth. Here's the ten. And as for the rolls, we'll
probably be doing a bunch next month. You'll get the call.' They
entered the store, and there on the counter, prominently displayed,
were some QRS rolls, played by Fats Waller.

'See that name, Fats?' said Cook. 'That's worth more than three
dollars.'

7

In June 1920, a young Negro of light complexion arrived in town from Atlanta, Georgia, fresh from a Southern University, and hoping to enrol in NYU in the fall, for further study. A fine pianist, this man was seeking suitable employment to carry him through the summer months. An opening at the Pace and Handy Music Publishing Company presented itself, and the youth, whose name was Fletcher Henderson, took the job immediately. Starting right in as a pianist, he worked there until Pace left the partnership and went into his own business to produce the Black Swan label. Henderson went along with him to work as accompanist for the blues singers he was to record. At first, he hadn't quite the correct jazz sense necessary to back these singers, but he soon learned the technique from two girl pianists also employed by the firm. During the eighteen months that Fletcher was with Pace, he played for Ethel Waters' first record for Black Swan, *Down Home Blues* and *Oh Daddy*. Ethel was a young singer just out of Harlem, and currently working at Edmond's 'Bucket of Blood' cafe at 135th Street and Fifth Avenue. Her statuesque figure, combined with an almost aloof approach to her audience, gave her a unique place among the cabaret artists. Someone told Henderson to spot this girl's act at the cafe, and, struck by her performance, he contrived to meet her. Thus began a firm professional association lasting many, many years.

Pace soon formed a company of artists called the 'Black Swan Troubadours', which included Ethel, Fletcher, and a dancer named Ethel Williams. In New Orleans, on one of the company's tours, Fletcher heard and saw a remarkable young trumpeter whose power and style left a lasting impression on him – an impression he took back with him to New York. Later, when he formed his band, it was he who first employed Louis Armstrong in New York.

Fletcher led from the piano a seven-piece band in the 'Troubadours', and during their travels they played most of the country. Crowds of seven and eight thousand would turn out for their performances in such places as Fort Worth and Houston, and these shows naturally promoted a lot of sales for Pace's Black Swan records.

Being a trained and studious musician, Fletcher was by nature inclined in the band field to work towards arranged jazz, rather than rely on sheer improvisation, thus attending to dynamics and expression through instrumental group voicing and planned effects. Impressed by Jim Europe's tremendously successful band of World War I days and thereafter, he sought to bring similar qualities to his own band. This was a somewhat broad departure from the typical New Orleans pattern, featuring only head arrangements (sketchy arrangements in verbal form, usually applied to ensemble work at the beginning and end of a number), or total improvisation; and for long it was a subject of debate among the various older schools of jazz thought. Whether jazz can be truly and legitimately thought out in advance, and transcribed on to paper, or whether pure inspiration at the moment of playing remains the only criterion by which the music may be properly judged – this was long a matter of heated discussion, particularly where groups of instrumentalists are involved larger than the traditional five or six with which pure jazz has been associated. The fact remains that the various Henderson bands were studded with the names of star musicians, and his records have left us with much jazz that is good and some that is superlative.

In 1921 he formed his first band and they made a string of titles for the Black Swan, Paramount, and various other smaller labels. In September 1923, the band cut their first sides for Columbia, with this personnel: Joe Smith, Elmer Chambers and, sometimes, Howard Scott on trumpets; Teddy Nixon and Chink Johnson, trombones; Edgar Campbell, Don Redman, Coleman Hawkins and Billy Fowler, reeds; Charlie Dixon, banjo; Ralph Escudero, tuba; Kaiser Marshall, drums; and Fletcher Henderson at the piano. Fletcher also used a violinist in the band, Allie Ross by name, but he didn't record as the acoustical system in use in those days was unable to cope with stringed instruments. This was also the reason why the band used a tuba, instead of the stringed double bass.

While rehearsing one day, before a recording at Columbia, a call came through for Fletcher. He went out of the studio and picked up the receiver. It was Sid Weiss, owner of the Club Alabam. He was quick to the point. There was an opening for a band at the Club, and he wanted to hear Fletcher's outfit in audition. Henderson said that they were up to their necks in record dates and weren't looking for any other work at the moment. He then hung up after thanking Weiss for the offer. A few moments later the phone rang again and Fletcher again rose from the piano bench. It was Sid. He pleaded with Fletcher, who was short with him. 'I'm in the middle of a record date, Mr Weiss. Sorry.'

A third call, a third interruption, and Weiss finally won out. Tired after auditioning a dozen odd bands, he was determined to get the Henderson group. Fletcher agreed and was then dismayed to hear that he was to come over right away for an audition.

'I'm only using six men on this date – not enough to give a fair idea of what we can really do,' he told the impatient Weiss.

'Okay, get the rest of them and come on over here right away.'

Fletcher called the rest of the musicians together and they went to the Club Alabam. They stayed there six months. They would, no doubt, have stayed longer but they came to the parting of the ways when the owner, wanting Coleman Hawkins to step up his performance a little, behind a blues singer, told a waiter to get him to do it. The waiter approached Hawkins and delivered the message, intimating that there would be a little extra in his pay if he did as requested. The tenor man readily accepted the proposition. The waiter reported the deal to the Boss but Weiss, having no intention of handing out any more money, flew off the handle and demanded that Henderson fire Hawkins. Fletcher replied by throwing the entire band's notice at him and, a couple of nights later, took his men out of the Club and over to the Roseland ⟨'23 – '31⟩ where Charley Burgess had been hopefully waiting for him. Thus began a record stand at a Broadway location for a single band. From 1923 to 1931 the Henderson band made jazz history at this prominent dance palace on the Great White Way, interrupted only by occasional trips and brief summer tours. In a memorable three days at the Roseland, they engaged in a battle of music with the Jean Goldkette organization – a battle so memorable that it attracted almost the whole musical world during its run. Fletcher Henderson and Jean Goldkette would alternate engagements at the Roseland and in Detroit, passing each other *en route*. Going into Connie's Inn in 1931 meant a long interval of eighteen months away from their old stand, but, following this spell in Harlem, they returned and played the Roseland for one to three months a year until 1936.

It was inevitable that Fletcher and Fats Waller would come into contact. One night, while playing the Savoy Ballroom in Harlem, after closing up at the Roseland, Fletcher was approached by a friend who suggested that the big fellow at the edge of the crowd be asked to sit in. Fletcher looked over and beckoned Fats, whose reputation was already known to him.

'You like to sit in? How 'bout it?'

'Yeah, *man!*' was the eager rejoinder and, lightly mounting the stand, Fats strode over to the piano. In a matter of seconds it became obvious to the leader that here was a man who could sit in with his band any time. Fats stayed most of the evening and had a ball. His friend, Don Redman, who did many of the band's arrangements, also played alto and he was delighted to have Fats there.

Of all the trumpet players who graced the Henderson band there are two who merit more than casual reference. The first was Joe Smith, whose story reads like a legend. Joe, born in Ripley, Ohio, was brought up on a farm with his two brothers, Luke and Russell. The two elder boys were given instrumental lessons, to the consternation of Joe who seized on a battered mellophone and practised alone while his father taught the others the fundamentals of music. Any day you passed the Smith barn you could hear the brassy tones emerging from the old building and resounding across the fields. Russell Smith, in pursuit of a career as a musician, went to New York where he eventually joined the Fletcher Henderson band. Joe wanted to go along with him but hadn't the money for the trip. Soon, however, he decided to make a break for it and set out without funds, begging rides and playing the mellophone on street corners to make enough money for food. He slept in fields, barns and occasionally in a farmhouse, his precious instrument beside him. One day he found that somewhere along the road he had lost the mouthpiece of the horn, and spent hours retracing his steps in frantic search – but without result. Then a bright thought came to him. At a farmhouse, he begged an empty thread spool from the lady who answered the door and carefully whittled it into a mouthpiece. Using this home-made attachment, he reached New York, where he became the mainstay of the Henderson band from its earliest days. Joe Smith is perhaps most famous for his sympathetic delicate work on so many of Bessie Smith's great recordings.

The other trumpet man, or, more correctly, cornet man, was the man who made the most powerful impression on the band – he was, of course, Louis Armstrong. Fletcher, hearing that Louis was in Chicago, made him an offer to come to New York, well remembering the dynamic horn which had commanded his attention in New Orleans a couple of years before. Armstrong arrived, eager to go to work in the big city, and expecting big things of the Henderson connection.

The initial reception that greeted the young man as he took the third trumpet chair at the Roseland can well be imagined. Here was Louis, the star improviser and *alter ego* of the great King Oliver, in the middle of a band which relied on careful rehearsals and to whom written music was of paramount importance. Fletcher demanded strict attention to the interpretation marks noted on all the arrangements. One day, shortly after Louis had joined the band, a rehearsal was scheduled at the Savoy. Fletcher had a medley of Irish waltzes called *Rose Fantasy* which he wished to sharpen up for the Roseland that night. In the score there was a passage where the notation called for a triple fortissimo on the brass, followed by a sharp diminuendo which brought them down to a pianissimo passage. The horns played the initial loud-voiced phrases and hushed appropriately as the next were reached. All, that is, except Louis. He was off on a wild ride by himself, and when Fletcher tapped for the band to stop playing, he stopped in surprise.

'Louis, will you kindly read the music?' Fletcher asked quietly.

Armstrong looked down at the printed sheet before him, and said, 'I *am* readin' the music, Pops!'

'That passage at the end – what does it say?'

'*pp*,' answered Louis confidently.

'Well, then, why didn't you play it that way?' Fletcher ran his hands through his hair.

'I did – don't it mean "pound plenty"?' asked Louis, innocently.

The answer broke everybody up, and in memory of the event Fletcher wrote a special arrangement of *Should I?* featuring a free-wheeling brass break for Louis in the middle of the number. On the sheet music was emblazoned, for all to see, 'Pound Plenty!'

Louis and Fats were introduced one day, during a jam session at the Hoofer's Club. They became firm friends and played many gigs, dances and even a few broadcasts together, under the auspices of Clarence Williams, who used them from time to time in his Blue Five.

*   *   *

Working for Fletcher Henderson at that time was a white arranger named Ken Macomber. He and Fats got together early in the big man's writing career, and, with Andy Razaf, were familiar sights at the white publishing houses, and at 'Uncle Tom's Cabin', the affectionate nickname applied to the Gaiety Theatre Building where the Negro publishing firms of W. C. Handy, Clarence Williams, and Perry Bradford hung out their shingles.

Ken tells of a day in the early Twenties that typifies the carefree methods of Razaf and Waller in their first years, when tunes were going for practically nothing. The three of them had met one morning at 45th Street and Broadway, Fats greeting them lustily with claims of 'a great tune' he had just composed. He hummed it to them a couple of times and immediately Andy had a title. As they strolled along to the Mills Music office, Andy was running the tune over in his mind, trying and rejecting lines and rhymes under his breath. Up the elevator they went, and into the publisher's office. The tune was demonstrated and sold; they collected their cash, and sped over to Shapiro-Bernstein, a rival house, where they also had an entrée. *En route*, Fats and Andy changed around the verse and refrain of the same tune and sold it a few minutes later to an enthusiastic buyer.

This selling of the same tune to a couple of publishers was perhaps just, in that it made up in some degree for the low cash payments usually made to the composers. They had no more qualms in selling the same tune to different publishers than the publishers themselves had in offering fifty dollars in payment for them. And it is no small tribute to the ability of Razaf and Waller that they were able to get away with it without losing the good faith and interest of the buyers. As Irving Mills put it: 'You never knew when they were going to come up with another big hit, so you *had* to buy them, even though you knew they probably had sold it elsewhere down the street, or even across the hall.'

At these demonstrations Andy was, as it has been said, the vocalist, but after listening to Fats' private vocalism one day, and noticing the expressive face, with heavy black eyebrows accenting each line, he suggested that Fats do the vocals as well as the playing. Fats demurred, being a little bashful about his singing. He felt that of all voices he had ever heard his was perhaps the least pleasing to the ear, and could see no reason why they should handicap themselves by giving up Andy's expressive way with a set of lyrics. 'You wrote them, you oughta sing them,' he claimed. But after a long argument, Andy finally won out, and Fats agreed to try it for a time. But only so that he could prove Andy was wrong, he told him.

The results were electrifying. As soon as Fats began to sing as well as play, the combination sold even more songs than before. Though they might have thrown the set of words and music together in a few minutes, thinking it was not really worth much trouble, they were surprised to find that, at the end of the demonstration, a smile would crease the publisher's face, and he would reach for his cheque book. Andy was soon able to slap his partner on the back, and say, 'I told you so!'

These early efforts by the team were light songs dealing with simple emotions. Andy would suggest a title and a theme, and they would let the mood of the moment dictate the type of song they wrote. If Fats was hungry, he would write a tune or suggest lyrics on that theme; if he was tired, he would write a tired tune. There was not a single idea that sprang from the lyricist's fertile imagination which would not bring fresh melody from Fats – his resource of melody was apparently limitless. One of Andy's fondest tributes to his friend runs to the effect that if he had desired, there is no doubt that he could have 'set the telephone book to music'.

But these days of scuffling around, and the permanent struggle for money to pay the rent, and in Fats' case to keep him in eating and drinking money, took heavy toll of his marriage. In spite of all his friends did in advising and pleading with him to attend more to his family obligations, Fats somewhere along the line felt that it had been a mistake to marry Edith. The simple home they had uptown became a place to eat and sleep in, and that was practically all. In spite of his pride in the young boy who bore his name, and who was now over three years old, the home steadily diminished in importance.

Somewhere in these months, the final break came. Fats and Edith, who had faced marriage with such high hopes, parted. With the severance of their married life, Edith retained the boy, and Tom moved out of the house, finding himself a place to live in Harlem.

Soon after this he was off to Philadelphia to play the Douglas Hotel in a trio, with Bobby Thompson on fiddle and Howard Hill on guitar. His abrupt departure from Harlem at this time may have been to forget his marital break-up, but he also did his best to forget his continued obligations in that quarter. Edith, without adequate funds, had to rely on family and friends. A settlement had been made, whereby Fats had agreed to pay about $35.00 per week to Edith and the baby, but from the first month, it seems, the payments began to fail, and when they came in at all, were never for the correct amount. At first Edith took no action, maybe unaware of her rights, or maybe retaining a spark of her old love for the wayward man.

After his return from the City of Brotherly Love, Fats was at once on the look-out for a steady job, and help came from a new friend of his.

For some time, Fats had been haunting Connie's Inn, the famous nightspot hard by the Lafayette Theatre in Harlem, and he was a familiar sight to the regular patrons, as he sat at the baby grand and played any tune they requested. Not a regular employee by any means, Fats nevertheless became to the Immerman brothers a sort of musical Man Friday who could be counted on to rehearse acts, write a tune or two, or play intermissions between the floor shows and the band sets. One of the customers was a Captain George H. Maines, a notable press agent on Broadway at this time. Maines and his wife were intrigued by the virtuosity of the portly pianist, and invited him down to their West End Avenue apartment. From there they proceeded to a friend's house, where a small organ and piano were installed. Although Fats wasn't able to read music very quickly at this time, Maines detected a goodly share of genius in him, and took it on himself to introduce him to Irving Berlin & Company, and to Harry Link, the publisher's representative working out of Santly Brothers, who had the reputation of being one of the most honest men in the business.

Maines was also in a position to help further. Meeting an old friend, Bert Lewis, 'The Southern Syncopater', on the street, he told him about Waller. Lewis, the current M.C. at the Kentucky Club, just off Seventh Avenue, at Times Square, was interested, and told Maines to bring Fats down one night. Maines did so and the big man made an immediate hit with the management, singing and playing, passing remarks to Lewis as he played, and generally having himself a ball. The 'Southern Syncopater', as he was generally called, sang a great many novelty songs, and he and Maines cooked up a good gimmick for Fats. Fats was to be billed as 'Ali Baba, the Egyptian Wonder', complete with Eastern clothes and a turban with an enormous 'jewel' in its centre. The story goes that one night Fats went out on to the street between shows, wearing the turban. He encountered Bert Lewis on the corner, and amid much ceremony they greeted each other in mock-Eastern fashion, while passers-by goggled at the impressive bulk and mien of the 'Egyptian', who finally burst out laughing at the ludicrousness of it all.

The house band at the Kentucky Club was well-known to Fats, the leader being none other than Duke Ellington. The night that Fats was auditioned for the job, Maines was approached by the debonair young leader. Said Duke, 'Friend, I can't have that man Waller in my band – that baby is liable to submerge me. I know his playing. I think he can't be beat, and I don't want to be the fall guy for his piano playing.' Maines and Lewis went into a huddle and came up with a deal whereby Fats would be used strictly as an accompanist, and as a soloist at other times. Everybody was happy.

A little later, Maines prevailed on a Prof. Hugo Reisenfeld, conductor of a theatre orchestra nearby, to book the entire

Kentucky Club show into the theatre. The show was billed in lights:

FATS WALLER AND SONGS

DUKE ELLINGTON AND HIS ORCHESTRA

MAXINE BROWN, THE SWEETHEART OF THE AIR

INA HAYWARD

ETC.

It was Fats' first appearance on Broadway. Indeed, the Kentucky engagement was his first downtown public appearance of any note.

George Maines also was instrumental in Fats' appearances on Radio stations WHN and WOR for broadcasts during these years.

The introduction to Irving Berlin was the renewal of an acquaintance that went back to Fats' early days in Harlem, and it wasn't long before he was making Irving's office a regular port of call. He particularly liked to sit at Berlin's special office piano and say to him, 'Now look y'here, see if you know what this is called.' Sixty-four bars later, he would spin around on the seat, and say to the infatuated listener, 'Well, then – how 'bout that! What was the name of that song?'

Irving would often have to shake his head, not recognizing the intricate melodic passages that Fats had played. With a burst of laughter, Fats would tell him that he didn't know one of his own tunes. He would play it over again, straight this time, and Tin Pan Alley's greatest tunesmith would have to smile as he saw his melody re-designed by Fats. It was a rare day for Razaf when he and Fats went down to the Berlin office to see Irving, for Andy has always regarded Berlin as the prince of lyricists.

For the next few years Razaf and Waller hit the publishers so often and so hard that everyone who had the experience of dealing with them has his own favourite story to tell. It is impossible to relate them all, but perhaps Harry Link's are typical of most. He used to say that on countless occasions when he was sitting by his open office window he would hear a booming voice echoing his name up from below. On looking down, he would see Fats and Andy standing by an open taxi, with nothing in their pockets but holes. 'Bail us out, Harry!' they would call, and invariably Link paid off the cab. When Fats and his partner had what they thought was a good tune, the subway was not for them – a taxi was the order of the day, and as much speed as possible through Central Park, even if they hadn't a cent between them.

If Fats ever found himself downtown without funds, Link was his soft touch. All he had to do was breeze through the outer office, into the inner secretary's office. His raised eyebrows would ask 'Boss in?' and without waiting for a reply, no matter what visitors Link had with him, he would go over to the piano, and start to play a medley of Harry's favourite tunes. This was the signal that Waller was in need of a little 'trash'.

Later in the Twenties, Link got himself an apartment in the élite Essex House, on Central Park South, and Fats often used the place for writing tunes. At one time, the publisher recalled, the Waller constitution was somewhat overburdened by the ill effects of prohibition gin, and its owner reluctantly decided to go on the wine wagon. Somebody told him that if you dropped a certain pill into a jug of wine it would provide the magic spark, making it almost as palatable as good hard liquor. So, armed with a gallon bottle of wine and a few of the wonder pills, Fats arrived at Essex House one afternoon, and proceeded to Link's apartment. He revealed his plans to Link, and retired to the kitchen to prepare the elixir. Link remained in his room, trying out some new songs Fats had just given him. Suddenly he was startled by a loud report, and a tinkle of glass – then silence! He jumped to his feet, but before he could reach the kitchen, the door swung slowly open, and Fats came through, shaking his head and muttering.

'Man, that's some powerful pills!' he declared. 'Don't you lay no more of that wine on me.' He promptly looked around for the gin bottle.

*   *   *

Another lyric writer with whom Fats collaborated extensively was J. C. Johnson. His first name being James, the similarity to

James P. gave rise to such confusion that early in his career he decided to use his first two initials only, professionally. He wrote some songs with Fats as early as 1923, and was already an established name in the music business at the time of his first contact with the jovial pianist. He was eight years older than Waller and had come up the hard way in Chicago, shining shoes and doing odd jobs whilst learning to play the piano. But after he got to New York and heard some of the wizards of the keyboard then reigning in that city, he gave up the piano in disgust and concentrated on songs and poems. He said that when he was feeling low and needed a good laugh, all he had to do was to read over the first set of words he ever wrote. He arrived in New York in 1915, and had his first material published three years later.

Johnson, Razaf, Edgar Dowell, and Spencer Williams were the principal lyricists with whom Fats wrote during these formative years. There were others, of course, and on nearly five hundred known compositions credited to Fats Waller, publishers' and producers' names appear as co-composers. These latter were, as often as not, courtesy credits, or given in order to obtain publication fees. In addition, much material written by Waller has never been published under his name. Rumour persists, and indeed Fats confirmed it during his lifetime, that at least three of the main hits of the Twenties are in reality Fats' own compositions, picked off publishers' shelves by hack writers and turned into great hits. This cannot be passed off as mere hearsay; it is due to the fact that Waller sold many tunes for trivial amounts, often surrendering all subsequent rights for ready cash. Andy Razaf can well remember the days when his partner would walk into a music office and say, 'I'll write you a song for $2.50.' Whatever he needed at that moment was to him sufficient payment, and buyers were not normally anxious to jack up prices for his benefit. When, later in his career, he did begin to realize the tremendous returns that were being made from these cheaply sold compositions of his, he began to re-appraise his value to himself and others. Harry Link and Irving Berlin were always eminently fair with Fats, the former claiming to have given him his first royalty contract for a song. 'Fats,' he said, 'didn't even know what it was to sell a song and continue to reap benefits from it, before I put him wise.' Further evidence in support of his claim to authorship of many 'anonymous' hits lies in the fact that many of them were written in the years when he and Razaf were partners. They did the scores for whole shows both in Harlem and on Broadway, for this was the time when he and Andy were selling melodies right and left. It is impossible, of course, to list these lost songs by name but it is fortunate that he left behind him compositions which match and, it is hoped, even surpass the stolen ones. Such tunes as *Honeysuckle Rose*, *Ain't Misbehavin'* and *Black And Blue* – all from the same period – will surely perpetuate the memory of their composer when the men who performed petty thievery on his works will be long gone and forgotten.

During this period Fats continued playing at the Lafayette and doubling Connie's Inn, sometimes going out on short tours with a show from the theatre and then back for more weeks at the organ. One day Frank Schiffman was standing at the back of the theatre, leaning against the wall, as Fats rehearsed the day's routines. The music seemed to be more beautiful than ever, thought Frank. . . . Suddenly with a discordant crash the music stopped. Schiffman looked quickly towards the console to see what had happened, but there was no one there. Puzzled, he walked down front and became aware of another man striding down the next aisle, holding a piece of paper in his hand.

'Anything I can do for you?' asked Schiffman.

'I'm looking for Thomas Waller – I just saw him at that organ.' The man's eyes strayed over the stage.

'What do you want with him? Maybe I can help,' commented Frank.

The man turned out to be a process server and had an order for Fats to appear in court. Edith's patience had given out and she had sought the aid of the law to try and get her overdue alimony paid. Fats didn't show up at the Lafayette for two days, but when he saw Schiffman, he explained his absence. 'When I saw that man comin' down the aisle with that little bitty piece of white paper in his hand, man, I decided to get while the goin' was good.'

Thus began the open season on Fats Waller for process servers. Always in arrears, and deeply resentful of the fact that Edith had called the law into their affairs, he stubbornly resisted the demands

93

put upon him. Perhaps these episodes robbed us of a lot of music which might have been written but for this continual hounding. It is not unreasonable to assume that Fats' working days and nights were taken up with less productive activities because he was aware that, the more money he earned, the more would be taken off him for the support of Edith. But in all justice she cannot be condemned for trying to hold him to the line agreed upon.

There are quite a few stories which tell of Fats' troubles from this quarter. This one comes from Sammy Smith:

Waller had been picked up by detectives and incarcerated overnight. The word spread quickly among his friends and about fifteen of them, led by Fletcher Henderson, went to try to bail him out. Knowing that the presiding judge of the court where Fats would have his hearing was a friend of Sammy Smith, they hurried over *en masse* to the NVA Headquarters. On finding that Sammy was over in Newark they decided to camp in the lobby until he returned. Hearing of Fats' trouble, Sammy agreed to do what he could. Next morning a disconsolate Fats faced the prospect of a term in jail. As he entered the courtroom and made his way to the bench, he didn't see the additional figure sitting by the judge's side. He didn't know that Sammy Smith, an old baseball battery mate of the judge's, was once more calling the signals. The judge nodded as he listened to the voice on his right.

'Your name is Thomas Waller?' came the voice down to Fats' ears like Fate itself.

He nodded and said, 'Yes, your Honour,' in a low voice.

'Case dismissed,' came the voice again, with finality.

Slowly the lowered head came up in disbelief and as he saw Sammy, Fats broke into a big grin. 'Thank *you*, your Honour.' The judge coughed and rustled some papers. 'Next case,' he said.

Another story about Fats' trials comes by way of Ken Macomber, Spencer Williams and Perry Bradford. It is one of those tales which are almost too good to be true; it may have been built up by many jolly tellings over the years but it is certainly worth re-telling:

Fats, it seems, was caught again in the toils and eventually sentenced to serve some time in the Raymond Street jail; bail was fixed at five hundred dollars, and his pals set about raising some money to release him by selling songs and borrowing from here, there and everywhere. Finally they had the required sum and rushed post-haste to jail. They were led along to Fats and there, in a cell that the Taft Hotel would have been proud to call a room, sat their friend. A fine cigar was in his mouth, a glass of amber liquid in his hand, and against the wall reposed a new upright piano. With Fats was a well-dressed and jovial man who greeted them with a wave of his glass. Fats grinned at his thunderstruck friends but when they told him they had raised his release money, his face fell. Beckoning them quietly to a corner of the cell he said in guarded tones, 'Now latch on, you men. Just you take that money and get the hell out of here!'

'Why?' they chorused.

'Well,' said Fats, 'you see that guy there? He's a millionaire and he'd rather sit here in this cooler than give his ex-wife the satisfaction of paying her the money she demands. We're sure living in style – we got steaks and we got all we want to drink. We near got everything. He got that piano brought in and he likes to hear me play! So you go away with your cash. Come see me later – much later.'

*   *   *

The Big Town was still roaring towards the climax of the Twenties. Jazz was rampant, and the Charleston, Black Bottom, and bathtub gin held sway. Night clubs and theatres were reaping a golden flood and men struggled with each other for control of the various entertainment empires. Night clubs in Harlem were no less affected than others, as the beer barons fought to sew up for themselves these lucrative bistros. On Park Avenue, it became fashionable for the socialites to hire for their parties the cream of current uptown entertainment.

The great Bojangles, Bill Robinson, was one of the most popular entertainers of the day and naturally a prime favourite of the Four Hundred, whether in the fabulous apartment houses of Park Avenue, or the luxury of Long Island North Shore Estates. Fats became a favourite accompanist for Robinson on these choice outings and there was plenty of recompense for them both. The first time they attended one of these social gatherings Bill danced his heart out for the guests and Fats played tune after tune. As the evening wore on towards morning, Fats began to fret about his money. 'Hey, how about my gold?' he asked Bill in a loud stage whisper.

'Now, listen to that,' cracked Bill to the crowd. 'Some people can't trust nobody!' Thrusting his hand into his pocket, he pulled out a few bills and passed over to Fats the promised twenty-five dollars. Then, as an afterthought, he tossed over an extra ten dollars saying, 'Here, boy – here's a tip for yo'self.'

Fats grabbed it up and shoved it in his pocket. Directly they got outside after the party Bill collared Fats and said, 'Here you, Filthy, gimme back that ten. I overdid myself just now.'

'Ten?' said Fats with raised eyebrows. 'I ain't seen no ten, no sir!'

Willie Smith and James P. were also great favourites at these lavish affairs. It was at a party given by Charles M. Schwab at his famous Riverside Drive mansion that Willie 'The Lion' remembers Fats at the piano beginning to 'make with the jive'. As he relates it: 'James was always so modest. He wouldn't act funny at all, just always relied on his playing. He always used to say, "What do I have to do for them besides play?" That was enough for him and I guess it was enough for the customers, him being James P. But I had my own act, and I poured it on 'em, even as I still do now. When Fats came along, he took that West Indian dialect from James and ran away with it. This night at the Schwab party, Fats was in that little chapel half-way up the main stairs where Mr Schwab had that organ. You couldn't keep him out of it. Some place it was. We did lots of parties there, for the cream of society. Well I was there, as usual, mugging while I played. I'd roll my eyes on 'em, and talk and grunt all the while, and get a lot of laughs. Fats was playing the other piano at the time. When I had finished I said to him, "Filthy, why don't you do that stuff like I do? You know, that stuff you do at the rent-parties uptown."

'Fats hesitated and said, "Willie, I'm not sure I can do it here with all these people. They might not like it. You can really lay it on them – you know it's okay for you to do that stuff. But maybe not me."

'So I told him, "Now's your chance to start, Fats. Go on, let 'em see what you can do." And he went out there and knocked them dead.'

Willie 'The Lion' and Fats were also teamed up at an exclusive party given by Mrs Harrison Williams some years later. Along about the middle of the evening, the hostess looked over at her pianist 'boys', and noticed that Willie was out of cigars. She brought over a box of high-priced panatellas, and 'The Lion' lit one, putting away a few for later reference. A few minutes later one of the more stuffy guests made his way to where 'The Lion' sat, and interrupted his playing with, 'Look here, my man, you can't smoke in here. You're one of the entertainers, and don't think you've the right to fill the air with clouds of cigar smoke!'

Without losing a beat, 'The Lion' kept on playing. His eyes looked straight ahead, and his cigar wobbled as he talked and puffed.

'Now, listen. You're gonna get in my hair, and I might lose my good ways.' His eyes left the piano before him, and looked around for a waiter. Beckoning one over, he said, 'Will you please call Mrs Williams – this man is annoying me.'

Fats' rumble echoed, 'Yes, yes, you call Mrs Williams over here.'

A few moments later Mrs Williams forever endeared herself to her 'boys' by stopping the music and announcing to the guests, 'There are a couple of fine fellows here playing the pianos for your entertainment. They are my friends, and I expect to see them treated as such. Anyone who doesn't like this knows where the door is.'

Another host for whom Fats played, from 1927 to 1930 on his memorable New Year's Eve parties, both solo and with pick-up bands, was Otto H. Kahn. He always paid his entertainers well – and in gold coin, to boot.

*   *   *

1925 saw Fats Waller again on record. Perry Bradford with his Jazz Phools, a recording band, used Fats and James P. Johnson on twin pianos on a date for Vocalion. The numbers made were, *I Ain't Gonna Play No Second Fiddle*, and *Lucy Long*. Besides James and Fats, Louis Armstrong, Charlie Green and Don Redman were on the sides. It was Louis' last New York record date before he returned to Chicago. The young trumpet player had knocked them cold in New York in spite of the confinement of Fletcher Henderson's written arrangements which had to some extent restricted the freedom play of his improvisations. He was now off to the scene of his first Northern triumphs, but he was not going back as second trumpet man to Joe Oliver, nor to play third trumpet in a big jazz band; he was now looking forward to a new career as band leader in his own right. He carried with him the promise of Ralph Peer that as soon as he got to Chicago, an Okeh recording contract awaited him, under his own name. Peer had learned a lot about what was good jazz since his early days at Okeh.

8

Things were now beginning to break for Waller in a much bigger way. Though financially tied by the bondage of his alimony payments he still kept up with his downtown connections, and his beloved, vibrant Harlem never let him down. Plunging anew into the swirl of house parties and jam sessions after hours at the clubs, he rejoined James, Willie, Brooksy and the others in endless rounds of the houses. At any hour of the night they would knock on an apartment door and continue to do so until someone answered. Then Lippy's voice would crackle out: 'Open up there. I got James P. and Fats with me.' It was like an open sesame – the words were infallible – the doors would open and the fun began. Lippy always made sure there were plenty of luscious queens on hand at the parties, the boys from all around came running, and a party was on.

Harlem in the Twenties was well supplied with houses of prostitution. It was no secret that many prosperous New Yorkers were constantly calling at the luxurious palaces of sin which, under official condonation, were reaping their share of the money which flowed into Black Manhattan. Perhaps no other place in town was as popular as an establishment known as the 'Daisy Chain'. Located for most of its life in the West 140s, this good-time house had a long Harlem history, and has been perpetuated on record by Count Basie's *Swingin' At The Daisy Chain*. Its proprietor, the attractive Hazel Valentine, was also the subject of Fats' own *Valentine Stomp*, dedicated to her – a piano solo regarded as Waller at his best and most typical.

The 'Daisy Chain' moved at one time to 101 West 140th Street, where it was popularly known as the '101 Ranch' after an early New Orleans house. Harlemites also knew the place as 'Paris in the Spring', and its star attraction for many years was a girl with the provocative nickname of 'Sewing Machine Bertha'. A great favourite among the patrons, Bertha is still mentioned with affection when the good old days are spoken of. The 'Daisy Chain' wasn't entirely commercial either, for rumour has it that the standard rate was five dollars, with your money back if you weren't satisfied!

It was only a matter of time before this celebrated whore-house claimed the attention of the piano-playing professors and, in fact, almost the entire Harlem musical set. Boasting a fine grand piano in the parlour, the house was the scene of many a memorable jam session. Inspiration ran rampant, with the dusky beauties crowding round the piano when they were not otherwise engaged, and of course there was always plenty of gin on hand to 'fluidize' the evening. Many of the hit songs of that period got their start in the 'Daisy Chain' and the famous W. C. Handy was once inspired to remark: 'If Fats Waller could be locked up in a room at the "Daisy Chain" with a piano, a bottle of gin and several beautiful chicks, he would certainly come up with some of the most beautiful music written this side of Heaven.'

Hazel Valentine was a warm friend of many of the pianists and other musicians of Harlem, and Fats is said to have paid the rent at the 'Daisy Chain' on more than one occasion when things weren't going too well.

James P., with a few hit shows behind him, was now fairly affluent. He had bought a Cadillac on the instalment plan, and one bright spring afternoon picked up Fats and a couple of others. They drove over to the 'Daisy Chain' where James honked the horn until Hazel came out of the front door and got in the car. They set course for Mount Vernon and Gregory's, a popular stop-off, but first they had to go through the Bronx. At the wheel, James P. seemed anxious to beat all the lights and get over the Grand Concourse with the least possible delay. The others didn't ask any questions, merely sat back and enjoyed the breeze, but soon the reason for his haste became very apparent. At last a red light forced him to halt, and from an auto dealer's establishment on the corner two men ran over and, without waiting for any explanations, showed their credentials and, with no further ado, re-possessed the car. The occupants had to make their way back downtown by subway, swearing it was the last time they'd take a ride with James P. But James P.'s misadventures with cars continued. On another occasion he and Fats had been holed up in a Harlem spot for about three days having a ball. James' wife, Lil, who had secretly been taking driving lessons, decided she would teach her husband a lesson. Spotting the car, she drove it off from the front of the place they were in and when at last Fats and James emerged into the sunshine they were appalled to find the car gone. After a frantic and fruitless search they trudged back home to find the car neatly parked by the kerb. James P. thought it wiser to hold his tongue and ask no questions.

For some time the Lafayette had been putting on short-run musicals. James P. Johnson had written a great deal of music for these shows which were complete stage shows. Leonard Harper, an up-and-coming Negro producer, who later went into Connie's Inn with outstanding success, was one of the men who staged these productions. Others were Charlie Davis and one Carey. The theatre owners decided in 1926 to do a revue and they didn't have to look far for a composer. Fats had been hobnobbing with the vaudeville stars, Ralph Cooper and Eddie Rector, and was often to be found drinking at William Blackie's, a bar adjacent to the theatre. A favourite drink of the house was top-and-bottoms, a potion which consisted of blackberry wine and gin. Over a few of these imaginative concoctions with the team one evening, Fats was assured he would get the assignment to write the score. Accordingly, in company with Spencer Williams, Fats worked out the songs. Featuring a hit song *Señorita Mine*, which swept over the country under the banner of the Clarence Williams Music Publishing Company in a remarkable climb to popularity, the show, 'Tan Town Topics', was a notable local success. It was indeed unfortunate that all the Lafayette Theatre's productions were doomed to such a short happy life – around three or four weeks – in the Harlem theatre, then perhaps a couple of weeks on the Eastern Negro Theatre circuit and that was all.

Fats also did the music for a show called 'Jr. Blackbirds' – a show whose title capitalized on a great hit of the moment. In this year the Lew Leslie production entitled 'Blackbirds' had hit the Alhambra Theatre in Harlem and had played there for six weeks to packed houses. Its star was the incomparable Florence Mills, whose début in 'Keep Shufflin'' five years before had started her on her dazzling career. Florence was as beloved of the Negro race as anyone has ever been, and it is true to say that the adulation which followed her every show, whether it was downtown or in Harlem, surpassed anything before or since. Her performances were true magic – a singing and dancing comedienne with a most vital personality, she used to great effect a sweet melodious voice with a diction that was clear as a bell.

Leaving the Plantation Club, 'Blackbirds' played the afore-mentioned Alhambra and eventually went on tour. The show and its star were immortalized in Europe, playing five weeks in Paris and six in London where an enchanted Prince of Wales attended the performance no less than sixteen times to applaud 'little Twinks' as he called Miss Mills.

*   *   *

One of the regular patrons of the Lincoln Theatre where Fats now doubled in addition to the Lafayette, was a pretty 16-year-old girl named Anita Rutherford. A carefully brought up girl, she was only allowed to go out with one boy, and so, with her young man of the moment, she visited the local showplace to see the stage and screen attraction of the week. As she entered she was spotted by Fats standing in the rear of the orchestra section. He watched her intently as she sat down and tried to remember where he'd seen her before. He thought it had been at a party in a friend's house. Before the show started Anita sat and chatted with her friend, now and then turning round to see if there was anyone behind them whom they knew. Suddenly she spotted a figure waving to her – it was Fats Waller, seated at the organ. He gave her a disarming smile which she answered hesitantly. Later that week she bumped into Fats again. He asked her if she remembered him and expressed his desire to take her out. Flattered by the attentions of the famous young musician and charmed by his expressive features, Anita agreed to a date, insisting however that he should call at her home and meet her family. A fast Waller courtship ensued, although Anita was soon well aware that Tom was not entirely free of obligations. His alimony payments were a constant drain on his somewhat erratic income and in spite of the way he laughed off his debts, she pressed him to take the matter seriously, trying to explain the grave trouble which might otherwise result.

This young girl was probably the best thing that ever happened to Fats Waller. Wise beyond her years, and ably advised by her mother, she resolved to marry Fats but only if a lot of changes were made. She sought the advice of Captain Maines, now a close family counsellor in addition to the intensive work he did for Fats' musical career. Maines' advice was that she should by all means marry Fats for it was obvious he needed someone to straighten him out. His career, although pursuing a haphazard course, was gaining momentum in spite of the vicissitudes which beset him, and Maines foresaw a great future for him. A contract which he held with Fats to manage him for life, lay on his desk; it was never enforced.

'Anita is a lovely young girl, Fats,' he said; 'she wants to marry you but I don't want her to get hurt. You know what happened before. Do you think you can make it stick this time? Do you want anything permanent out of marriage?'

The answer tumbled out immediately: 'Sure I do. I love Anita – I wouldn't hurt her!'

'I believe you, but this time I want to see you get a proper start. Here's what I'll do, Tom. I am going to release you from your obligations to me as your manager, and let you go ahead – seriously now – and save your money. I want you to settle down, and put enough cash together to buy a home. Ten thousand should do it. I also want to see you start a family. What do you say?'

Fats agreed this was what he wanted, so, promising to keep up his alimony payments, he went to Anita. For the first time in his life Fats was truly in love. His attraction to Edith had been greatly coloured by the loss of his mother, but this seems to have been the real thing from the first, and his love for Anita continued throughout the rest of his life.

He now plunged with renewed vigour into his work and, spurred on by the new impetus, he began to toe the line. They first went to live with Anita's grandmother, who by all accounts was quite an enterprising old lady. Her place at 107 West 133rd Street, just a block from Fats' birthplace, was a combination lunchroom, barbershop and poolroom. The whole house was owned by the Rutherfords, who let out some of the twenty-six rooms to others.

Now not even his own piano-playing was satisfactory to Fats, and he began to make regular trips to the great teacher, Leopold Godowsky. He took courses in advanced harmony along with James P., who was always a real student of the piano.

But money was short, and Fats was desperately writing new tunes, with or without Andy's lyrics. One day, sitting discouraged at the food counter of Jess Wynn, 'The Hamburg King', next to the Rhythm Club on 132nd Street, the door opened and in walked Don Redman. Immediately sensing Fats' depressed attitude, he said softly, 'Hello, Fats.'

Looking up, Fats brightened immediately. 'Hey, Don – have a seat and buy me a hamburger.'

After putting a couple of them away, he said, 'C'mon in the back room. I got something for you.'

Jess Wynn had a piano in the back room of his restaurant, and Fats sat down, unrolling a bunch of sheet music as he did so. Without hesitation he played over eight numbers, all of which he had just written. Don was enthusiastic. 'They're great, man. What're you goin' to do with them?'

'Sell them to you,' was Fats' retort. 'Don, I need money fast. How about buying these? You can have 'em for ten dollars a piece. They'll be great if you do 'em up for Fletcher. They'll be big hits, man. I know! C'mon, Don, take them.'

Don looked at him. 'Fats – you been drinking.'

'Not much, Don, just a slight touch of those liquid ham 'n' eggs.' He gestured with the music. 'How about it, will you take them?'

'No, Fats, I won't take them. You take them down to Fletcher yourself when you're back on the ball. Don't sell 'em cheap, Fats. Now let's get out of here.' They went out into the air, and parted with a handshake.

The very next day, Fats took off for Fletcher's house, and the band leader, after listening to Fats playing his new numbers over on the piano, bought most of them at a fair price. Don Redman did arrangements for all of them and a number of them were eventually recorded. Fats claimed that some of his tunes were later, with altered titles, credited to Fletcher as composer, but whatever truth there may be in this statement, it is certain that he and Fletcher were at this time close friends. Fats was called in as pianist on several of the Columbia dates and appeared intermittently with the band for years. Fletcher knew his own limitations as a pianist, and certainly recognized Waller as the great musician he was.

Waller numbers incorporated into the Henderson band book, and also recorded by the band, were *St Louis Shuffle*, *Whiteman Stomp*, dedicated to the popularly named 'King of Jazz', himself an enthusiastic Waller fan, and later *Keep A Song In Your Soul*, *Crazy 'Bout My Baby*, and the catchy *Stealin' Apples*.

With Ken Macomber, Fats laboured long and hard at the Roseland in the middle and late Twenties, writing tunes and arranging for the big band, which from time to time did battle with such rival orchestras as the aforementioned Jean Goldkette orchestra, and others of that period. All the big bands played the Roseland, and the Henderson organization took on all comers.

In this same year Fats came into contact with a publisher named Joe Davis. Davis, who hadn't done business with Fats before this, later figures prominently in the Waller story. He was a white publisher who early hopped on the Negro jazz bandwagon and became a steady buyer of Waller-Razaf-J. C. Johnson material.

In the meantime, Ralph Peer, now owner of the Southern Music Company, had induced the Victor Talking Machine Company to take over his publishing house as a subsidiary, and retain him as President and General Manager. In this capacity he reaped a large harvest. Apparently the Victor Company went into the deal with their eyes wide open, for the contract giving Peer a royalty of 2 cents per record on all those featuring Southern Music (Peer) copyrights didn't, on the face of it, look too extravagant. The company reckoned that race discs might sell 20,000 copies a record and that on that figure Peer might make a good income, but when the record sales went up into figures like 700,000, Peer's income skyrocketed. He later was able to buy back his own publishing company.

Before this happened, however, the Victor company placed the management of the race and hillbilly series also in Peer's hands. He quickly remembered his friend from the Okeh days: Fats Waller, the unpredictable. This proved for Fats a fortunate connection, for race records were not being pushed to any great extent by Victor, which favoured the rising hillbilly field, and in consequence,

Waller, together with Fletcher Henderson, McKinney's Cotton Pickers and Jelly Roll Morton, was the mainstay of their race label.

His first Victor recording was made on 17 November 1926, and it remains one of his historic sides: *St Louis Blues*, backed by his own *Lenox Avenue Blues*. The Victor people had bought an old church in Camden, New Jersey, which contained an organ on one side of the large hall, and a Steinway concert grand on the other. One microphone faced the organ chamber; another stood by the piano. Beside the Steinway was an additional console organ, convenient for recording piano and organ together, or organ and band. On this equipment, then, Fats played the immortal old tune. It was rendered in a drag-tango-tempo which made W. C. Handy exclaim with delight when he heard it for the first time.

At home, Anita was delighted with the change that had come over her husband. He seemed to have straightened out considerably, and was now facing up to his responsibilities as never before. His nightly crawling with the cronies continued, but his daylight hours were more productive, and sage advice from Maines, Peer and his lyricists Razaf and Johnson, who had before fought a losing battle against his waywardness, straightened him up to some extent. So his career continued apace.

Nevertheless, the Waller idiosyncrasies still came to the fore in many ways. In his usual airy, off-hand fashion, he continued to sell songs to publishers without bothering to tell them that a rival had just bought the same song down the street.

J. C. Johnson recalls one occasion on which Fats breezed into a music publisher's office with an idea, which he demonstrated briefly. The publisher liked it and paid Waller for it on the spot. With a hearty 'See you tomorrow with the music!' Fats was off with the cash for a little refreshment. The next day he came in again, and the man requested the manuscript of the song he had bought the previous day.

Waller's brow furrowed. He said, 'Oh, that one? Well – I guess I didn't think that one was good enough for you. But here's another one – much better, just you listen to this!' And without any preparation, he sat down and picked out a catchy tune on the piano which the man truly did like better than the one he had heard the previous day. This was typical of the disarming quality which

Fats possessed all his life. Nobody could ever really get angry with him and stay that way. Pulling a stunt like the one mentioned would have blackballed most writers in Tin Pan Alley for life, but Waller made a habit of such pranks. He thrived on innocent fun, embarrassing though it might be for the other person. Coupled with his likeability was a sheer genius which shone through everything he did, and preserved his standing throughout the years.

His good friend Spencer Williams now left Harlem and the United States for Europe, going over to Paris with Josephine Baker, a singer and dancer who had knocked the New York audiences cold a couple of years before when she appeared in 'Chocolate Dandies', a Sissle and Blake production. Spencer found a lot to his liking on the Continent, and he spent a great deal of the next twenty years in France and England, writing material for Miss Baker, who had become a blazing star in the French musical firmament. He wrote the music for the 'Revue Nègre' in Paris, which was produced at the Champs-Elysées Theatre, and had a ten-month run. In 1927 Josephine went into the Folies Bergère, for which Spencer wrote material as well.

Early 1927 found Fats recording prolifically. Not, as yet, under exclusive contract with Victor, he nevertheless recorded for them more than for any other company. On Victor, his organ playing, at which Peer considered him a genius, is prominently represented. Such fascinating titles as *Soothin' Syrup Stomp*; *Sloppy Water Blues* and *Rusty Pail*, both blues numbers written by Fats; and others such as *Stompin' The Bug*; *Hog Maw Stomp*; and later with Morris' Hot Babies *The Digah's Stomp*, a version of the old rag classic, *The Dream*.

Fletcher Henderson used to tell this story about Fats. One day when Fats was in the studio, he recorded an anonymous tune he had written, or maybe made up in the studio on the spot. After the cutting he was approached by the studio manager who wanted to know what the title was.

'Title?' rumbled Fats. 'I guess we'll just call that one *Thundermug Stomp*.' His eyebrows were raised in innocence.

The man filled out the record sheet accordingly. Then, puzzled, he turned round. 'By the way, Mr Waller, what is a thundermug?'

'My, my, don't you know what that is?' incredulously replied Fats. 'Was you brought up in the country?'

'Why, yes, as a matter of fact, I was.'

Fats' nose wrinkled in a smile. 'Well then, I suppose you had one of them under your bed – did you not?'

The man caught his meaning and without another word took out his pencil and drew a line through the word on the record sheet.

'Guess you'll have to think up another title for that one, Mr Waller,' he said with a smile.

Other organ solos from this period were *Sugar* and *Beale Street Blues*, both done at the same session. He also made another pair on this same date, featuring him playing the same tunes on organ as a background for vocals for Alberta Hunter, but they turned into virtual organ solos in themselves, such is the length of his part on these sides.

On this day, 20 May 1927, on which the old church seems to have rocked most irreligiously, a new band recorded for the Victor label. It was Thomas Morris' Hot Babies, a pick-up group which included the leader on cornet, Charlie Irvis on trombone, and Eddie King on drums. Fats played organ in combination with the band, creating what is probably a jazz recording first. The selections were *Fats Waller Stomp*, *Savannah Blues*, and *Won't You Take Me Home?* The vital music that is displayed on these Hot Babies sides is in no small way due to the indescribable hot quality that Fats manages to coax out of the pipe-organ. He was undoubtedly the most successful jazz organist of that time, standing head and shoulders above all other competitors.

It becomes apparent with a minimum of observation that Thomas Waller's love for the organ as an instrument exceeded his relish for the piano. Whenever possible he would use the organ in recordings, and he approached it with what seems to have been almost reverence. Each time he threw the switch and sensed the mighty response awaiting the touch of his fingertips, he felt inspired. Undoubtedly the true nature of the man emerged from behind that hilarious crust that made his name synonymous with joviality and jive, and communicated itself to the fortunate listener each time he recorded on organ. The two sides of Fats Waller's character are clearly etched in the grooves of his records by comparing, for instance, any of his torrid band or piano pieces with the touching series of spirituals he recorded in England for HMV in 1938.

It is asserted by Charles Edward Smith in the *Yearbook of Swing* (Downbeat Publishing Co., 1939) that sometime during his Victor recording career Fats made a series of records which were never issued. They comprise one of the most extraordinary sets of recordings that he ever made, and it is to be hoped that eventually they will be found and released to a public that is now more than ready for them. Bach's Fugues in D Minor and B Minor, Rimsky-Korsakov's 'Flight of the Bumble Bee', 'Spanish Days' by Friml, and Liszt's 'Liebestraum', were all played, both as originally written, and also in the typical Waller manner. An unconfirmed rumour has it that these Waller recordings were suppressed at the request of one of Victor's top artists – an organist. Perhaps timidity on the part of the recording company in holding back these precious masters was excusable at the early date on which they were made, but to keep faith with the millions of Waller fans, the RCA Victor Company should now take immediate steps to place them on the market as they have so generously done with his other works.

In the spring of 1927, Fletcher Henderson and Fats went to college, playing various fraternity dates at Princeton and Yale Universities. Fats, with his ferocious mugging at the keyboard, panicked the collegians and gained for himself a new and loyal following of youthful fans.

*   *   *

In the same spring Anita announced that she was going to have a child, and she and Fats were jubilant.

In May came an unexpected new opening – a job was offered Fats in Chicago at the Vendome Theatre. Fats' friend, Louis Armstrong, was making history playing in the pit band led by Erskine Tate, and he and his wife, the former Lil Hardin, offered to put up Anita and Fats in their home for as long as they wished to stay. Consequently it wasn't long before they boarded the train and headed for the mid-western city.

The fresh air of the Windy City blew all the alimony troubles out of Fats' mind, and, with a fine jazz band in the pit, and an inspirational Louis with whom to duet during intermissions, life indeed was swinging.

Erskine Tate was one of the most prominent leaders in Chicago and was at this time doing a marathon stint at one location. He opened with his large orchestra at the Vendome in 1918 and stayed there for nine years straight. Besides Louis and Fats, he employed from time to time in his band such artists as Omer Simeon, Earl Hines, Teddy Weatherford, Darnell Howard, Buster Bailey, and Jabbo Smith. The usual procedure for a show was that the Tate band, for the opening and during intermissions, would play some very arranged selections bringing in anything and everything from light classics to musical comedy selections but also giving his star soloist a chance to shine. Then as a finale the band would really romp and let go with a genuine torrid jazz session. The band performance lasted for an hour. In addition they often accompanied the silent films as well. Fats was a feature on the organ as well as the piano, bringing to the Chicago audiences a little genuine Lenox Avenue music – he was as resounding a success as he had been at the little Lincoln Theatre in New York.

After hours, there was plenty going on. Louis was doubling over at the Sunset Cafe, Calumet and 35th, where he had succeeded the Carroll Dickerson band, with whom he played for some time. His new band, which included Earl Hines, Honoré Dutrey, and Tubby Hall, was the first band which Louis actually fronted, and Fats lost no time getting over there each night, after the Vendome closed its doors, to sit in with this wonderful group. The band featured two pianos on many occasions, a musician named Hansby playing opposite Hines. Earl also played with Tate at this time, having succeeded the well-remembered, but little recorded, Teddy Weatherford. Weatherford left Chicago at this time for the Orient, where he died during World War II.

When Fats walked into the Sunset Cafe, booming a greeting to his friends, a piano was always vacated for him. What a shame it was that he never recorded with this historic little band! The piano that Fats performed on was placed above the band, and one night when everything was rocking solid, some local song-pluggers, according to long-established custom, approached Louis with a new tune. He took the parts, glanced at them and then passed them around to the sidemen. With no rehearsal the band went into it, and by paying strict attention to the music they got the first chorus off like a dream. The second time round, Louis picked up the beat a little, and they all began to give the number a freer interpretation. Towards the end of the first eight bars, third time round, a certain amount of disorganization was apparent and polyphony flew out of the window. Seated at the grand piano, Fats then ventured some new exploratory harmonies. Finally he raised his eyebrows and started desperately crashing out great chords, in an effort to try and regain the lost melody. As the music faltered and died away to a whisper, he sighed, and then, leaning over to the rest of the band, said, devastatingly, 'Pardon me, boys, but what key're you all strugglin' in down there?' It broke up the house. Louis and Earl split their sides, and are still laughing at it to this day.

The good times in Chicago came to an end for Anita and Fats in a rather disconcerting way. A man showed up with a warrant for Thomas Waller's arrest on a complaint that his alimony was in arrears. He was taken back to New York and had to face music of quite a different kind. Anita, with the baby, which they had named Maurice, was left stranded in Chicago, and eventually her mother had to rescue her 17-year-old daughter and baby grandson.

This blow was a bitter one for Fats, for, more than the previous court proceedings, this one struck at his new love, and threatened to jeopardize his new family life. Henceforth, he was determined to resist by any means in his power the claims that Edith made upon his income. All his resolutions were put aside, and he refused to abide by the legal settlements which he had previously agreed upon. His payments continued to be erratic and often non-existent.

Hauled into court to answer the new charges brought by Edith, Fats was disconsolate, but he was again lucky. The judge gave him a long lecture on the serious nature of his position, but announced that no further action would be taken if the payments continued as previously agreed. Fats, turning to his father who had accompanied him to court, gave him a hug. The older man patted his son on the shoulder and they walked away together.

*　　*　　*

Back in New York, Fats' first job was with Victor. A special day's recording was set up at Camden, the music to be in memory of Florence Mills, who had died two weeks earlier of appendicitis. The whole Negro world mourned her, and her funeral had been the scene of tumult and an unbelievable demonstration of grief.

Singers Bert Howell and Juanita Stinette, the latter of the vaudeville team of Stinette and Chappelle, made the trip to the studio with Fats, who was accompanied by Anita and baby Maurice. At the studio, Ralph Peer asked Anita if she and the baby would like to stay whilst Fats recorded. Anita was enthusiastic, and promised that the baby would be kept very quiet.

Juanita Stinette sang *Florence*, with a soft organ background by Fats filling out the side reverently. Bert Howell followed this with a tune specially composed for the occasion and called *Bye-Bye Florence*.

The session finished, Peer came over to Anita, and patting baby Maurice's head, said, 'What a well-behaved little boy, Anita! He's been so good and quiet this afternoon, I want him to have this,' and he gave her a cheque for ten dollars.

More recording followed on 1 December 1927: a set of six sides – four with Thomas Morris' Hot Babies, and two organ solos, Spencer Williams' *I Ain't Got Nobody* and the aforementioned *Digah's Stomp*.

By the end of that year Miller and Lyles, who had a not too successful show running called 'Rang-Tang', were laying their plans for another Broadway show in 1928 and looking for a backer. One came soon, from a notorious source. A great admirer of the famous team was the gambler Arnold Rothstein who in recent years had been secretly backing big shows on the Main Stem and who was reported to have put up much of the money for 'Runnin' Wild' back in 1923 – the show that introduced the Charleston. Knowing that the team were now short of an 'angel' and wanting to see them back on Broadway, he decided to finance their new comedy, 'Keep Shufflin'. Con Conrad, a Harlemite, was something of an entrepreneur himself, handling several vaudeville acts and staging various shows here and there. It was he who acted as adviser between Miller and Lyles and Rothstein, and who became the show's producer. Back in 1921 in England, Miller, Lyles and

Conrad had got together and vowed that some day they would do an all-Negro show on Broadway – a show in which they would all participate. So was born the idea for 'Keep Shufflin'' – an idea which now, seven years later, was to come into being. Resolved that this show should have the best of everything, Rothstein had Conrad scout around for a writer who could turn out a real hit score and it was to James P. Johnson that Conrad went first. Johnson's lyricists and co-writers at this time were Henry Creamer and Clarence Todd. Fats was also approached, and as he was in dire need of work, the offer could not have come at a more opportune moment. He and Andy Razaf were commissioned to do half the tunes for the show.

Before it actually got under way, however, James P. had to finish rehearsing another opus, 'Messin' Around'. This show, with a score by himself and Perry Bradford, and dancing staged by George Rector, didn't open on Broadway until April 1929. As a whole, it got disappointing reviews, but the music was praised by all the critics.

The new show was whipped into shape in good time, and contained tunes galore to gladden the hearts of the first-nighters. It opened at Gibson's Theatre in Philadelphia prior to its New York début, and besides the two star comedians, a tremendous success was scored by a singer named Jean Starr, who sang what was regarded as the hit song of the show, *Give Me The Sunshine*, a tune written by Con Conrad.

There were twenty-two musical numbers in the show, and among them were some of the most pleasing hits ever written by this great battery of composers. Johnson, Creamer and Todd made history with *Sippi*, while Fats and Andy contributed, among others, the catchy *Willow Tree*.

Opening in New York on 27 February 1928, at Daly's 63rd Street Theatre, scene of the immortal 'Shuffle Along', the show delighted critics and audience alike. In this musical play, the comedy team of Miller and Lyles carried the show, with other talented performers in the cast, notably John Vigal and Clarence Robinson, prominent as juveniles, a smooth dancer, Byron Jones, and Blanche Calloway, sister of the then unknown Cab.

The book had been written by the two principals, and much to their surprise it was immediately hailed by the critics as broad satire slanted towards the impracticability of Communism. Flournoy Miller denied that any political implications had been planned, and claimed that the whole thing merely originated from a simple idea they had had one day. The happy coincidence, however, didn't worry them in the least, and it was perhaps responsible for some of the success of the show.

The plot roughly was that two lazy-bones, Steve Jenkins and his pal Sam Cook, thought they had found the easy way to a life of wealth and plenty. Enlisting a group of workmen in their new 'Equal Got League', they promised riches for all. Resolving to blow open a bank, they started to figure out who should be the lucky one to do the dynamiting. Steve Jenkins (played by Miller) hit upon the idea of staging a battle royal to see who was the most fearless. No sooner had he proclaimed himself the referee, when his partner hopped on the bandwagon, and proclaimed that he was the vice-referee. In the mêlée that follows, Steve is knocked out, and the subsequent scenes dealt with his dreams of the developments which would ensue after the bank had been robbed. After living in riches and splendour for a few days, with everybody running about loaded with bills and gold pieces, the city's utilities start to fail, the stores close, and transport lines stop running. Money becomes worthless, Steve sees the utter futility of the scheme, and awakens to a complete turnabout.

During the early stages of the show, Miller, who was completely unaware of the power of their backer, became very tired of his continual interference. One evening, after a particularly hectic day, he strode into Rothstein's office, and confronted the gambler.

'Mr Rothstein,' he began, 'I'm mighty tired of hearing "Mr Rothstein says do this and Mr Rothstein says do that." Who the hell is running this show, anyhow?'

A tough-looking bruiser seated at the back of the office leaped to his feet on hearing Miller's rough treatment of his boss, and his hand plunged into his coat pocket. Rothstein merely smiled broadly, and motioned for the man to sit down. The man sat, and Miller went on, railing at the man behind the desk. Every time his voice hit an excited peak, Rothstein just grinned again.

When Miller had finished, he turned and walked out of the

room, slamming the door behind him. Rothstein just smiled. Back with Lyles in their dressing-room, Flournoy told his partner that he had really told that Rothstein guy a thing or two, and recounted what had happened.

His partner, hearing him out, turned pale, and sat down suddenly. Looking at the ceiling, he then slowly proceeded to explain to Flournoy Miller the facts of life in the underworld, and Rothstein's exalted position therein.

But despite his fearsome reputation, Rothstein was by all accounts an eminently fair and generous man, particularly with the show people in 'Keep Shufflin' '. He was a strange man, from whom you could borrow a thousand with never a mention of repayment; but woe betide anyone who forgot to return a half-dollar he had borrowed!

Fats and James P. were not long in finding out where the money was coming from, and, meeting Rothstein one afternoon, Fats arched his eyebrows at him and said, 'How 'bout lettin' us have a little trash to get a cab uptown, Mr Rothstein? We are temporarily embarrassed.'

Rothstein opened his wallet. 'Sure, boys,' he said; 'how much?'

'Oh – a double sawbuck'll do us.' James nodded affirmatively.

Rothstein looked up. 'That much for just a taxi ride?' he asked quietly.

Fats took a look at the gambler's eyes, and stuttered, 'W-well, how about ten bucks?'

'*How much?*' The voice was no longer inquisitive.

'H-how 'bout a fast finn?' Fats faltered, coming down fast. Rothstein softened, and handed the boys five dollars.

On one occasion, however, the boys fared much better. Running into Rothstein backstage one day, Andy and Fats caught him in a giving mood. Fats, as usual, tried to hit him flippantly as ever for a little money, and nearly fell flat on his back when Arnold said, 'Sure, boys, how about five hundred apiece?' Outside, they caressed the folding money, and Fats said to Andy, 'Man! That is sure that goose who lays them golden eggs!'

*   *   *

Fats and James, in addition to writing some of the score, also showed their talents on the keyboard in the intermission between the acts. The programme read: 'In the orchestra – on the white keys, Fats Waller – on the black keys, James P. Johnson – on the bugle, Jabbo Smith'.

The band which Johnson led during the show took a breather at the interval and the powerful James P. and his partner, the rotund Fats, took over on the twin grand pianos. Much has been written about the fabulous virtuosity of King Oliver and Louis Armstrong when they played together on the bandstand of the Dreamland Cafe in Chicago; they played as one man, and their cornet duets became justly famous. None the less, the piano duets, as performed nightly at Daly's Theatre, were also fully worthy of the same praise. *Dippermouth Blues* was the vehicle used by the two cornetists, and *Sippi* now became the tune talked about all over town; and particularly the versions as played by Johnson and Waller.

Beginning with a straight version of the melody, they quickly followed with chorus after chorus of variations, improvising, creating as they went along, and playing as if the four hands were guided by one brain. The oneness that always characterized the playing of Johnson and Waller really came to full flower at these sessions. Alternating the melody lead between them, they nightly took *Sippi* further along the jazz road than *Ol' Man River* himself had ever ventured. The audience were loath to leave between the acts, so sensational was the playing of these two musicians, and the bars did the worst business on record. It became a kind of rent-party *de luxe* – in strange surroundings, to be sure, but as truly jazz as if it had emanated from the cellar of Pod and Jerry's.

Spectacular displays were also put on by a drummer known as Battleaxe, whose gyrations and antics delighted the audience, and by Jabbo Smith with some beautiful trumpet playing.

But every night Flournoy Miller had to work hard to get the boys out there. Often, the comedian recalls, he would get off stage as quickly as possible after the curtain fell, and dash down to their dressing-room, only to find them just standing there, hands clasped behind their backs, smiling happily.

'You're on,' he'd call. 'Come on, get out there!' He would look around for the bottle he knew was there somewhere.

Fats and James P. would assure Miller that the last thing they wanted to do was miss the intermission.

'Well, let's go!' and Flournoy would leave the room with them, only to return as soon as they had reached the pit. Hundreds of times he turned the room upside down in his quest for a bottle; but he could never find it. Waller and Johnson were pastmasters at gin-concealment.

Sippi and *Willow Tree* were in such demand that Victor decided to record a band version right away. James and Fats did their double piano act but their playing was so restricted by time that it bore no resemblance to what they did in the theatre.

*　　*　　*

1928 saw a gala night at Carnegie Hall to mark the 25th Anniversary of the writing of *Memphis Blues*. William C. Handy, the famous 'Father of the Blues', presented a programme of blues and jazz, together with some Negro spirituals, using an orchestra of forty pieces, and a mixed choir of twenty voices.

The feature of the concert was to be an ambitious rhapsody recently written by James P. Johnson, entitled *Yamekraw*. It was James' musical impression of life in the notorious black quarter of Savannah, Georgia, known as the Yamecraw district, and the composition had already drawn wide acclaim and had been made the subject of a Vitaphone short film, with an all-Negro cast, including Johnson himself. He had intended to play the piano part at the Carnegie Hall concert himself, but because no substitute could be found it was impossible for him to get away from his conducting at the theatre.

'You go ahead and take over, Fatness,' he said, disgusted with his luck. 'If I can't do it, you might as well. You know it anyway.'

Fats dashed over to the Hall for a rehearsal, and in addition to the selections he was to play on piano and organ, he satisfied the promoters of his ability to perform James P.'s colourful rhapsody. He was in for a busy evening.

Friday, 27 April 1928, was a night to remember in more ways than one. Wind and rain lashed up and down 57th Street like a tropical hurricane, but nevertheless the house was well filled.

Opening with a number called *The Birth Of Jazz*, performed by the choir armed with tom-toms, the show quickly got into its stride. W. C. Handy took up his position in front of the orchestra, and Fats played *Beale Street Blues* on the organ, with orchestral accompaniment. This was followed by a group of spirituals arranged by Mr Handy; then a blues medley in which *Yellow Dog Blues*, *St Louis Blues*, and *Beale Street Blues* were featured – the last number being sung by the composer's daughter, Katherine E. Handy.

Other acts included J. Rosamond Johnson and Taylor Gordon, who sang a group of spirituals; 'Dusty' Fletcher's character songs; a cake-walk demonstration; and a performance of Will Marion Cook's 'Exhortation'. Fats played *Yamekraw* just as James P. would have liked, backed by the large orchestra, and the concert was a rousing success, both artistically and financially. Fats lit out for the theatre and found his friend just emerging.

'How'd it go, Fats?'

'Fine, wonderful, perfect – we killed them over there – it was solid, man!'

* * *

The year wore on, and the two pianists worked nightly at the theatre. It seemed that *Willow Tree* and *Sippi* would get stale and that nothing else could be done with them, but they were still requested each night, and Fats and James P. somehow managed to make new things happen to them.

In June, Fats left the show, to take a job playing the organ at the Royal Grand Theatre in Philadelphia. This was one of the last times he would be playing for the silent films, for sound movies were beginning to come in very slowly. The larger theatres with pipe-organs were the ones which first installed the new systems, and with the advent of the new medium the organ as a means of entertainment started to fall into disuse.

In the weeks that Fats and Anita spent in the City of Brotherly Love, the seemingly inevitable happened once again. The payments to Edith fell in arrears, and real trouble greeted Fats on his trip homeward, quite unable to meet the outstanding debt which had accumulated in his absence. The court this time lost patience with him, and he found himself behind bars on Welfare Island, in jail for alimony arrears. It was no mere overnight stop, and this time his friends could not help. This time there was no party-throwing ex-commissioner of the city to share steaks with, no gaiety, no music – Fats was in prison.

While in prison, Fats suffered another blow with the news of his *July '28* father's death. He was offered the opportunity of attending the funeral, but declined, not wanting to enter the church under police escort.

During the weeks that he spent in jail, Anita and her family were not idle, and good friends made the rounds, trying to collect the money to secure his release. The debt ran into four figures, an amount not easy to come by. Loyal Captain Maines added his influence, and the fund grew, but it seemed an impossible task.

On 4 November, a man who might have been well able to help Waller was shot in the Park Central Hotel and died two days later in hospital. Arnold Rothstein had lost his last trick, and with his passing went any hopes of money from that quarter. In fact, he owed Waller about a thousand dollars at the time of his death – a debt which was never collected.

But later that same month the singer, Gene Austin, a long-time friend of Fats' and a keen admirer of his work, hearing that he was again in jail, awaiting bail, rushed to court with the necessary cash.

'This man,' said the judge sternly, pointing to Fats in the dock, 'has been before this court too many times for failure to pay his alimony dues – this cannot go on any longer.' And then, looking at Gene Austin, 'Is there any special reason why I should release this man on bail?'

Austin, somewhat taken aback by the question, as he had expected no difficulty in 'springing' his fat friend, thought quickly and replied, 'Well, your honour, I do have a record session this afternoon, and if this man is not there to play the piano for me, it will put quite a few other musicians out of a job – and jobs are hard to come by these days.'

'Well, if that is the case, I will accept bail,' said the judge, 'but . . .' and he went on to give Fats a severe lecture on the errors of his ways.

Gene Austin used Fats on his session all right, but it is a sad commentary on the affair that the other musicians he had hired for the date refused at first to work with Waller, because of his colour. The record was eventually made with the accompanying orchestra grouped around one microphone, while Fats was placed at the opposite end of the studio by himself: an early and unhappy case of segregation.

The court after this kept direct contact with Fats, receiving his payments and transferring them to Edith. In future, they aimed at ensuring regular payments.

Shortly after Fats' release from prison, Anita gave birth to another son, who was named Ronald.

Thomas Wright (Fats) Waller, 1935. "I'm livin' in a great big way."

James P. Johnson

Andy Razaf

Willie (The Lion) Smith

Mary Lou Williams

Corky Williams (at piano) and
Russell Brooks

Count Basie

Duke Ellington

J. C. Johnson · · · Fats and Myra Johnson

Spencer Williams and Fats at Brighton, England

"Spreadin' Rhythm Around." Fats in the film *King of Burlesque.*

Fats and Lena Horne in his last film, *Stormy Weather*

"Havin' a Ball." A party after the show.

At Bricktop's, Paris, 1932. Fats, Spencer Williams, and Bricktop at right.

Fats with Les Hite (left) and Frank Sebastian at the New Cotton Club
Los Angeles, California, 1932

Edith Wilson, star of
Hot Chocolates

Kitty Murray. "All That Meat and
No Potatoes."

Una Mae Carlisle. Station WLW,
Cincinnati.

Don Redman. Fats' friend and band
leader.

Myra Johnson, Fats, and Lew
(Blackbirds) Leslie

Aboard *Ile de France,* 1939

Anita and Fats with author sailing up the Clyde, Scotland, 1938

Fats at the organ in London

Fats and the Danish musician, Sven Asmussen

"Are you all there, Fats?"

Curtain call at the London Palladium

Adelaide Hall, star of *Shuffle Along*

Fats and Bill Robinson stalking Lena Horne on *Stormy Weather* set

Fats, the English gentle-
man

Fats at the Yacht Club,
a New York night spot

Fats on a Mexican holiday

"Yeah, yeah, yeah! Fats was a solid sender." Louis Armstrong with the author.

Party at The Nest, London. Fats with Spencer Williams, Reginald ("Serenade to a Wealthy Widow") Foresythe, Adelaide Hall, and Anita Waller.

First television show, London at BBC's Alexandria Palace Studio

The band in *Stormy Weather*

Fats' big band on tour, Dallas, Texas, 1940

Fats and his son Maurice

The last Victor Record date for Fats and his Rhythm with the Deep River
Boys

9

Now that he was out, fortune once more smiled on Fats. Connie and George Immerman, the operators of the famed Connie's Inn, next to the Lafayette Theatre, and friends of Fats from his earliest days, had for years been accustomed to his constant attendance at their club and had often used him as a featured artist between shows. Almost from the first day the club had opened, early in the Twenties, Fats had been in the habit of dropping in and playing the piano in the afternoons, and some time before he joined the cast of 'KeepShufflin' ', he had started to urge the Immermans to get an organ installed. He was amazed when eventually, taking him at his word, they bought a new, piano-shaped Estey with built-in pipes. This little organ became famous at the Inn, mostly because it was never played by anybody except Fats Waller. It became his baby, and he soon taught it to talk.

As soon as he was out of jail, he sought out the Immermans, who assigned him to work with Andy Razaf writing the music and lyrics for a new floor show, 'Load of Coal'. Razaf, knowing his partner's weaknesses only too well, resolved that this time Fats' good-time Harlem acquaintances were not going to prevent the show being completed on time. He thereupon suggested to Fats that the place to work was at his mother's house in Asbury Park – strategically adding that he had never tasted food like his mother made. Fats, whose first inclination had been to celebrate his return to civilization with a little party-making, finally succumbed to Andy's blandishments and they journeyed to the seaside resort. True to Andy's promise, the table was laden with Fats' very own favourite dishes. Andy had hired a small upright for the occasion, and they lost no time in getting to work.

'Now, here's the set-up,' Andy began. 'We've got a show to write. There's a spot in the programme for a ballad, another for a soft-shoe routine, and a place for a good rhythm number. Let's go from there. Which shall we do first?'

'Perfect!' said Fats, chewing on a fried chicken bone. 'How's this?' He played a scrap of melody.

Andy nodded eagerly. 'Go on,' he said.

Fats repeated the phrase, then played it over again, then added another phrase. In another minute he had completed eight bars. In an hour he had the ballad completed, and Andy had a lyric ready. They called it *My Fate Is In Your Hands*. Fats ran through the second one in short order. A catchy piano melody, to which Andy's words soon followed, gave birth to *Zonky*, a strong rhythm tune. Only an hour and a half had elapsed since they had first approached the piano.

Finally a piece for the soft-shoe routine, and Fats, dwarfing the little instrument, looked up at the ceiling in concentration. His fingers strayed over the keys, trying out little fragments of melody, until finally he struck one a little longer than the rest. 'Wait!' cried Andy. 'Play that again.'

Fats obliged, playing the little theme with fuller chording, and an added bass line.

Andy hummed for a moment, and said, 'How about this – "Every honey-bee, fills with jealousy, when they see you out with me".'

Fats finished the middle eight bars, and there was the last number almost complete. Another hour's work polishing what they had done, and Fats rose from the piano.

'Andy,' he said, 'I gotta go back to New York. I just remembered I got a heavy date.' A wink of his eye. 'See you tomorrow in Connie's.'

Andy tried to persuade him to stay, but nothing he said would dissuade Fats from leaving. Andy went back to finishing the lyrics for the last of their three numbers, and he smiled to himself as he played over the new melody. Fats had left, but he had had him pinned down long enough to get the show written. As he worked on the last number they had done, still incomplete in melody, and lacking most of its lyrics, he liked it more and more.

Several times he thought he was on the right track and then tore up the lines he had written. Then he began writing furiously for the idea which had been so elusive suddenly came to him. It came quickly now – a final touch on paper and he ran over to the phone and asked for New York.

'Hello,' he called. 'Is Fats there, Anita?' He listened a moment, then shook his head and called another Harlem number. 'Tell Fats Waller to come to the phone, please,' he asked the answering voice. He soon heard Fats' voice and began to talk rapidly into the mouthpiece. 'Fats? Listen, I've done the rest of that last number we did. You don't remember the melody? Lord, man! Good thing *I* do.' He hummed the melody over the phone. 'Now get this. Every honey bee, fills with jealousy, when they see you out with me, I don't blame them goodness knows, Honeysuckle Rose.' Fats' reaction was enthusiastic. Andy then sang the next four lines and added, 'Here's the bridge – give me a tune – I don't remember that middle eight you wrote for it.' He talked the lyrics, then listened intently as his partner's voice came back at him with a tune. Mentally he combined tune and lyrics, then nodded. More came and he said, 'Wait a minute, Fats, I want to try that on the piano.' Setting the phone down, he ran to the keyboard and picked out the tune, singing the lyrics as he went. They fitted. Elated, he dashed back to the phone. 'Got it, Fats, see you tomorrow.' Fats had hung up!

'Load of Coal' was a great success at the Inn – its music justly became famous, with *My Fate Is In Your Hands* assuming the proportions of a hit song which outlived the memory of the show which gave it birth. *Zonky* enjoyed some popularity and the enormous popularity of the third number *Honeysuckle Rose* is well known. It seems strange, looking back, that this, the best loved number of the three written that day, was then looked upon merely as an unimportant soft-shoe number backing for the chorus. Inauspicious though the presentation was, the number sold itself to the publishers and was plugged along with the more immediately popular ballad. Its début on the air, at about the time the show opened, took place on the Paul Whiteman 'Old Gold Show'. This broadcast rivalled the B.A. Rolfe show for Lucky Strike cigarettes, and featured the fast brassy arrangements beloved by its sponsor. Whiteman's show was slanted to draw listeners from the rival radio show, by playing, in slower tempo, each selection more or less as it had originally been written. Harry Link took Fats and Mildred Bailey over to audition *Honeysuckle Rose*, and the good Mildred rocked them with her version of the new song. No one asked any questions and it was

123

scheduled for broadcast. The subtle lilt which Miss Bailey had imparted to the tune was preserved in the band arrangement, and they were all set.

Just before the show, however, somebody higher up, for some reason, reversed the scheme of things and the Old Gold Programme was completely re-vamped so as to model it more closely to that of their rival. The shuffling rhythm of *Honeysuckle Rose* was now played double time and was horribly mutilated. The song, according to Harry Link, who was in a position to know, was set back fifteen years. It was not until years later that it came to public notice in a Hollywood production. A major film studio included it in a big musical and Andy Razaf was astounded, and not a little incensed, at the way the film treated the story of its creation. The song was depicted as having been written in jail by a white composer. Razaf immediately brought this to Fats' notice but Fats merely shrugged his shoulders and said, 'What's the difference? It's all good publicity, ain't it?' Andy didn't see it that way, however, and immediately wrote to the company concerned, claiming that the film episode was a gross misrepresentation and a most unpleasant reflection on himself. Even now, the memory of that presentation still angers him, especially the way the studio's representative tried to explain away the whole affair in the pages of *Variety*. The article written in answer to Razaf's letter chided him for 'poor sportsmanship' and suggested that he should be proud to have had his song featured so prominently. His answer is simple still: 'I wonder how they'd have been able to placate Irving Berlin if they'd presented a scene showing *Alexander's Ragtime Band* as being written by a coloured boy behind bars.' The point was well made and the flurry is just one more in the long list of injustices perpetrated in the past on the Negro writer whenever an opportunity arose.

As 'Load Of Coal' came and went, Fats was writing more and more material at the Inn. When the next show, another revue, went into planning, he and Andy were ready with a couple of bales of music. This opus was to be entitled 'Hot Chocolates' and was staged by Leonard Harper who had been associated with the Inn for some time. A large cast of entertainers was involved and plenty of music was needed.

While rehearsals for this show were in progress, Ralph Peer sent a young Chicago musician to get Fats Waller organized for a coming record date in the Victor Studio. The musician, Eddie Condon, has given a hilarious account of his difficulties in organizing this session in his autobiography *We Called It Music*. The story is well and truly told, and the Waller talent for procrastination and complete unconcern has never been more aptly described. One can imagine the frustration of the young guitarist as he realized that trying to get Fats on the ball was something a lot harder than it seemed at first.

These jaunts to the Victor Recording Studio were the bane of Peer's life, and it can readily be understood why he stuck someone else with the job when it was realized what it took to get Fats and Thomas Morris' band moving. On their record dates in Camden, Peer would have to get up very early in the morning at his New Jersey home, drive up to Harlem to pick up Fats – probably either asleep or else still going strong on the piano at some night club – then collect the rest of the band. Then, while Peer drove south for several hours, a heap of humanity snored in the back seat with a couple of quarts of gin stored under the seat for future warming up of the boys at the old church studio.

But as soon as they had got there, unpacked their instruments, and wet their whistles, they were ready – and, as the records prove, really ready to go!

On the Condon date some of the most immortal sides in the Waller list were recorded. There is not a single recording from that date which can be called secondary. The dynamism of the little combination as it turned out *The Minor Drag* and *Harlem Fuss*, both composed on the way to work, is tremendous. Then, as if that were not enough, there is Fats' scintillating attack on *Handful Of Keys* and *Numb Fumblin'*. The former was perhaps Fats' best piano solo and definitely his own favourite amongst the numerous piano sides he recorded.

Among the performers in 'Hot Chocolates' were several names who later gained much theatrical prominence. It was in fact a real 'star-maker'. One of the juveniles was the late Eddie Green, famous as the waiter in radio's 'Duffy's Tavern'; another player was the late James Baskette, much later the endearing Uncle Remus in Disney's

'Song Of The South'; and a youthful Cab Calloway also made his name in this show. The band who played at the Inn was led by LeRoy Smith and a brand new addition to the floor show was Fats' old friend, Louis Armstrong. Just fresh in town from Chicago, Louis and a small group had been booked into Connie's by Tommy Rockwell. Alternating with the Smith band, he was a fresh attraction to New York audiences, having been away for four years. His throaty voice did wonderful things to the Razaf lyrics, and his golden trumpet, which had succeeded the earlier cornet, reached to every corner of the lavish club with its glorious tone.

The show played the Inn for some weeks, and then to the delight of the cast it was booked into a downtown legitimate theatre as a full-sized revue. Fats and Andy, who had already written most of the score for the show, were now hard at work on another song or two for the downtown production. But the ease with which ideas flowed from these two songwriters was quite extraordinary.

'No one to talk with, all by myself,' sang Andy Razaf one afternoon in Fats' apartment. He paused, thinking hard; then, his face brightening, 'No one to walk with, but I'm happy on the shelf . . .

'There, Fats, what do you think of that?'

'Make like you're dead, man!' replied Fats, who was idly picking out little snatches of melody on the piano.

'Ain't Misbehavin'!' Andy leaped out of his chair to fetch pencil and paper. 'Da-da-da-da-da-da,' he mused. 'Gotta get something for that part.'

Fats repeated the little theme he had been playing as the Razaf hand scribbled, 'I know for certain, the one I love – I'm through with flirtin', it's just you I'm thinkin' of . . . Ain't Misbehavin''—' Then he was stuck again. 'Fats, that theme has to be emphasized by the last lines of those two phrases. Now what can we say . . . wait a minute now . . . da-da-da-da-da . . . savin' myself for you. How's that?'

'Fine, wonderful, perfect,' said Fats, now thoroughly alert. He sensed that here was something that he liked very much. From there on it was easy.

'Get that melody down on paper,' Andy said. 'You know you

have a memory for tunes, which is as full of holes as a cullender.'

The finished *Ain't Misbehavin'* went into the revue and became the hit tune of the freshly vamped show. It was performed by Cab Calloway on the stage at the Hudson Theatre, and also by Margaret Simms. But, as sung and played by a white-tuxedoed Louis Armstrong who performed from the orchestra, the song was a smash hit from the word go.

Louis credits this song as giving him a big boost along the road to fame – it was certainly one of his first great hits.

Walter Winchell's column some years later told a supposedly factual tale of Fats' having written the song in jail, but although it is a good story, it is completely without basis in fact. The title and lyrics were in their entirety a creation of Razaf's, and, although the melody line may in some form or other have occurred to Waller during his incarceration, the finished product was assembled in Fats' apartment one afternoon.

Ironically enough, however, the song's title does seem to be a perfect theme for Fats. The story of his life is vividly portrayed by those two simple words and it is hard to believe that he did not think them up himself. His irrepressibility and complete abandonment to life's seamier side combined with his boundless good-nature made him the living personification of a man who might sing *Ain't Misbehavin'* – with eyebrows raised in joyful innocence.

*   *   *

'Connie's Hot Chocolates' opened at the Hudson Theatre in New York on 20 June 1929. It ran for 219 performances before going out on the road. Each night after the show at the Hudson, the cast with one or two exceptions headed for Harlem and played the show all over again at Connie's Inn. They worked themselves to the bone but their efforts paid off for the show received wonderful notices from the very first night. A contemporary review, by F. P. Dunn, Jr, was as follows:

The latest addition to the long string of Negro shows, 'Hot Chocolates', which came to the Hudson Theatre last night, proved to be a colourful, fast-moving, spirited and expert display of Afric accomplishments, especially in the dancing line. These young bloods of Harlem can dance, and they do, with an immense amount of energy and willingness.

Most of the performers in the show are on the entertainment staff of Connie's Inn, a Harlem night club, and after the curtain rings down on their Broadway performance, they go uptown and do most of it all over again. If they always pour as much energy into their work in the theatre as they did last night, I cannot for the life of me see how they can do anything more uptown than stagger across the floor. But it seems that they do.

The show in the Hudson does not go in for music very heavily. There is a song called *Ain't Misbehavin'* on which much reliance is placed. Almost everybody in the show sings it at one time or another, and as there are a good many in the show, the song gets sung pretty often. It is tuneful and pleasant, and I should feel like giving everybody a great deal of credit for it, if it only were not so strikingly reminiscent of something I seem to remember from a year or so ago. Never mind what.

What the show does go in for, and perfectly grandly, is dancing. On the stage they do practically every kind of dance that ordinary mortals could not even think of trying to do. The girls' chorus is pretty and well-trained and puts its heart and soul into its work. But it has to defer before the marvellously rhythmic clogging of a team of eight young men who seem to be the answer to the question: where do the street corner dancers of Harlem go?

Before the background of these two choruses glide three performers who really make the show. First of all is one 'Jazzlips' Richardson, a powerful man with a gleam in his eye, who comes out alone, and perfectly calmly, almost without visible effort, does an utterly unbelievable acrobatic dance. I have not seen anything more rhythmically gymnastic. Last night he literally stopped the show. Then there is a lithe crazy little person known as Baby Cox, who insists on singing pathetic songs slightly off key, and then suddenly begins to caper, for all the world like a monkey on a stick. And finally, there is one Louise Cook, who, while representing the Goddess of Rain, does just such a dance as grandfather used to sneak off and see at the county fair.

The whole show has pace and enthusiasm and enough talent to make it the best Negro revue since 'Blackbirds'. There are even one or two decently funny sketches, and the lapses from good taste are few. And by the way, the report that the show was postponed from last Monday so the cast could have their gold teeth out is a base canard!

From the 'New York Age' review of 'Connie's Hot Chocolates' by Robert Garland, *New York Telegram*:

With most of its gold teeth and no little of its tediousness removed, Connie's new tanskin revel is a far better show than it was a couple of weeks ago in the Bronx Windsor Theatre. Nowadays, at the Hudson, Hot Chocolates is faster, funnier, and a good deal franker.

As goes without saying, the dancing is marvellous. There is, of course, no Bill Robinson and no Earl Tucker, but there're the Eight Bon Bon Buddies who make 'Sweet Savannah Sue' and 'Say it with Your Feet' snappier than it could possibly be without them. And there's Baby Cox, who uses her voice badly, and feet superbly, and, much too close to morning, there're the Three Midnite Steppers who, earlier in the evening, would take the house by storm.

If the rest of Hot Chocolates lived up to its dancing, it would be a show of shows. But the rest of Hot Chocolates does not live up to its dancing. Some of it is plain, ordinary torso-tossing from the downtown burlesque shows. Some of it is childish prattle in connection with the 'Wedding of the Rabbit and the Bear'. Some of it is dubious, not to say dirty, wisecracks in connection with a female and the poolroom papa of whom everyone has heard.

The piece at the Hudson gets under way in an excellent likeness of Connie's not-uncelebrated Inn, where 7th Avenue and 131st Street come together. There you're face to face with head waiters, waiters, doormen, masters of ceremonies, guests, entertainers, members of the orchestra, and the likes of them. And, as I mustn't forget to mention, Paul and Thelma Meers. Paul and Thelma, without warning, burst into 'The Waltz Divine' You will, I fancy, like it.

Soon, however, the club revue comes into its own. This club revue is an enlargement of the floor show which has brought fame and fortune to Connie and Connie's Inn. That is to say, George Staton, Ernest Taylor and William McKelvey sing *Pickaninny Land*, Russell Wooding's Jubilee Singers sing *The Song Of The Cotton Fields*, Margaret Simms and Paul Bass sing *Sweet Savannah Sue*, and the entertainment is under way. The chorus, of course, is helpful.

Follow in the order named, 'The Unloaded Gun', a fairly funny sketch in which Eddie Green, Billy Maxey, and Jimmy Baskette are leading players; the 'Say it With Your Feet' of which I have spoken;

an embryonic song success, known as *Ain't Misbehavin'*, sung by Margaret Simms, Paul Bass, and Russell Wooding's Sextette, and a satire on prize-fight promotion, which is nicely stressed by Jazzlips Richardson, Billy Higgins, and the aforesaid Mr Green.

And so from 8.30 to 11.45, it goes. In the 'Goddess of Rain', Louise Cook does what she can to make the Irving Place Theatre safe for 44th Street. Assisted by an undressed but earnest chorus, she succeeds. In 'Southland Melody', Russell Wooding's Jubilee Singers sing snatches of *Carry Me Back To Old Virginny*, *Old Black Joe*, and the *Comin' Home* which somebody has fashioned out of Dvorak's 'New World Symphony'.

In 'Jungle Jamboree', Baby Cox and the Hot Chocolate Drops try to be as much like *Diga Diga Doo* as possible. In his own dancing speciality, Jazzlips Richardson is the outstanding feature of the evening. If you'll pardon the exaggeration, he is unbelievable. 'That Rhythm Man' with Jimmy Baskette and the entire company brings the first act to a close. In these ears, 'That Rhythm Man' would be more effective without an accompanying orchestra.

In the second stanza, Mr Baskette and Mr Green are funny, in a quiet way, mind you, as clerk and customer in a telegraph office. And Edith Wilson is excellent in a song known as *Black And Blue*, and dirtier than desirable in *Traffic In Harlem*. Dolly McCormick and Madeline Belt aren't bad in *Can't We Get Together?* Billy Maxey and the much-mentioned Miss Wilson flirt with the police in *Poolroom Papa* – one of those songs which are supposed to mean two things, but which only mean one.

On second thoughts, Hot Chocolates remains fast, funny and frank. It's only fair to tell you that even if it is no second 'Blackbirds', the audience adored it, crying aloud for more, and more, and more.

Louis Armstrong entered the show after the first reviews had been written and gradually worked himself into a bigger feature, finally emerging on to the stage to do *Ain't Misbehavin'*. At the time the quoted reviews were printed, he was not actually in the show, and thus is not mentioned.

The music was extremely well received, and the haunting *Black And Blue*, as sung so effectively in the show by Edith Wilson, deserves a special word. Written about the same time as *Ain't Misbehavin'* this standard is perhaps even more a perfect wedding of words and music than its more famous companion piece. Razaf's lyric pen has never shown to better advantage than in the plaintive:

> 'Cold empty bed – pains in my head;
> Feel like ol' Ned – Wish I was dead. . . .
> What did I do . . . to be so Black and Blue.'

Waller's relentless and rather oppressive blues line carries the words through the thirty-two bars as if cast in the same mould, and today only re-affirms the complete compatibility of these two great talents. But this song too has its little prologue.

During the preliminary rehearsals, a discussion of a certain spot in the show took place between Razaf and one of the production men. 'Andy, here's what we want,' the man said. 'When the curtain rises this little gal will be in bed under a white counterpane, with only her dark face sticking out over the sheets. Now we need a number for her to sing – something about how tough it is to be coloured. You know what I mean – something funny.'

The man was serious, but Andy and Fats resolved that they would give him the song he wanted about the trials of being a Negro, only it wouldn't be all that funny. Razaf's lyrics to *Black And Blue* assume a powerful dignity when delivered by a Negro – and always will.

In late July, the show held its first midnight matinée, played almost entirely for the benefit of other show people, busy themselves from early in the evening to midnight.

Amsterdam News, Wednesday, 24 July 1929. Writer on local daily:

There's still night life in them side streets off Broadway. On Tuesday night, or rather Wednesday morning, the grand old Hudson, the proud and haughty theatre that housed such gems of the drama as 'The Third Degree' and 'Brewster's Millions', rocked as it never rocked before, and with a dusky interloper known as 'Hot Chocolates'.

Broadway may be changing, but there's still enough of the population willing to sit up until three in the morning, a hot July morning, mind you, to prove that the old days haven't entirely departed. It was a stylish gathering, representative of the opera, society and stage. From a seat in the first row, Bill Robinson was recognized and applauded – he leaped to the stage and he danced. From a seat in the second row was spotted Ethel Waters who, when spotlighted, sang from the aisle.

This festive occasion marked the first midnight performance of Connie and George Immerman's speedy revue. It is their first time away from Harlem, as far as show business is concerned; and it must have been gladdening to their hearts to hear their three practically unknown stars applauded almost beyond endurance. Baby Cox, Edith Wilson, and the jungle headliner, Jazzlips Richardson, all new to Broadway, earned another notch in their belt of glory. Among the stage folk present were Eleanor de Cisneros, Fritzi Scheff, Fay Marbe, George White, Esther Howard, Zolya Talma, Valerie Valaire, Blanche Ring, Mabel Withee, Horace Braham, Emily Ann Wellman, Teresa Maxwell Conover, Verree Teasdale, Libby Holman, Barbara Clark, and a generous smattering of the 'New Moon', 'Show Girl', 'Follow Through' casts and the entire company of 'Journey's End' and 'Street Scene'. N. T. Granlund of the radio, Harry Hershfield of the comic strip, and the Singer midgets, and Park Avenue hobnobbed in the foyer between the acts.

Louis Armstrong had to work really hard in those days. He played the Hudson Theatre, being a featured soloist from the pit, and also doing a speciality in company with Fats and Edith Wilson called '1000 lbs of rhythm', while his own band would be uptown, entertaining the customers at Connie's Inn. The bandstand was shared with the band led by the LeRoy Smith outfit after the downtown show had ended. Concurrently with 'Hot Chocolates', Armstrong played a spot at the Lafayette Theatre in a couple of revues, and was also at other night spots for brief shows.

Fats' career proceeded apace this summer. One day he ran into Harry Link in a publisher's office.

'Hey, Fats! What you got there?' Link nodded towards a manuscript under Fats' arm.

'Oh, just a little bit of music, Harry. Gonna be a big hit, I expect – well, one never knows, do one?'

'Let's go over to my place.' Link opened the door, and they both went out and across to the Santly Brothers Publishing Company.

'Now, let's hear that song,' Link said, as he cleared some music from the rack of the office piano.

He listened intently to the tune Fats played and shook his head in admiration. This guy Fats was really terrific – there seemed to be no end to the tunes he could turn out.

'Good, Fats, how about us doing this together? I'll get Billy Rose to get some lyrics out on it.'

Fats nodded approval. 'Sure, sure, Harry,' he said, 'but we gotta get a little loot first.'

Link with a grin obliged.

The number became another Waller hit in this, his most productive year. It was called *I've Got A Feelin' I'm Fallin'*.

Another day, Link was visited in his office by a Cleveland club owner in search of new talent for a new show he was putting on.

'I've got to get the best available talent.' He looked at Harry, who picked up his phone. He called an uptown number.

'Who's that? Fats? Good. Listen, I want you to help a friend of mine from Cleveland. He's looking for some fine Harlem entertainers for a new show he's putting on – can you help?' He listened for a few moments and said, 'Great! We'll meet you there as soon as we can get away tonight. Be looking for us.'

That night, as their taxi drew up outside Connie's Inn, Link pointed out to his friend the premises over the Inn. 'That's the Entertainers' Club,' he said. 'If you don't find what you want here, there just isn't anything to be had.'

Fats was there to greet them as arranged, as he knew that this, of all the Harlem spots, was where the best talent was to be found. This was where show people gathered and one never saw a sloppy act. When show people perform for each other they are always their own severest critics. The reward for a good show was handsome, for appreciation from fellow artists meant more than the applause of a huge audience. Consequently everyone tried harder and often surpassed themselves. After watching a couple of dozen acts the man from Cleveland was ecstatic. He hired ten acts on the spot, some twenty-two people, and after telling them the set-up he spread a little advance money out amongst them. 'And here's the money for their train tickets,' he said to Link; 'they must leave Monday, ready to open Wednesday night.'

Link, happy at the good showing the acts had made, passed them over to Fats and made him responsible for getting them to Penn Station on time.

The following morning, at the last minute, Harry called Fats. 'How's everything coming?'

'Fine, wonderful, perfect,' came Fats' old tag line. 'Don't you worry yourself 'bout a thing.'

At train time, Link stood waiting at Penn Station with twenty-two round-trip tickets in hand. Eventually four people joined him, but he looked around in vain for the rest. They were not to be seen then, or for some time after. Once again a promoter had made the fatal mistake of giving an advance.

Another time Fats was booked into the Regal Theatre, Chicago, but half-way there he decided he was lonesome for Harlem so he de-trained and went back home. These peccadilloes of his were not calculated to inspire the greatest trust in his reliability, but somehow he managed to emerge with a whole skin and his independence intact every time. Nick Lucas, the 'Singing Troubadour', has a favourite tale of Fats' party habits. It was late in the year and in New York the party season was in full swing. Lucas had run into Fats in Tin Pan Alley and asked him what he was doing that night.

'Big Party, Nick.'

'Well, Fats, how about coming over to Newark earlier in the evening? I've invited a bunch of friends over to my house. They'd love to see you.'

'Okay, man,' said Fats, 'but I gotta get back early. I've been asked to this big society hop and Mr Waller needs the trash.'

That evening he and three other boys showed up at Lucas' house and were promised $100.00 between them. Nick had just bought a new piano and Fats' big bulk soon occupied the piano stool. His three musician friends tore the top off the music, and the apartment. The ample supply of gin provided by the astute Nick was enough – the other party was forgotten. Festivities didn't break up until very late, and next day Lucas surveyed his new piano, now sadly in need of a repair man. The sixty-odd empty bottles told their own mute tale.

In August, Fats recorded six piano solos. They included his new song, plus *Ain't Misbehavin'*, and *Sweet Savannah Sue, Love Me Or*

Leave Me, *Gladyse*, and *Valentine Stomp*. Another session that month produced *Waitin' At The End Of The Road* and *Baby, Where Can You Be?*

The following month he went over to Okeh for a session with Don Redman, Coleman Hawkins, Benny Carter and company. A couple of sides were made and released under the name of 'The Little Chocolate Dandies'. The titles were *That's How I Feel Today* and *Six Or Seven Times*.

Another notable session from this period was a record date he made with the 'Buddies' on 30 September, when, besides Fats, there were such illustrious names as Jack Teagarden, Otto Hardwick, currently away from the Duke, Gene Krupa, Al Morgan and Charlie Gains. They cut *Lookin' Good But Feelin' Bad* and *I Need Someone Like You*.

He also sat in with McKinney's Cotton Pickers for three sessions in November and recorded more piano solos in December when he cut *My Fate Is In Your Hands* and *Turn On The Heat*. On the 18th of the same month, a set of four numbers by the Buddies was made at Victor, including *Lookin' For Another Sweetie* – which tune has come down to us as *Confessin'*.

Thus ended a truly big year for Fats, when upwards of thirty separate recordings were made – it was also his peak year for the production of hit tunes.

But in spite of all this, Fats still lost his head on occasion, and 17 July 1929 turned out to be one of the blackest days in his career. On that day he sold outright to Irving Mills, all rights, title and interest in the following compositions:

Sweet Savannah Sue	*Snake Hip Dance*
Jungle Jamboree	*Say It With Your Feet*
Poolroom Papa	*Offtime*
Ain't Misbehavin'	*(That) Rhythm Man*
Dixie Cinderella	*Wedding Of The Rabbit And The Bear*
My Man's Good For Nothing But Love	*Laughing Water*
Sweet Devilish Thing	*You Slay Me*
Pickaninny Land	*Black and Blue*

Waltz Divine   *I'm A Stationary Woman Look-*
Can't We Get Together?   *ing For . . .*

For this impressive list of hits it is reported that Mills gave
Thomas Waller the sum of $500.00, but it is not known if this was
the final payment of a series, above and beyond royalties already
received. It is probable that Fats, plagued by alimony claims at this
time, quite failed to foresee the tremendous future value of such
tunes as *Ain't Misbehavin'* and *Black And Blue*.

One of the engagements that Fats enjoyed most in the whole
year was his annual guest appearance at the famed Paramount
Theatre organ. Here he sat in for his friend and admiring contemporary, Jesse Crawford, who held down the job at this choice spot
for some time. For this happy little gig Fats received the good
salary of $750.00 a week. But even more important, perhaps, was
the fact that his success at this theatre was duly noted by the
Paramount people who, because of this, made a radio artist of him
the following year.

10

Harlem was now at the zenith of its popularity. The fashionable crowds congregated there nightly, and business was booming. Connie's Inn was doing the lion's share of the big trade, closely followed by the Cotton Club and the Savoy Ballroom. Fats would spend many of his afternoons at the Inn rehearsing new numbers, going over acts with Leonard Harper, and sometimes swopping stories or just listening to some of the many musicians who dropped in to pass a few hours. A frequent visitor was a young 19-year-old girl from Pittsburgh, Mary Lou Williams. A fine pianist, with a prodigious memory, she first met Fats when Leonard Harper brought her into the Inn one day and introduced them. Fats, she says, armed with the usual jug of Old Grandad, was writing some music for the show, whilst regaling the chorus lovelies with such a selection of *risqué* stories, and off-beat remarks, that they could hardly dance for laughing. Leonard Harper, who was producing the show, asked Fats if he had written any music yet. Fats without a word got to work on the piano, and rattled off six or seven tunes, without apparent thought or effort. They were all good melodies and Mary Lou's ears were working overtime. When the rehearsal was over, Mr Harper bet Fats she could sit down and play every-thing from memory that Fats had just written. Fats at once took the bet, and the young girl was pushed on to the piano stool. With some concentration, she managed to get through nearly everything she had heard.

Fats was astounded, and before she could stop him, he just picked her off the piano stool and threw her up in the air, saluting her with a mighty hug and a smacking kiss as she landed back in his arms.

'Fine, wonderful, perfect!' he roared.

No wonder the boys around that time used to call him the OAO (one and only).

Mary Lou Williams was soon in the big time, joining Andy

Kirk's outfit in 1929, for whom she arranged and composed in addition to playing piano in the band.

The little white organ that the Immermans had bought for Fats was now, together with the man who played it, famous all over town. The Inn patrons were alternately charmed by the dazzling floor show and the musical interlude played by Fats on the Estey. A split bottle of White Rock cost a dollar, and, with whatever particular brand of vice they chose to add from their pocket flasks, the customers came back night after night, week after week for more. Connie's was always careful not to get entangled in the Prohibition laws and the owner never made a practice of selling liquor to the regular customers. But they did offer them the cream of the current talent. The renowned Bojangles, Bill Robinson, made frequent appearances at the club, and Connie recalls that he insisted always on being introduced from his table and then being 'persuaded' to dance by the M.C. Thus Robinson was not billed in advance but preferred for some reason of his own to act as a visiting celebrity.

Outside on the street, the corner of 131st and Seventh Avenue, was the real centre of show life. Besides the Inn, and Small's Paradise a couple of blocks away, there was the Entertainers' Club, a Chinese restaurant, the Lafayette Theatre right next door, and the Tree of Hope. This landmark, which was at one time a flourishing tree growing up through the pavement, became a lucky symbol to the show people of Harlem. And when it died and its branches no longer held leaves, it still remained something sacred. Nobody in his right mind would pass the Tree and neglect to rub its trunk and wish for luck, least of all Thomas 'Fats' Waller, a devout superstitious believer. In later years the Tree became crowded by new streets and deeper pavements but, to save the day, and the Tree, Bill Robinson personally financed its removal to the centre of Seventh Avenue, where it still remains to this day – a short stub of a trunk now, but still available to all the superstitious who pass by, and a reminder that this corner had once known glory.

On the main thoroughfare an assorted collection of characters, the like of which the world had never seen or ever will see again, just stood about and talked or promenaded up and down in the

Manhattan night. On every corner brightly-clad entertainers, still wearing their stage make-up, rubbed shoulders with furtive-eyed dope peddlers who kept the reefers moving from hand to hand. Talent scouts from out of town were always to be seen, and an innumerable variety of dusky folk who had gravitated to the metropolis from all quarters of the States in search of a little or a lot. One of the more picturesque legendary characters was an eight-foot giant Negro weighing 793 pounds, who earned good money by just walking up and down the street advertising London Character shoes. He was well paid and no wonder, for his feet were size twenty-six. His job came to an end when for a bet he ate a full pound of salt – it was his end too!

Amongst the new musicians in town was a New Orleans drummer well known to Louis Armstrong, Zutty Singleton. Zutty had worked his way to Chicago via the riverboats, and it was while playing with Charlie Creath's band on one of these trips that he met and married the leader's sister, Margey Creath – herself a musician. The first night in New York, he sought out Louis and they started the rounds.

Seated at a table in a restaurant in Harlem, Louis spotted Fats. He greeted them with a hearty welcome and as soon as Louis introduced Zutty, the two voices started on the jive talk in a way that only Louis and Fats could talk. Louis told Fats that Zutty was one of the best drummers in New Orleans. It wasn't long before Fats had promised Zutty to fix him a record session as soon as the chance came.

As it happened, it wasn't long in coming but it was perhaps in some ways the strangest session ever recorded by either of the two jazzmen. Mr Loren Watson of Victor called up Fats one evening, and told him that there was a guy in town who wanted to record with Fats and his pals the following day. 'Get a couple of guys together and come on down,' he said. Fats, always allergic to rehearsals and never too inquisitive about programming, said, 'Fine! Be there!' He thought a minute, called Zutty, telling him where and when, then gave Duke's great cornet player, Bubber Miley, a call. 'Don't know what it's goin' to be, but there's some of that good gold going, so just you bring your horn.' Miley agreed.

As it happened, they got there on time, but even Fats' eyes goggled when he saw, standing awaiting them in the studio, a large Scotsman clad in kilt and sporran, and with a set of bagpipes under his arm. Mr Watson welcomed the three musicians, then rather hesitantly said, 'This gentleman wishes to make some jazz records with you on the bagpipes. The records will be for his private use only – they will not be released.' The three stunned musicians nodded.

After some discussion as to the tunes to be played, the session finally got under way. To the amazement of Fats and Bubber Miley the piper played jazz, and knew what it was all about. Hot bagpipes was not exactly what they expected, but the music began to sound better and better the longer they progressed. Zutty laid down a solid beat, and with Bubber's growling horn and Fats' pretty figures on the piano, the jive was really jumping. On playback, they were astounded at the good jazz that had been played, and so finally they cut a few more. Later that evening in Harlem, Fats and company found themselves telling their story to unbelieving ears, and it was a long time before they could get anybody to take the story seriously, there being no proof. The records and the piper disappeared, and were never heard of again by either Fats, Bubber or Zutty – but the last-named still sticks to the story that this was a session that really happened. The records, if they still exist, probably remain the proud possession of some Scottish collector, who, if he chances to read this, might do jazz a service by making them available for issue.

*   *   *

'Hot Chocolates' finally closed in New York and went out on the road. It carried Fats along with it doing the Louis Armstrong spot, *Ain't Misbehavin'*. Cab Calloway and the Russell Wooding's Orchestra also went out on the road.

When the show hit Pittsburgh, Anita called Fats one evening long distance and was dismayed to hear from one of the cast that he wasn't available. Smelling a rat, and knowing her husband like a book, she immediately hopped a train to the steel city. She took a cab to the theatre from the station, and arrived during the last act. Fats was on his way out of the pit when he was stopped by a stagehand, who said, 'Man, you's for it!'

'What you talkin' 'bout?' asked Fats as he hurried towards his dressing-room.

'Anita – *Honey*!!' he exclaimed, as she stepped out from behind the door. He herded her into the room, then looking out at the cast, most of whom had congregated in the passage, he announced to one and all, 'If *anybody* comes to look me up, just you tell 'em I am tied up with my *wife*.' He closed the door, 'Now listen, honey, I can explain everything . . .'

*   *   *

The momentum of the fast-moving year 1929 carried Fats along on its crest. He turned out another series of top-notch songs, of which *Blue Turning Grey Over You*, with splendid title and lyrics by the inimitable Andy, was an outstanding success. *Prisoner Of Love*, not to be confused with the Russ Columbo hit of the same name which it preceded, was also written at this time, as was *Keep A Song In Your Soul*. Most of Fats' material this year was published by Joe Davis, who put the pianist under contract for a considerable time. The deal called for first crack at anything that was composed. Fats was also expected to provide a piano accompaniment for anyone who visited Davis' office, trying to sell him new material or to demonstrate their voices. His hours were from ten to five, and he was on a weekly salary, plus royalties for his tunes. However, as was his habit, he was continually bootlegging tunes, so that the contract was in essence merely a reminder for whom he was working.

One of Fats' most attractive piano solos is called *Alligator Crawl*. This was composed as far back as 1927 and was entitled variously *House Party Stomp*, and *Charleston Stomp*, before Davis gave it its final name. He also handled Fats' memorable *African Ripples* and the piece which many consider Fats' best composition, *Clothes-Line Ballet*. Certainly it is lyric in quality and ranks high among the best melodies the composer ever wrote.

With Joe Davis working conditions weren't bad at all. Fats found himself right in the heart of the music business at the most productive hours, and part of his deal with Joe was a bottle of gin at the start of a composing session, and another of Old Grandad with which to finish it. He was always sure of a market for a good tune and could always bring in his friends on the deal when a set of smart lyrics was needed, or one of them needed money.

Nevertheless Joe was a hard-headed business man and didn't put up with too much nonsense when it involved financial loss. It took all of Fats' talent to wheedle out those necessary extras for 'worthy causes', but Fats was a really powerful motivator when the occasion demanded. Joe remembers one particular occasion when Fats came into the office accompanied by a beautiful young coloured girl. Before Joe even had time to open his mouth, Fats laid such a sorrowful tale on him that in spite of his better judgment, Joe found his hand heading towards his wallet. He still hopes he really did help that lady in distress, but has often wondered just who reaped the benefit of his generosity – maybe it was both of them.

*   *   *

The Regal Theatre engagement of 1929, which Fats had abandoned when half-way there, now came up again. The management, notwithstanding his previous failure to appear, booked him in again, in 1930. Accordingly Fats and Anita, who was now able to go on the road with him more often (the two children being old enough to be left at home with their grandmother), once again took the train out to Chicago. The Windy City was at this time in the middle of a wave of gangsterism, and the young Anita was involved in a hair-raising experience outside the theatre. She was just leaving the stage door entrance one night and had emerged into the alley, when she was seized by several gunmen. They had mistaken her for one of the showgirls and they marched her towards the street where a sedan car with open door awaited. Luckily a quick-witted doorman spotted who she was, and called out to the gangster, 'Hey, you know who that is?'

One of the men advised him to mind his own business and pushed Anita on. She, poor girl, was speechless with fear.

'That's Fats Waller's wife!' persisted the doorman.

Hearing Fats' name they stopped and took a closer look at her. 'This ain't the one we want,' the spokesman said. He looked at the others and then said to Anita, 'If you don't want any trouble, I suggest you forget all about this.' Without another word they boarded the car and were gone. Whom they were really after and why was never discovered, but Fats, when he heard what had happened, told his wife, 'Never you mind, 'Nita – they wouldn't hurt you. I worked for those hoodlums in one of their clubs once.'

This contact with the underworld was in those days something of a necessary evil in show business. Entertainers wanted none of it, but it had to be; they either played ball or didn't get work. In addition there was always the threat of 'liquidation' if anyone talked too much. Most of the big night clubs were owned by racketeers, beer barons, or vice lords. In the New York area Dutch Schultz controlled a large piece of the business, one of his rivals being Vincent 'Mad Dog' Coll. The two gangs were incompatible in Harlem, and shooting affrays were not uncommon on the busy streets at night. It was this rivalry that contributed largely to the closing down of Connie's Inn in the early Thirties.

'Mad Dog' Coll it was who conceived the idea of kidnapping Connie Immerman and holding him for ransom. He knew if the job was done properly there was a lot of money to be made, and so one quiet night he put his crude plan into execution.

Don Redman, whose band was playing at the Inn (thus being the last band to do so), was standing at the back of the club, waiting to go on stage. It being summer, he stood with his back to an air vent, enjoying the cooling draught. Suddenly a voice from the other side of the aperture called, 'Jay, where's Connie?'

Without knowing to whom he was talking, Don replied, 'I dunno – George's here, though, if you want him.'

They did want him if George was the only brother there, and so he was grabbed, taken off, and held for three days. In the meantime his mother waited frantically for news. At last a contact was made and a sum named. Arrangements were made for the transfer, and George was duly delivered back at the Inn. But the police were there and, before any further transactions could develop, shooting started, and the kidnappers were forced to flee without their loot. This terrible experience affected George's weak heart and was no doubt a contributing cause of his premature death.

The direct result of this kidnapping was that Connie and George decided to give up Connie's Inn and they closed the place in 1932. Later they invested money in the Cotton Club downtown on Times Square, re-entering show business in less hectic times and in a more healthy neighbourhood. Fats was a steady figure until the very last day when the Inn was finally shuttered – playing both the little organ and the piano in the way only he knew how.

About this time Fats secured through his various friends a spot on the Columbia Radio Station WABC in New York. He was featured on the Paramount-Publix show, 'Paramount on Parade' – a combination musical programme and fashion talk, the latter by Marion Burton. Starting 8 December 1930, it was planned for thirteen weeks, with air time from noon to 12.15 every Monday, Wednesday and Friday. The show caught on and was quickly expanded to a half-hour after only four weeks had elapsed. When the thirteen weeks were done, the show was extended for another thirteen. It finally ended in June 1931, following which Fats went straight into a new series entitled 'Radio Roundup', starting 18 June. The music heard on this show was by the Claude Hopkins Band, who had the Roseland booking at the same time.

This valuable radio experience was but a foretaste of what was to come, when Fats would reach, via the airlanes, that vast unseen audience that as yet scarcely knew his name. The work sharpened his performance to some extent, for this was no visual show, and no amount of mugging and leering here would help sell Waller to his audience. So a new side to Fats' performances began to emerge – once again, as in the early days when he and Andy Razaf were selling their songs, he began to sing. Certain credit for this must go to Joe Davis, who sought to expand Fats' personality on records to the point where he had something to offer other than the excellence of his piano playing.

The first instance of Waller's voice on record is a date for Columbia Records, whereon Fats does marvellous things with *Royal Garden Blues*, *Dallas Blues*, and *I'm Crazy 'Bout My Baby*, playing and singing with the Ted Lewis band. Benny Goodman remembers the occasion well, as he recounts in his autobiography *Kingdom Of Swing*:

... On one occasion Lewis got Fats Waller, Bud Freeman, Muggsy (Spanier) and myself for a date – the only time, so far as I can recall, when the four of us were on a record together; and we turned out at least one record that was worth remembering. This was a coupling of *Dallas Blues* and *Royal Garden Blues*, on which Fats plays some wonderful piano and also sings some swell stuff. If you've ever seen Fats, you know what a great big good-natured guy he is and the kind of piano he can play when he's feeling right. This was one of those occasions, all right, and even the fact that Lewis leans over and pulls that 'Is Everybody Happy' stuff in the middle of one of his solos, doesn't throw him off.

This particular date took a little promoting on Davis' part. He first had to talk to Frank Walker, boss at Columbia Records, who then had to convince Ted Lewis that Fats Waller was just the pianist he needed for this date. The results more than justified the effort, and Fats was such a hit that Columbia hastened to record him alone. The following week they had him cut *I'm Crazy 'Bout My Baby* and *Draggin' My Heart Around*, entitling the record 'Thomas "Fats" Waller (singing to his Hot Piano)'.

In 1931 a pretty definite pattern of jazz in New York had come into being. Big and small bands held sway at countless nightspots, and most of the big names were in the Big City to stay. Not a lot of new talent was coming along, though bandsmen such as Chick Webb, Benny Goodman, Tommy Dorsey, and John Kirby – even if not yet in their full stride – were fast becoming known in and around New York music circles. The original crop of jazzmen who nursed the art from its swaddling clothes and made it into a lusty and productive business were mostly still around. Some, unhappily, were dead – Bolden, Keppard, Rappolo, Tony Jackson, Bubber Miley – and some had left the scene: King Oliver, Jelly Roll, etc. But this year brought a totally new man to the fore. A pianist hit the town like a clap of thunder. His name was Art Tatum.

Tatum grew up in Toledo, Ohio, and received his early professional experience in the local area around Toledo and Northern Ohio generally. Reuben Harris and Bernard Addison heard the 18-year-old kid in Toledo and told him to pack his bags and get to New York. He did, and got his first chance when he came East as accompanist for Adelaide Hall. He played the Lafayette Theatre with Miss Hall, and in a few days his name was being noised up and down Seventh Avenue as the greatest new jazzman to hit the street for many years. Most people in those days who heard his phenomenal technique were at first unbelieving and then completely dazzled. Tatum brought a new trend to jazz. A fertile brain guided nimble fingers in miraculous runs and odd harmonies, and broken time-patterns were his stock-in-trade. Like James P. Johnson before him, he fathered a new school of piano players. His ideas in harmonic progression have come, in recent times, to be taken for granted, but one has only to listen to his early piano records to realize the impact this man had upon jazz piano playing.

Naturally, such a bombshell could not go unnoticed by Tatum's competitors, and the piano-playing hierarchy, represented by James P. Johnson, Willie 'The Lion' Smith, and Thomas 'Fats' Waller were not long in seeking out the newcomer. Fats arrived backstage one night before the midnight show at the Lafayette Theatre and extended his hand. Art, who knew full well the prowess of this young fellow before him, was reserved in his manner, not feeling fully on a par, professionally speaking, with Fats. He didn't realize that in a couple of earlier shows that day his playing had so amazed certain spectators that they had headed for where Fats might be found and spread the word.

'Say, man, they're all talkin' 'bout you around here. Where's you come from so sudden?' Fats wanted to know.

'Oh, I just came in from Ohio . . . Toledo.' Tatum was warmed by the welcome.

'Mind if I stay back here and catch the show?' Fats raised his eyebrows. 'What're you doin' tomorrow night after you're through?'

'Oh, I don't know – just fool around, I guess.'

'Okay – you're comin' out with us guys. We'll show you all the spots around here.'

So it was agreed. The next day's show over, Tatum was greeted as he left the stage by his new acquaintance and an older man whom Fats introduced as James P. Johnson. Others also hovered around in the background, and were duly introduced – Seminole, Earl Wiley, Lippy. The Harlem boys were out in force. They were to need force, too.

'Where'll we go first?' Fats wanted to know.

Tatum quietly interjected, 'Listen, fellows, I'm staying with Reuben Harris while I'm in New York – can you wait till I pick him up?'

'Reuben? You stayin' with him? Swell, man! We play at his place all the time.' They set off.

A couple of stopping places for a drink, and they finally reached Reuben's and routed him out of bed. Next stop was a place called Morgan's, a bootleg joint that kept late hours, and boasted a good piano. This was a special event, and the New York contingent seethed with excitement as they thought what they were going to show this fellow from Ohio. But as they walked along, chatting merrily and joking about the beauties they jostled on the sidewalk, Fats was a little dubious. Although, when backstage, he had not really heard Tatum play anything excepting backgrounds for Adelaide's singing, something in what he heard even in that subdued performance had hit him hard. He had told James P. the following day that this Tatum guy was terrific. James had laughed it off.

'Listen, Fats,' he had said. 'How you goin' to tell how good he is if you haven't heard him play out on his own? Any guy can make it look good when the singer's got the crowd jumpin' already.'

'You wait, Jackanapes,' Fats had said, unconvinced. 'Maybe this guy's goin' to surprise us all.'

'I sure hope he does, man.' James had smiled. 'We ain't had much excitement around here for a long time.'

On their arrival at Morgan's, they were greeted and treated by the few inside, but quickly headed right through for the piano.

Drinks were ordered, and Seminole sat down at the keyboard. The little man was in rare form and his rock-steady beat brought shouts of encouragement from the rest of the musicians present. Reuben Harris, sitting next to Art Tatum, smiled confidently. His boy from Toledo was really going to spring it on them, he told himself.

Lippy, eyes sparkling, began to chatter encouragement: 'Beat it out there, now. Beat it out!'

'C'mon, Art, you take over now!' Fats called from behind a glass of gin. 'They got the thing warmed for you.'

Tatum looked over at the piano, and Seminole looked around questioningly. He arose from the stool, and Tatum, nodding his assent, proceeded to the instrument. Everybody was laughing and talking, but as soon as they saw the newcomer make for the piano the chatter ceased. They waited expectantly.

Tatum spread his hands out over the keyboard, feeling out the instrument. Finding the tension of the keys to his liking, he nodded ever so slightly and rippled a short series of runs. He played around with effortless grace for a short time, gaining speed and tempo. A breathtaking run that seemed to use up every note on the piano, led into a familiar theme – *Tea For Two*. But something strange had happened to the tune. Just as suddenly as he gave them the melody he was out of it again, but never far enough away from it to render it unrecognizable. Then he was back on it again. The right hand was playing phrases which none of the listeners imagined existed, while the left hand alternated between a rock solid beat and a series of fantastic arpeggios which sounded like two hands in one. His hands would start at opposite ends of the keyboard and then proceed towards each other at a paralysing rate; one hand picking up the other's progression and then carrying it on itself, only to break off with another series of incredible arpeggios. Just when it seemed that he had surely lost his way, Tatum came in again with a series of quick-changing harmonies that brought him back smack on the beat. His technique was astounding. Reuben Harris stole a look round the room. Everyone was exactly as they were when Tatum first sat down. Fats' drink halted on its way to his lips, Fats sat as if turned to stone. A wrinkle had appeared between his eyes as he half frowned, half smiled at what he had heard. Nearby, James P. was likewise transfixed, small beads of perspiration showing on his forehead.

Art finished and quietly got up. He smiled and offered the stool to the next man. For a minute nobody moved, then James P. figured that it was his turn. He got up quickly and lost no time in starting in on one of his own specialities. There was no relaxing now. He tried the old reliables *Shout* and *Keep Off The Grass* and he played his best. Fats followed with his *Handful Of Keys* which drew a few cheers, but nothing could take away the feeling that Tatum had the edge. Art returned to the piano and played a version

148

of *Tiger Rag* which left the audience limp. James P. tried his best to save the day for Harlem with a brilliant rendition of Chopin's *Revolutionary Étude*. It was the last stop James could pull out, and Tatum appreciated the performance with warm praise.

None the less, the locals had been cut and they knew it. It was an established fact that they had been beaten at their own game by the boy from Ohio and they wanted to make the most of it. James, Art and Fats rolled out on to the Avenue, arms around one another's shoulders, looking for audiences. All down Seventh Avenue they roamed, then turned off on West 133rd Street, visiting in turn Pod and Jerry's, Brownie's, and the Nest. At every stop delighted crowds applauded the new top pianist – it was a night long remembered by all concerned. James P., reminiscing about it afterwards, simply said, 'When Tatum played *Tea For Two* that night I guess that was the first time I ever heard it really *played*.'

Art's stay in New York that first time was all too brief, and it was only on odd occasions that he was seen for some time after that. But it wasn't very long before he made his first records and so became known to a much wider public.

*   *   *

If you had wanted to hear Fats Waller in the flesh in 1931 you would have had to hop a subway or hail a cab, late in the evening, and proceed to one of the better basements in the Village, the 'Hot-feet Club'. This place with the fascinating name was a bustling bistro, located at 142 West Houston Street. It attracted some of the best crowds making the nightly trek to this district of artists and models. These were the depression days and only the brave, with large resources, were able to make regular ports of call to this type of club. Fats was playing in a neat little band led by Otto Hardwick, Duke Ellington's alto man who was out on his own after breaking away from the Washingtonians. The band seldom included the same musicians two weeks in a row but Fats stayed on for about six months. Others who drifted in and out of the little band were Wayman Carver, flute and alto; Chu Berry on tenor; Garvin Bushnell, alto; Ted McCoy, baritone; Tiny Walters, saxophone; Herbert Cowen, drums; Doctor Rhythm (John Sansome) on banjo; and a West Indian named Freckles who added to the already extensive reed section with his clarinet. The two Albertas, Prime and Hunter, took care of the blues singing and a torrid 'Hotcha', Drusilla Drew sang the rhythm numbers.

The Hotfeet Club was a mecca for the depression-day musician and was considered possibly the best spot in the Village. It was owned jointly by a man named Walsh and his partner whose only name apparently was 'Rubber'. The club successfully featured rather naughty and lively fare and it attracted many political and social luminaries, of whom Jimmy Walker was not the least known. The place opened at 11 p.m. but didn't really get under way until much later. Waiters and entertainers would sit around taking it easy, while up on the bandstand the musicians would relax with a couple of drinks and a little light jamming. As soon as the doorman sighted a customer coming, he would yell through the door, and the band, the waiters and entertainers would immediately electrify themselves into action. By the time any customer had reached the hat-check girl, and long before he had taken a seat, a torrid revue would fill the floor with every indication of having been in progress for hours. The patron would be ushered to a seat in the dimly-lit club, given a drink and treated to a really splendid spectacle. The show was in reality non-stop, unless the place suddenly found itself out of patrons; when everybody would sit around again until a warning from out front nudged them back into action.

Financially, the club paid the performers well – tips averaged as much as thirty dollars a night which about equalled a week's salary. Sometimes the tips were so lavish that the musicians had to be hunted out and reminded that they also had a pay-check coming. One of the favourite tip-extracting stunts, calculated to appeal to the basic weakness of any liquor-loaded male, was a table-to-table collection. One of the singing waiters, with a curvaceous dancer in tow, would make the rounds holding a large galvanized can, the sung tag-line being 'Stick out your can – here comes the garbage man', as the dancer provocatively wiggled her rear. As the tip fell into the can, she would oblige with a 'bump' as thank-you.

Fats, in addition to his piano playing, did a little miniature cabaret act of his own. Between numbers he would introduce a couple of stories – the broader the humour, the more the customers loved them.

'A cow accidentally ate a bee, and the bee got so mad it swore to sting the cow in its stomach. However, on the way down, it fell asleep; and when it woke up, the cow had gone.'

Or, 'I used to be a porter on the Pennsylvania Railroad, and every time we passed through Newark, I'd lean out and kiss my girl as we went by her home. However, this time I didn't know we'd overshot the place, and I kissed a mule twenty miles down the road. That wouldn't have been so bad, except the mule was going the other way.'

This kind of patter, plus Fats' version of Andy Razaf's *My Handy Man*, then a current rage, sent his stock soaring in Greenwich Village. 'Doctor Rhythm', another character who worked the club, and who was part Japanese, was also responsible for some of the most bawdy songs imaginable, such as *Baseball Blues* and *Still Playin' The Horses*. The 'Doctor' started playing banjo at the tender age of 4, when he played on the corner of Sixth Avenue and Fifty-third Street as an accompaniment to his cousin who shined shoes. As a child he went on the stage with Bert Williams in 'Blossom Time' and at 15 was on the road with J. J. Chester's medicine show. In the mid-Twenties he replaced banjoist Bobby Robertson in Jelly Roll Morton's band and played with Edgar Hayes' band at the Alhambra Theatre, and Fess Williams' Royal Flush Orchestra before he joined the cast at the Hotfeet Club.

While Toby Hardwick was at the Club, so it is told, he had the great satisfaction of cutting the band led by his former employer Ellington, at a benefit show at the Astor Theatre. His group consisted of five saxophones, no brass, and a rhythm, inspired by the mighty Waller left hand. The Hotfeet boys had the mighty opposing band hung, drawn and quartered, and it is said that it's the only time the great Ellington band have ever been bested in a battle of music.

The demise of the Hotfeet Club was caused by the same thing that killed Connie's Inn. Walsh, the principal partner, decided to open a similar spot in Chicago, but the local gangsters did not open their arms to his coming, and Mr Walsh's body was brought back to New York two weeks later. The Hotfeet Club was buried with its owner, and Fats and the others were out again looking for a place to perform.

One of the biggest parties of the year took place in Harlem around this time. It had always been the fashion to throw a big celebration for any musician who really was making good, and the honoured guest this time was Duke Ellington. A basement club was hired and the élite of the jazz music world were all invited. Liquor was flowing freely and the party was in full swing, with Fats, Willie 'The Lion' Smith, and many of the Harlem regulars whooping it up at the back end of the room. The rumpus evidently carried a long way because at the very height of the festivities a whistle blew in the street above. A hoarse shout of 'cops', out went the lights – and a mad scramble for the stairs followed. 'The Lion', realizing that discretion would obviously pay more dividends than valour, beat it quickly out of the back door. He found himself in a dirt yard full of garbage cans stacked against a lone tree barely visible against the moonless sky. With a look behind him, and his ears attuned to the sounds coming from the basement below, he quickly made for the tree.

Scuffling up the slim trunk, he threw his leg over the lowest branch, and drew back amongst the leaves and hoped he was hidden from below. He held his breath and listened intently – immediately sensing he was not alone. But he almost fell out of the tree as a deep voice came down to him from the branches above. 'What's up – a bull after you, man?' They were never discovered, but to this day Willie wonders how Fats made it up that tree as quickly as he did.

One of Fats' own parties turned out quite differently. On 21 May 1932, his birthday, he was throwing a shindig at his Harlem apartment and had many honoured names as his guests – the Dorseys, Jimmy and Tommy, Eddie Condon, 'The Lion', Carl Kress, Zutty Singleton, James P., to mention but a few. The evening had proceeded with great success until about five in the morning, when there was a thunderous knocking on the door. The tumult died slowly, and fell away to silence as the door was opened to reveal a scowling patrolman. 'Now how about breaking this up before I run you all in?' asked the law. 'Nobody in this block has been able to get a wink of sleep with this racket you're creating – break it up now, there's good fellas.'

With an apologetic smile, Fats stepped forward and began to explain. It was his birthday, and a fellow never knew but what he might not have any more birthdays, and besides, these were old friends who didn't often get together. Everybody was having a good time, nobody was disorderly, and hadn't he heard that music on his way up – it was solid, real solid, man. 'Just you take the weight off of your two feet, John Law,' Fats invited, 'and treat your ears awhile. Here, have a glass of this fine liquor. Take off your jacket and that heavy pistol belt. That's it, relax. Re-lax, man. Now, Mr Waller will lead our brothers here into another chorus of that righteous music – take it away, men.'

The music recommenced, the patrolman's feet kept time to the beat, and in a short time a homely Irish grin spread over his face.

11

In July, Spencer Williams, who had been back in New York for a spell, once again felt the call of Montmartre and the Paris nightlife. Spencer, he decided, was nowhere unless he got out of New York quickly and returned to France. Resolved to go with all speed therefore, he took a quick stock of his finances. Not enough, something had to be done. Write some songs, maybe. He pondered a while, and decided to call on Fats. Maybe he'll work with me. He knew he'd like Paris, and wondered if Anita would let him join him. It was worth a try, so before another day had passed, he gave Fats the idea. Fats' eyes gleamed at the prospect.

' 'Nita, honey,' he said when he saw the mood was right, 'I'm goin' on a little vacation with Spencer just to pick up some trash, y'know. Now, I won't be gone long, be back in a few weeks. Now he and I, we got a lot of songs to write so I'm goin' to be up for a while tonight. You go back to bed, Spencer's comin' over soon. Yes, 'Nita, we is off to Paris to find some of that old, original French gold.'

There was not much Anita could say, for she saw Fats' heart was set on the trip, so she gave her assent. That same night Spencer came over to 135th Street, and they started in high good humour writing a few saleable things to finance their trip – and a marathon session it turned out to be. During that night and in the succeeding two days, they actually wrote twenty-seven tunes and sold them all! Only one, however, *Down On The Delta*, ever saw publication.

It was early August when they finally set sail, and Fats and Spencer threw a big shindig on the eve of the sailing. Among the guests were W. C. Handy and his daughter Kathleen, and the party lasted all night, eventually ending down at the pier where the *Ile de France* was tied up. Most of the guests looked somewhat bleary-eyed in the bright morning sunshine, but they all managed to raise a ragged cheer as the liner cast off.

It didn't take long for all on board to realize that they had a couple of uncommon passengers amongst them. Fats from the very first day at sea was at the piano in the saloon, and he and Spencer never tired of giving special ship's concerts. Happily, Fats was a good sailor, and he roamed the decks keeping everyone amused day after day. The generous draughts of wine and whisky, brandy and champagne, that he accepted were enough to have flattened a lesser man, but Fats thrived on the liquid fare and, no matter what the weather, always remained on an even keel. Spencer, not to be outdone, kept pace with him, and by the time they reached France, the liquor locker must have been considerably depleted.

Once in Paris, Spencer was naturally at home, and he lost no time in arranging quarters for them at a little hotel in the Rue Pigalle. This was right in the middle of the artists' quarter of Paris, where they were surrounded by innumerable little cafés and restaurants which amply supplied their needs for food, drink and even companionship. Fats plunged into the Paris night life with typical abandon. No prohibition, and above all white and black mixing indiscriminately and with a freedom that came like a breath of fresh air to Mr Waller. Fats' own favourite spot became La Rumba, situated in the same street as their hotel. Other spots which often saw the lusty pair were Cabaine Cuban, Gavarnies' Melody's Bar, L'Enfer, and Boudon's Café, where they frequently ate, and the celebrated Bricktops, where for many years the red-headed Negress Ada Smith made travelling Americans feel so much at home. Time meant as little here as in Harlem; even less, if possible – nothing much happened until after midnight, and Fats and Spencer would entertain, and be entertained, through the hours of darkness, threading their way from place to place along the narrow streets, admiring the food, the wine and the women with equal fervour.

With the eye of a connoisseur, Fats quickly became acquainted with many of the more attractive female jazz lovers. It was lucky Anita wasn't around, for he was to be seen with one or two on his knee almost any hour of the night, and sometimes when over-filled with *vin rouge*, he didn't even care if they were lovers of jazz or not – bring me a dozen of those French mam'selles, would be his cry! He knew his stay in Paris must be all too brief, and he was eager to taste its pleasures to the fullest extent.

It was on this visit to Paris that Fats met up with a man who was to become one of his most loyal and vociferous supporters, Hugues Panassié. This jazz enthusiast, whose studies into the then new music were way beyond anything of a like nature in the United States, was completely enchanted by his first meeting with the frolicking pianist. He has written extensively of Fats' piano greatness, and was fortunate that he met Fats at this time, for shortly afterwards Panassié's *The Real Jazz* was published and included a spendid tribute to Waller. He wrote an amusing account of his reactions to Fats' and Spencer's visit to Paris, in the *PL Yearbook of Jazz, 1946*:

We agreed to meet again the day after the next at 'La Rumba'.
He was there from a half-an-hour after midnight. I had nothing to complain of: he played a great deal, for he was equally fond of taking his part in an orchestra and giving solos. I found almost as much pleasure in watching him as in listening to him. His appearance when he played was a complete reflection of his style. The body leaned slightly backwards, a half-smile on the lips which seemed to say, 'I'm really enjoying myself; wait a bit, now listen to that, not bad, eh?' He rested his hands on the piano and hardly moved them at all, his fingers alone seeking out the necessary notes.
He only raised his hands a very little from the keyboard. Thus the incredible power of his playing proceeds not so much from the rapidity of his attack as from its heaviness. Its force is not nervous at all, but muscular. Instead of bringing his impetus from a height to strike the keys brutally, rather does Fats attack them very closely, and seems to want to bury them in the piano. This is surely why his playing, in spite of its terrific force, appears so much more placid than that of other pianists.
It is well-known that Fats is not only a magnificent improvisator but also one of the best and most famous composers of jazz. Some of his pieces have been great successes, played by all the orchestras. I was not backward in asking him to interpret some of them, especially *Ain't Misbehavin'* and *Handful of Keys*. When I asked him to play *Sweet Savannah Sue*, however, I was most surprised to see that he could not remember it at all.
Something that struck me about Fats was that, far from forgetting music when he stopped playing, he loved it so much that he lived it every instant. At 'La Rumba' while he was sitting at my table and

talking to me with one ear, he continued to listen to what they were playing behind him, so that at any given moment he might break off in the middle of a sentence, exclaim, 'What a pretty piece that is!' get up, go and find out the title and then come back and tell me it as he sat down again.

Fats also had very good taste, a taste extremely superior to that of most jazz musicians. Here was no grave theorist, though, pronouncing sententious aphorisms on his art. He lived music constantly but thought on it never, and it was only by questioning him that one had the opportunity to hear him make some exceedingly intelligent observations.

In reality, he loved life in all its aspects, he loved to laugh, he loved to drink – and couldn't he drink! I have never known a man able to imbibe so much at one time.

It was this very side of his personality that has caused prejudice against him on the part of many jazz students, who, passing their time in building up intellectual theories to prove that the art in which they are taking an interest is as profound in its way as the music of the classical masters, are deeply shocked by the records of Fats wherein he sings with a spicy *canaillerie*, enriching the miserable text of the American songs with phrases of his own ludicrously comic invention. How many times have I heard it said that the buffoonery of Fats' vocal choruses was of an inadmissible vulgarity! How can these unfortunates who moan, and with good reason, at the inanity of American songs, not by contrast admire Fats who, well aware of that inanity, but obliged to perform these pieces, turns them completely into ridicule by his remarks, or by the emphatic or farcical manner in which he declaims them.

This marvellous humour of Fats' vocals one often finds again in his piano solos, for instance, when he follows up a lightly touched little phrase in the upper register of the piano with a few violent chords which are like a *blague*. Those who disparage Fats make this another grievance against him. My God, how these people detest laughter, all that is joyous! Why must they attach importance only to those things which have a serious air (as they call it)?

It has been said of Fats that he was a santé [tonic]. Impossible to find a truer word for him. In everything he did can be recognized an indomitable vitality, an easy force sure of itself, a joy in living which really do you good. That is why all the jazz musicians liked so much to play with him, to feel behind them this solid rock-like support, voluminous, unchanging. As in addition to all this Fats was a grand creator, an admirable piano technician and had the greatest possible swing, it is no exaggeration to say that he was one of the four or five great personalities in jazz music. Here was one of those rare people whom one could not misunderstand without misunderstanding the music of jazz itself.

Also in France at this time was a young medical student from New York, John Theobolds, who was then completing his studies at Lyons. One evening, wandering around Montmartre, he heard some piano that sounded right out of Lenox Avenue. He looked up and saw he was outside the Club L'Enfer. He hastily opened the door to behold the bulk of Fats Waller at the piano, surrounded by a covey of French chicks, and several empty bottles. As he stood watching, quite enraptured by the music, a voice boomed out, startling him: 'Hey, Boy! You play this thing?' Involuntarily, Theobolds nodded his head and then at once regretted his action, for he knew that after this man his playing would sound like someone's five-finger exercises badly played. But Fats leapt up and ushered him to the piano stool with a 'Take over a while, young man, won't you? I've gotta dance with some of these French queens.' So saying, he grabbed the nearest girl and headed for the small dance floor.

But all this partying was costing money, and even although lots of drinks were on the house from the grateful managements of the various clubs lucky enough to have their customers entertained gratis, something had to be done. Spencer had charge of their finances but their expenses ran to thousands of francs a day – drink was never cheap in La Belle France! After six weeks had gone by, the Williams finances were in sorry shape and Fats, without further funds, saw that his little sojourn was about to wind up. So, without Spencer's knowledge, he wired Saul Bornstein, of the Irving Berlin office, for funds. Saul had been his private banker on many occasions and he came through with the passage money.

On what proved to be their last evening together, Fats and Spencer were eating, as often, in Boudon's. Towards the end of their meal Fats suddenly raised his eyebrows provocatively. Spencer turned to look for the girl and saw she had responded to the Waller high sign. She consented to leave with Fats, and Spencer shrugged and waved them off before resuming his dessert. It was the last time he saw his friend for six years. Once out of the restaurant, Fats took the girl by the arm and said, 'I gotta go someplace. Now just you go back and tell him I went back to the hotel.' Fats hated good-byes and this was his way of getting out with the least possible ceremony.

When Spencer saw the girl return he asked what had happened. She told him as instructed by Fats, and a worried Spencer made for the hotel without delay. But Fats and all his things had gone. He had packed and caught the milk train out of Paris to pick up his boat at Le Havre.

*   *   *

Back in New York among his friends, a big party was given in his honour. James P., Eddie Condon and Bud Allen were amongst those making the official greeting and, as Fats would have said, this party was a real 'killer'. Some really serious drinking took place, so much so in fact that even the honoured guest himself ran out of breath. In the middle of recounting to his eager listeners some of the lusher and pleasanter aspects of Parisian life, the heat and the liquor and the excitement suddenly became too much even for him. With all speed he made for the bedroom where he promptly passed out cold on the floor. James P. and Bud frantically tried to rouse the inert form and finally, after much puffing and grunting, they got his eyes open and his brain working again. 'Hey, Fats, wake up!' said Bud worriedly. 'You got company. You can't treat 'em like this. You're the host, man!'

Fats rolled his bloodshot eyes and the Waller brows contracted. With a mighty effort, he gave some thought to the problem. 'Okay, man,' he said, after some deliberation. 'You be vice-host, I quit the job,' and without another word lapsed again into unconsciousness.

Later the same night, or more correctly the next morning, he was himself once again, so much so in fact that he persuaded all those still making sense to accompany him to Luckey Roberts' St Nicholas Avenue apartment. Here the party received fresh impetus!

*   *   *

In late 1932, Fats took on a manager – the first full-time agent he ever had. The man was a shrewd man in show business named Phil Ponce, and was the father of the celebrated singing team, the Ponce Sisters. With a theatrical background that stretched back over a great many years, Phil was an ideal manager for Fats. He took over the management of the unpredictable pianist at the behest of Marty Bloom, who was now trying to get out of his obligations and was clearing the way for his next stop – the production of the floor shows at the Sherman Hotel's Panther Room in Chicago.

The first thing Ponce did to try and get his new charge started in the best possible way was to establish Fats at the great radio station in Cincinnati, WLW, which blanketed a large part of the country in its programming. Fats was hired for a one-shot appearance, but it went so well that Ponce was able to secure a two-year contract. This opened up a new and untouched section of the country to Fats. Before this, the only means of spreading the irresistible Waller magic abroad had been by means of his gramophone records. His piano rolls had lost much of their attraction, the player-piano being no longer in vogue, and there was a vast untouched public who were quite unaware of Fats' entertaining abilities. WLW could be the means of making his name a household word. Ponce realized that radio offered the greatest possibilities for Fats' particular style, for whilst the visual appeal of the artist was not to be denied, his unique voice and sparkling keyboard style were a natural for radio.

Anita and the two boys accompanied Fats out to the Ohio town when he began work in a new programme to be called 'Fats Waller's Rhythm Club'. Included on the same programme were the white house band and the Southern Suns, a Negro singing group, four men and a girl, all members of the same family. The show was announced by Paul Stewart who later went into motion pictures.

The programme would open to the strains of *Underneath A Harlem Moon*, and then swing into *I Got Rhythm*, introducing each performer in turn. The show was built around a very simple 'plot' – the Deacon, as played by one of the Southern Suns, preached to a Sinner, who had confessed his uncontrollable addiction to that 'Devil's Music'. Whilst the Deacon, in stern terms, lectured the

Sinner, Fats, playing softly, insinuated his seductive music into the discussion. A little more of Fats' piano music and the Deacon found himself under the spell. The show wound up in a good old jive session, with all the stops pulled right out.

This show clicked from the start and, thanks to the excellent production, lasted a year. In the Christmas week of 1932, Fats was told of a young girl named Una Mae Carlisle, who had been a great hit at a summer resort. The show had finished and she had returned to her home in Xenia, Ohio. Fats was especially interested when he heard that she was an exceptional pianist, and he immediately got in touch with her, asking if she would like to come on out to Cincinnati and do a Christmas week radio show with him. Actually the girl was still in school, but with her mother's consent she made the trip, accompanied by her sister. Fats was rehearsing when she arrived from the station, but he stopped on seeing her, and at once set her to work. She went on the air that night at nine o'clock playing the piano, with Fats accompanying her on the organ. Fats was enchanted beyond description by her playing and they didn't leave the studio that morning until the early hours.

Una Mae at once abandoned all thoughts of returning to her home, and when her mother finally found her, she was holed up across the street from where Fats was staying. Una Mae put up such a fuss that her mother finally agreed that she could stay in Cincinnati and work on the radio show, if she agreed to live with some friends of the family. So Una Mae found herself a steady fixture both at the radio station and with Thomas 'Fats' Waller. He took an intense interest in this pretty young kid who played the piano so strongly in his own style. Fats, of course, brought her along the road to maturity in his own way. She probably didn't get to bed as early as a young girl should, and she coughed and spluttered over her first drink, some of Dr Ross's corn whisky which Fats experimentally placed before her. But, despite these drawbacks, she certainly learnt a lot about jazz.

The Waller Rhythm Club eventually became such a hit on the air throughout the Midwest that the RKO Circuit booked it complete as a vaudeville attraction. Paul Stewart worked out the scripts and sketches and the show opened at the Cincinnati Palace.

Paul recalls that Fats was rather self-conscious at first, but the huge audience was a ready-made one – they knew just what to expect and the show was received with enthusiasm. As the show progressed Fats grew increasingly more at home, and the tour was off to a good start. The band used for the show was part of Clarence Page's outfit, operating under Fats' name.

But as time went on, Una Mae became more and more involved in her feelings towards her pianist partner. As an artist she loved him dearly, but his wilfulness infuriated her so much at times that they quarrelled violently. Once, when the show was in Indianapolis, she drank some oil of wintergreen in an effort to make herself sick and scare Fats. These tantrums punctuated the no doubt close attachment that really grew up between them – Fats was now 29, twice her age, but still he was only a big kid at heart. Anita and the children had returned to New York during the vaudeville tour.

Some weeks later, in Youngstown, Ohio, the road manager flew the coop, taking with him the proceeds from the past engagement plus all the advance money. The show was completely stranded. A cousin of Una Mae's helped them back to Cincinnati, where they were able to resume the radio show and also do three or four weeks in a club. Between them they bought a car, and when a booking for a big country club date in Louisville came through, they resolved to drive down. Fats said he'd stop by early the next morning for her, and they'd be on their way. At six-thirty she was waiting, but no Fats. Eight o'clock, nine, ten passed, and at eleven she called a cab, and drove to his house. The garage was open, but there was no car to be seen. Una Mae immediately took off for the station where she caught the first train for Louisville. Arriving in town, she asked a redcap for the name of the best available hotel, and, on checking by telephone, found that sure enough Mr Thomas Waller had registered there within the hour. A few more inquiries took her to a corner where the local musicians used to hang out and there she saw Steve Dunne and Earl 'Inky' Tribble, two of the musicians from the Clarence Page band.

The two musicians, knowing Una Mae's temper, instinctively ducked as they saw her coming. 'Oh-oh, look y'here, here comes Sister Gizzard-Lip,' they cried, and were off down the street. At that moment Fats and the 'Deacon', with three fancy-looking dames, zoomed around the corner in the familiar black and yellow automobile. Una Mae, sizing up the situation at once, marched into the middle of the street and stopped the car. By the time she had run out of breath, the others had all dispersed, and Fats was reduced to a jelly. 'I was comin' by to get you, Baby, I really was, but somehow I just got late. But I knew you'd get here all right!' It took all Waller's wiles and fast talking to cool her off this time, but by the time the show was due to go on he had won her round again.

One of the less exciting sides of the WLW radio programme was Fats' participation in the 'Moon River' late night show. A long-time favourite in the Midwest, this programme had become a sort of institution. It began around one o'clock and continued until half past, featuring uninterrupted organ music, romantic and classical. It was always a perfect programme for lovers, and had no doubt been the inspiration for countless proposals, and other romantic nightly interludes. Coming from one of the largest contemporary studios in the country, 'Moon River' was announced with a minimum of words, but the music was selected with the greatest possible care. Seated at the giant Wurlitzer organ, Waller was allowed to follow his own inspiration for half an hour, and this was in some ways, musically, one of his most deeply satisfying times. Always an ardent organist at heart, Fats really enjoyed these quiet moments, with the subtle tones of the organ bringing into his mind and soul memories and inspirations. Cares dropped from his shoulders as at no other time. It was a rare period in his life, as, completely alone, with no madding crowd beating at the bandstand, he was able to play the music he loved upon his favourite instrument.

It was hard to reconcile this mood-invoking organist of the small hours with the same artist who conducted the rollicking swing programme from the same station earlier in the day. All mention of the artist's name was therefore eliminated from the programme sheets. But a somewhat jarring note to these idyllic moments was added by Mr Clark of WLW, who related some years later that although the music was all he could wish for, he could never get over his annoyance at Fats' habit of tossing empty gin bottles into the organ loft. All good things must come to an end, and Waller's stay at WLW drew to a close. A misunderstanding with his manager, Ponce, brought the engagement to a halt, and Fats returned to New York in 1934.

He started off this year by playing a few Harlem spots, notably Pod and Jerry's. One evening he made his way downtown to the President Hotel, just off the main theatre district in Manhattan, where he had been invited as a guest to the opening of a new cellar spot which was to feature a restaurant with music. Willie 'The Lion' was to open the place, which was to be known as 'Adrian's Tap Room', and to be operated by Adrian Rollini, the famous bass saxophonist and xylophonist, who had formerly had a spot at the Whitby Hotel on 45th Street, between 8th and 9th Avenues, known as the Whitby Grill – a place which had become a favourite musician's hand-out and stopping-off point for entertainers of all types. 'The Lion' had been the feature there, and, from the opening night at Easter, the place had been jammed. Eighteen months later, the least expired and, owing to the proximity of a Catholic school, was not renewed. Adrian searched for a long time for a suitable spot to continue his successful venture, and finally settled on the President – but with some misgivings. When he first saw the place it was a dubious-looking basement, filled with junk, but by hard work they got the place ready for the opening. By ten o'clock many notables in the music world were on the club floor, talking and drinking, but there was no sign of 'The Lion' anywhere. Many of Adrian's guests were only too happy to make music and finally, at half past eleven, in strode the unmistakable form of Fats Waller. Looking around at everyone with a big grin, he caught sight of a thoroughly upset Adrian Rollini. 'Hi ya, Boy!' he hollered. 'What's the matter with you, man – you look sad.'

'Your buddie Willie The Lion has let me down, and this is my opening night,' was the answer.

'Don't you fuss yourself, Mr Rollini, The Lion is probably tied up with that other job he had tonight. I'll work for you. How about that!'

Fats played at Adrian's Tap Room, on and off, for six months. He never made it a full-time job, but he did manage to spend some parts of his nights there, playing the piano and jamming with the many musicians who nightly came in flocks, eager to have a blow.

Fats would pick up about $65 a week and tips – a sum Rollini blushed to mention, for Fats was rated well above this amount for a single fifteen-minute broadcast in those days. But the Tap Room needed a piano tuner's continual attendance, for Fats gave the 'box' a real work-out.

A great attraction at the Tap Room was a delightful series of song battles between Martha Raye and Ella Logan, two up-and-coming young singers who would take turns singing against each other just for the hell of it. Tommy Dorsey and Edythe Wright also used to entertain the customers, and the late hours found Rollini's place a veritable Who's Who of Music, with sidemen from all over town *1934* converging on this little bistro for their musical kicks.

Like the Hotfeet Club back in 1931, the Tap Room made capital out of a talented group of waiters who would switch from table service to the shim-sham at a moment's notice and would lead gay lines of patrons and musicians in and around the tables and out into the street and back again in a dance which forecast the later, more famous conga.

Fats' CBS sustaining programme in New York this year forced him to quit the Tap Room engagement as the broadcasting company didn't approve of the situation. Nevertheless, the two arrangements did overlap for several months before CBS cracked the whip.

Rollini replaced Fats with another fine pianist, Putney Dandridge. His little band kept the customers well pleased, notwithstanding Putney's unfortunate habit of falling asleep while playing. Adrian said, 'There he'd be – playing one minute, and you'd turn away for a bit. When you looked at him next, he'd be nodding, his hands still on the keyboard. I'd go over and tap his head lightly to rouse him and he'd come back playing even before his eyes opened!'

*   *   *

One of those lucky breaks which so often shape careers was responsible for a New York radio connection for Fats at this time. Sherman Fairchild gave a swank birthday party for George Gershwin, and Paul Whiteman, who was providing the music, asked Fats and 'The Lion' to come along as entertainers. Arriving at the plush Park Avenue apartment, they peeked into the living-room and saw a host of Broadway-ites, including Harold Arlen, Vernon Duke and the guest of honour. Fairchild spied them immediately and called, 'Come on in, fellows. How about a few tunes?'

Willie, outspoken as always, said, 'Fats, how 'bout you goin' in there and starting off? I want to check the place awhile.' His eyes roved round the room, seeking out the bar.

'I don't want to go out there all alone,' said Fats. 'Come on out an' let's do some together.'

'No,' 'The Lion' countered, 'you best go out alone, an' don't you take that piano back in the corner neither. Play that one out front.'

Fats knew just what was in 'The Lion's' mind. A jealous man where his music was concerned, Willie wasn't going to risk any of the visiting songsmiths present stealing his stuff. Later in the evening he told Fats so, whereupon Fats replied in his carefree way, 'That's okay, Lion, they can steal all the stuff they want from me. Some day I'll be getting it all back again. Besides, I can spare it. There's more.' And there always was more.

The party started about eight-thirty and around ten o'clock in walked William Paley, head of the Columbia Broadcasting System. His young daughter was with him, and as soon as she entered the room she began to notice things. It wasn't long before her attention was focused on the rotund pianist who was mugging and laughing his way through a song. Running across to her father, she cried excitedly, 'Daddy! Look at that big man, isn't he funny? Look at his big shoes and those enormous eyes.'

Fats overheard what she said and, rolling his eyes and tapping his feet, he called, 'Hello, hello, hello – what's this?'

But his singing and playing also made an impression on the kid's father. Before the night was over Paley came over to Fats. 'Here's my phone number,' he said; 'call me tomorrow.'

Later that night when Fats reached home, he paused to write something on the door-jamb of the bedroom. From her bed Anita asked what he was writing.

'Don't let me forget this tomorrow, 'Nita. I may have a job on WABC!'

166

Sure enough it was true, for Paley had plans for sustaining a show with Fats as star. Later that day, when he called his programme director, he asked, 'Where are we going to put Fats Waller?'

'Mr Paley, we haven't room for him just now,' the director replied.

'Then make room,' came the reply.

So Fats was on the air again.

12

In the September issue of *Crisis* in 1934, the writer Roy Wilkins poured out his feelings ecstatically in a short piece on Waller after attending one of Fats' organ programmes over the CBS network. The piece contains several chronological and factual errors, all due doubtless to Fats' inability to remember dates and places, but the author's obvious enchantment with the informal rehearsal to which he had been treated reflects what often happened to listeners to this programme. Fats' début in New York in the spring of that year on a couple of sustaining shows brought an immediate and enthusiastic response from the listening public. The Cincinnati episode had sharpened him for this and he thoroughly enjoyed the work. In March he appeared on the 'Saturday Revue'; in April there were guest shots on Morton Downey's 'House Party' and the 'Columbia Revue', and in May, the 'Harlem Serenade', followed in June by Fats' own shows, 'Rhythm Club' on Monday and Thursday evenings, with an organ show on Saturday nights, and the 'Columbia Variety Hour' which was another forum for Fats. On every other Sunday night he was also a feature artist with Cliff Edwards, 'Ukelele Ike'.

One Saturday evening at the Paramount Building, where the organ studio was situated, Fats had a number of important visitors from the radio world. Agency executives and station men clustered about the large console as the big man warmed them with a selection of his specialities. Amongst them was W. C. Handy, at that time still blessed with his sight – he recalls the occasion as one of the most astounding he had ever seen.

'What a performance!' reminisced the Father of the Blues. 'Just imagine Fats sitting there with this crowd all around him, playing some out-of-this-world melodies. He would lift his right hand to take a draught from the glass of gin on the console, laughing at someone's joke, a cigarette perched on his lip, then without losing a beat or bar of melody, back to the drink again, and another draw at the cigarette, and a few more wisecracks. What co-ordination!'

In the midst of all this, Phil Ponce decided that this might be a good time for Fats to branch out again as band leader. A Victor recording contract was secured, agreeing to a three per cent royalty with an advance of $100.00 per selection. Fats hadn't recorded for Victor under his own name since 1930, when he did a two-piano duet of *St Louis Blues* and *After You've Gone* with Bennie Paine, so this was really the beginning of the big time. As early as May 1934, the familiar 'Fats Waller and his Rhythm' began to appear on labels. On this first date, the band consisted of Fats on piano and vocals; Herman Autrey, trumpet; Ben Whittet, reeds; Billy Taylor, bass; Harry Dial, drums. The guitarist was a kid still in DeWitt Clinton High School, Al Casey, who later became a regular with the Waller band and internationally famous with the instrument. Al had met Fats through the Southern Suns singers who had been with him on WLW and who were his aunt and uncles.

Appropriately enough, the first selection recorded by this recording band was a Razaf–Johnson (J.C.)–Johnson (James P.) number, *A Porter's Love Song To A Chambermaid*.

Assured of sales of their exclusive artist, Victor arranged another session in August and again in September. On the former date, Eugene Sedric makes his first appearance in a Waller band, on clarinet and tenor. The September date included some of the finest sides that Fats ever produced, the late Reginald Forsythe's *Serenade For A Wealthy Widow*; *How Can You Face Me?* (Fats' own composition and with lyrics by Andy Razaf); *Sweetie Pie*; *Mandy*; and one of Fats' most popular recordings of all time, *You're Not The Only Oyster In The Stew*.

In November, another two sets were recorded, making twenty band selections plus four piano solos of great note and extreme excellence. These are all pieces written while Fats worked for Joe Davis. *Alligator Crawl*, with its smattering of rare Waller boogie-woogie; the nostalgic and charming *Clothes-Line Ballet* (from the *Harlem Living-Room Suite*); the low-down, atmospheric ode to the reefer-smoker, *Viper's Drag*; and the scintillating *African Ripples*.

Around this time, Fats played a stage show at the Academy of Music picture house on Fourteenth Street in Manhattan, sharing the bill with the band of Charlie Turner who was currently appearing at the Arcadia Ballroom. Charlie, a bass player, had originally played tuba with the famous Alabamians, the band which Cab Calloway eventually fronted after his triumph in 'Hot Chocolates'. Turner's current band numbered about fifteen, including Hank Duncan on piano. This engagement set Ponce thinking – the fine reception which the entire band received seemed to spell possibilities for branching out. New York had acclaimed them – why not give the city and the rest of the country a chance to see Fats in action with a band? Charlie Turner was very keen on the idea and urged him to form a unit to go on tour. At length Ponce decided that it would be worth a try.

In early 1935 the band was first booked into the Meadowbrook on Pompton Turnpike, New Jersey, a spot where so many bands have leapt off into the big time. The date went over so well that they continued afield and made a short New England tour, including Boston and Providence. They wound up back home with an initial appearance at the 125th Street Apollo in Harlem, and at the Grand Theatre in Philadelphia. This was the beginning, and from here on Fats Waller was in the band business and life took on a hectic pattern that he had never known up to this time. Everything he had done before was easy compared to this – schedules, uniforms, arrangements, accommodations, transportation, musicians – all added up to place a strain on the ample shoulders of the big man. Most of the details, of course, were taken care of by Ponce's office and by the road manager and advance agents, but there was still a lot of responsibility. However, the valuable experience of Charlie Turner and Hank Duncan, both of whom had been on the road before this, made a world of difference.

The initial show they presented featured the band as an opener and provider of background music, with Fats as a featured soloist. One of the gags they worked was a mock piano battle between Hank Duncan and Fats Waller. With a deprecating smile and his eyebrows raised, Fats would look over at the slight figure seated at the band's piano. Duncan would immediately begin a hot chorus of *I Got Rhythm*. After another even better chorus Fats would say in mock astonishment, 'Say, this fellow really *can* play.' And the battle was on. They would take about two solo choruses each and then cap it off with a frenzied duet which wound up the number.

This little feature invariably went down well with the audiences. Henry Hank Duncan was a most talented performer who could invariably give his celebrated opponent a run for his money, having played spells with the later King Oliver Band and Fess Williams' Royal Flush Orchestra.

In addition to Duncan, who was also the possessor of a good singing voice, the band at this time included Herman Autrey and Sidney de Paris on trumpets; Benny Morton, trombone; Edward Inge, solo clarinettist; Rudy Powell and Don Redman on alto saxophones; Gene Sedric and Bob Carroll, tenors; James Smith, guitar; Yank Porter, drums; and of course Charlie Turner on bass.

Following this first tour, a call came for Fats from the West Coast and he left for Hollywood, where he worked for exactly one day for RKO in 'Hooray For Love' – a film which starred Gene Raymond and Ann Sothern, with Bill Bojangles Robinson an added feature. Fats sang one speciality number, *I've Got My Fingers Crossed*, and did a speciality *Livin' In A Great Big Way*, with Bojangles, using men from Les Hite's band – the pay, five hundred dollars, wasn't bad! He also worked with the same band at Sebastian's Cotton Club and, this being Fats' first trip to the film capital, Anita went along with him. Before they left, Fats was promised a part in a new 20th Century Fox film that was about to go into production, 'King of Burlesque', but in the meantime, there was work to do back in the East, so he returned to New York and rejoined the Turner band who had been playing the Arcadia Ballroom.

A tour of the Midwest started and, after a stop-off at Philadelphia, they headed for the Detroit area, where a record crowd of nine thousand people attended the show at Forest Grove. The crowd danced in three separate halls, with the music being piped from hall to hall by loudspeaker. Outside, the temperature had dropped to zero but inside the atmosphere was fair, and musically much, much warmer. The band now headed south, and the tour practically became a riot as record-breaking crowds stormed the doors of every place they played. On more than one occasion they played to crowds of over ten thousand people.

But Fats' unpredictable nature, which so endeared him to the vast audiences, began to work havoc amongst the promoters, and caused Phil Ponce undue worry. No matter how successful the tour, and how enthusiastic the audience, if Fats was in a wrong mood he would disappear and would fail to show up for the date. The panic would be on, with everyone scurrying around looking for the absent star, who, more likely than not, had cut off ahead to the next town on the agenda, there to cultivate a few supporters and get a few pints of 'Old Grandad' under his belt as an inoculation against the strenuous sessions to come.

One night at the piano, shortly after jumping a date, Fats became aware of a grizzled old fellow with chin whiskers standing before the bandstand. He peered through the smoky atmosphere at Fats, then at the portly Charlie Turner, with his bass fiddle, then back to Fats once more. Waller winked at Charlie, and in his calypso dialect, said, 'What's de matter wid him, ma'an?' It didn't take them long to find out, for directly the set was over, the old man jumped up on to the bandstand, walked up to Fats and slapped a summons in his hand.

Charlie says he never saw Fats look more crestfallen, as he saw the papers referred to a run-out on one of their dates. At Atlanta, Ponce called the tour off, Fats left for Hollywood to make the second movie, and the band returned to the Arcadia Ballroom.

This second film gave Waller quite an ambitious part in comparison with the previous one. As an elevator operator he had a small speaking part and also sang a number. The story concerned the trials of Warner Baxter, a theatrical producer on his last legs. Fats, who worked in his office building, puts on a show, with help from several other entertainers, which rebuilt the shaky business and assured the film of a happy ending. One item worthy of note is that, during the script reading, Fats insisted that the word 'Yassuh' be replaced with the more conventional 'Yes Sir'. Other little objectionable passages were also altered at his behest. Fats' overwhelming good nature and the kudos that is naturally accorded a great artist usually protected him from the shabby treatment often meted out to musicians on tour; nevertheless certain people and certain cities in particular even then made life hard on the Negro – no matter what his calling or stature in his profession.

Fats' first film, 'Hooray For Love' had its première in Philadelphia, and the band hit the theatre for the run, with Fats doing his memorable *I've Got My Fingers Crossed*, from both stage and screen. Then off again on a theatre tour.

Band tours are generally booked so that only theatres will be played on a given schedule, and rarely are one-nighters and dance dates included – these being handled on a separate tour. The latter are obviously the more gruelling, with accommodation sometimes difficult to come by. The major part of the day is spent in a bus heading from here to there, meals are grabbed on the run, and laundry and dry cleaning done when a moment allows. It goes without saying that nerves fray easily under the continual strain. Theatre dates usually last for three or four days, frequently for a week, and give the performer and musicians a much more stable existence. But even here, with anything between three and five shows a day, there is not much time to oneself.

In New York the Victor record people were goggle-eyed at the returns pouring in from the sales of the new Waller record series. The magic name of Fats Waller was surging ahead of all other artists in their catalogue. These weren't race records in the old Okeh and Black Swan tradition. Everybody was buying them. That stunning personality, coupled with the outrageous voice and those saucy asides, had hit the ears of the record-buying public like a bombshell. In fact, many people who had never bought a record in their lives were just buying Waller. Little men, big men, jazz fans and longhairs alike, it didn't make any difference – once you became infected with the Waller bug, you were hooked. Some took a little persuading, but if they were appalled by the revelry in *Oh Suzanna, Dust Off That Old Pianna*, or depressed by Fats' sobbing, *Somebody Stole My Gal*, they were sure to be won over by the subdued and charming *I'm Gonna Sit Right Down And Write Myself A Letter*.

If Fats had stopped recording right after that record and had disappeared from the jazz scene, a lot of good music and fun would have been lost, but no doubt his fame would have endured. It was this last-named song and the recording of it that put Waller and the band over the top, so to speak. In 1935 this song lay on a publisher's shelf doing nothing at all, but someone took it to the Victor studios while a rehearsal was in progress, and, looking it over, Fats agreed to record it.

They only had a piano copy, but Fats looked at it and shrugged his shoulders. He played it through a couple of times, pronounced a favourable verdict on it, and suggested the band get an arrangement worked up from which to cut a record.

But the studio manager wanted the tune done then.

Fats objected, but the number was made that self-same day, and it is hard to imagine a more finished performance. Waller played the melody to them three or four times and then the band played their appointed parts as if they had been playing the number all their lives. It is extraordinary to think that, only a few minutes before this, they had just made *Lulu's Back In Town*, one of those 'solid killers' to which this band of Fats' really did full justice. The change of pace and inventiveness of this little group of Fats' was astounding.

I'm Gonna Sit Right Down became a hit, but entirely because of the Waller version. It sold more records than any of his others and pushed the tune into top-rank rating, becoming so closely associated with him that many people thought he had written it himself.

If one looks at a discography of the Waller records, and sees the abundance of commercial tunes included, it seems strange today that he should have felt averse to recording some of the more successful songs, but the fact remains that many of these recordings were made against his better judgment. A case in point is the song *I'm On A See-Saw*, which he really tried to avoid, but in which he turned in a creditable performance, particularly the difficult vocal line. Another was *Big Chief De Sota*.

Actually, Fats was an excellent judge of what he could and what he could not sing. His own compositions, although often fitted with sentimental lyrics aimed at the popular market, were very singable, and even when Andy Razaf or J. C. Johnson incorporated some real sugary lyrics, Fats invariably pulled out all the stops and made a travesty of the whole thing. He knew his own voice and how ridiculous he could make himself sound playing the part of the anguished lover, so ridicule became his sharpest weapon. But, at the same time, he had the ability to put over an almost tender rendering, when he thought the mood and the song called for it. His melodious performances of such songs as *My Very Good Friend The Milkman*, *Rosetta* and *West Wind*, as well as the aforementioned *I'm Gonna Sit Right Down*, prove this point.

But it is as the master of hoarse, bawdy-toned, sixteen-cylindered jive that Fats is best known and loved by the millions. And at this period, the near flood-tide of his recording career, a fine procession of rhythm tunes were made by him and his little band. Imagine the fun and merrymaking that went into the following titles, all recorded in 1935 and early 1936: *Dinah, Take It Easy, There's Gonna Be The Devil To Pay, Somebody Stole My Gal, Truckin', Sugar Blues, Spreadin' Rhythm Around, The Panic Is On, Christopher Columbus, Big Chief De Sota, Black Raspberry Jam, Fractious Fingering, Latch On, Loungin' At The Waldorf*, and *Bach Up To Me* – the list could be much longer.

In the busy year of 1935, Fats invested some of the proceeds of his recent success in a Hammond organ. He had it installed in his Morningside Avenue apartment, and it is recalled that his elation with the new baby was only exceeded by the wrath of the neighbours after he had given it a full breaking-in work-out through to the small hours.

Fat's wardrobe was by now assuming heroic proportions – a necessary item in the life of a bandsman – and was indeed a far cry from the dim days when his baggy pants and tattered shirt had earned him the title 'Filthy'. His taste in fine clothes was not sudden, it was just a matter of economics, for Fats knew how to dress and paid well for the well-fitted suits which draped his large frame. He dressed his whole family equally well, and now, for the first time in his life free from the spectre of debt, he began to expand visibly. In 1936 he bought a new Lincoln, a custom-built convertible, priced at the dizzy figure of $7,200.00 and at last realized another youthful dream – he owned his own Lincoln like his old-time friend, Clarence Williams.

An interesting little episode occurred while the band was on tour in New England at the RKO Theatre in Boston. It was a Saturday and the I. J. Fox Fur Company sent a lad called Irving Siders over to the theatre to arrange with Fats for his appearance on the 'Fox Fur Trappers' radio show next day – the guest artist was usually obtained for this show from the current show at the theatre. Armed with ten dollars to buy whisky as an inducement (the boy had to get a passer-by to make the purchase for him) he studied the stills of the King of Burlesque outside the theatre so that he recognized his quarry. Once inside the RKO stage door, he was shown into Waller's dressing-room and handed over the bottles. These were graciously received.

'Do you want the whole band for the show tomorrow?' Fats wanted to know.

'Oh no, sir – just you, sir,' answered the kid.

'Fine! That'll be just dandy. Say, how'd you like to stay and see the show?' The kid nodded eagerly. It was late afternoon before young Irving decided he'd better get back to his firm. He told them Fats would appear next day and, having found out that Fats was married, intimated to his employers that Fats would appreciate a fur piece in exchange for the appearance. Accordingly, an in-expensive fur scarf was laid out for the entertainer. When Irving saw it, he protested that it wasn't good enough for Mr Waller's wife and, going down into the vaults himself, he selected a more appropriate item, a pair of crossed twin foxes. Given the okay to take it to the theatre, he hurried over with the gift without delay. The next day not only the leader, but the whole band showed up at the studio.

Unfortunately, just before the show, Fats broached the liquid inducer he had been given and for once got quite drunk. So lost was he that he made no sense at all and nearly completely lost the use of his legs. His valet, helped by Irving, wrapped a wing curtain around him and together they walked him to the waiting piano, concealing him from the audience until he was seated and had begun to play. Except for those backstage, no one was the wiser. He played as well as ever, but the directors of the I.J. Fox Fur Company were anything but pleased.

On the Monday Irving Siders got the sack and glumly hung around the theatre all day. On the Wednesday, when Fats at length spotted him, he asked him what the trouble was. When told, he smiled at the boy. 'Young man, you just come on with me and don't worry 'bout nothin'.' The kid stayed with the band through the rest of the New England tour until finally, in Chicago, Fats gave him his return fare to Boston. Siders, however, went to New York instead, and eventually entered the band-booking business with some success.

Life was a lot of fun for the band on these first tours. 'Fat Man' Turner, as the big bassist was known, used to engage in monumental eating bouts with Fats and Gene Sedric, whose build gained him the affectionate title of 'Honey-bear'. Charlie remembers that, whereas he himself would eat with regularity, Fats would go for long hours with little food and then suddenly lower the boom on his stomach with a gigantic spread. This habit gave him the edge on these 'chomping contests', and it wasn't uncommon for him to consume fifteen hot dogs at a sitting. One time in Providence, Rhode Island, Fats ordered steaks, one for 'Fat Man' and two for himself. When they arrived, they looked so huge Charlie asked if they were elephant steaks! But Fats went at them, and it seemed to Turner that the waitress had hardly had time to get back to the kitchen when Fats was calling for another order of the same size and quantity.

Even more impressive was his performance at Charleston, South Carolina. This was at a church affair where food was sold to enrich church funds. As the band played the last note of the evening, Fats dashed off the stand and over to the food counter, buying outright a twenty-pound fresh ham. Fancying some gravy, he also bought the pan the ham was in, a carving knife, and a gallon of mustard!

Earl 'Fatha' Hines also tells a tale about the man's capacity for food. One evening in Washington, D.C., a joyous reunion took place in a night-club dressing-room. The busboy arrived, bearing a tray of six hamburgers and twelve bottles of beer. 'Why, Fats, this is fine!' exclaimed the hungry Earl, whom Fats called his Jug Brother. Fats looked up quickly and said, 'Oh yeah, Earl; if you want some too, you'll sure have to wait, 'til we get some more. This little snack is just for me!'

*   *   *

It is strange that one of the most vital members of the Waller group is seldom mentioned. She is Myra Johnson, the dynamic singer who stuck through thick and thin with the band – staying with it until the end. Myra, a diminutive sepia bombshell who could rival her big partner in putting over a song, and who could whip up an audience to a virtual frenzy with her blues and rhythm singing, got her initial start with Charlie Turner's band at Small's Paradise. When that band was taken over by Waller, she left them and accepted an offer to go to Europe to join a Lew Leslie show. Later, back in the States, she was working a club in Atlantic City when it happened that Fats and company pulled into town for a dance date. 'Fat Man' Turner at once got hold of Fats' ear and gave the young singer such a big build-up that Myra was sent for at once. She listened to the proposition Waller and Turner made, but decided it might not be really as good as it sounded, so she turned it down and went back to the Club Harlem to finish out the summer. It wasn't until that fall (1935) that she finally accepted the post.

It didn't take her long to warm to the job, and she soon became invaluable in many ways. She acted as nursemaid, with medicine and pills, when any of the boys fell ill, and her voluminous travelling bag always contained such essentials as needle, thread and stocking caps. She quickly earned the admiration and companionship of the whole band and, except by Fats, who was apt to call her anything under the sun as the mood suited him, she was known as just plain 'Johnson' by the entire crew. As she felt more and more secure in her job she was inclined to talk to outsiders about it – and how much the band liked and depended on her. 'I'm the sweetheart of the whole band,' she confided to some fellows standing round the bandstand at a dance. She did not realize she had been overheard, until later that night, *en route* to Pittsburgh in a Pullman. The berths had all been made up and the gang was sitting around in the aisle in dressing-gowns, passing a bottle from hand to hand. Pretty soon Myra, fairly drowsy, flopped back into her berth and drew the curtain. To a man, the band got to their feet and, advancing on the hapless girl's bunk, threw aside the curtain and jumped one after the other on top of the tiny form. 'So you're the sweetheart of the band, eh, Johnson?' they cried. 'Isn't it wonderful?'

But in Chicago some time later she got even with them when they heard some unearthly sounds coming from her dressing-room in the State Theatre, as her voice moaned pitifully, 'Oh . . . Oh . . . Oh . . . Oh . . . Oh . . .' They all raced down the passage to help – 'You Great Big Beautiful Doll!' she finished, as she met them at the doorway.

Fats and Myra over the years developed some sparkling routines.

Each show would feature a duet and Fats would introduce her with 'Myrooooo, come hence, you wench!' or mutter into the microphone, 'Come here, you fine Arabian thing, you!' This expression was one of Fats' own special bits of jive, and references to Fine Arabian Love occur on many of his records. Myra's comely figure was often given the Waller nod, as with a sly grin he'd mouth into the microphone: 'and bring those fine Arabian cement bags with you.'

Their version of *Two Sleepy People* (or, as Fats preferred, *Two Sloppy People*) really wrecks the lyrics: 'Do you remember the reason why we married in the fall? . . . It was a shotgun wedding, you know . . .' and 'I remember the nights I used to kiss you in the hall (and, baby, that wasn't all) . . .'

Then there was the memorable *Shortnin' Bread*. The regular lyrics finished with a fast series of rhymed verses sung by Fats, typical of which is the following:

> 'Oh, Momma, Momma, don't run so fas';
> You're gonna show your big fat—'

*   *   *

In these early years, the band went through frequent minor changes in personnel, but the instrumentation remained the same, and the regulars, Herman Autrey, trumpet; Al Casey, guitar; Eugene Sedric, clarinet, and tenor sax; Charlie Turner, bass; and Wilmore 'Slick' Jones, drums; were nearly always there. Drummers Harry Dial, Arnold Bolden, Yank Porter, and Art Trappier; John and James Smith on guitar; trumpeter Johnny 'Bugs' Hamilton; and Cedric Wallace on bass (engaged later); were all alternate members of the band as it continued to tour and play dance dates. There was also the enlarged road band which fulfilled theatre and dance dates and which used various other musicians to bring it up to size. This band, however, despite its showmanship, could never match the intimacy and swing of the small group, which did most of the recordings and the small club dates. The fact that, over a span of almost nine years, this little unit remained remarkably stable, and survived a couple of break-ups, only to reform months later with no difficulty, remains a tribute to the magnetism of working with Thomas Waller and to the fine musicianship of all the individual members, many of whom must have many times refused offers of less gruelling schedules to join other outfits. Certainly men like Casey, for instance, who was rated the nation's top guitarist, warranted positions as more than sidemen. Indeed, since 1943, Sedric, Casey, and Cedric Wallace have all had their day as leaders of their own outfits, with varying degrees of success. However, the adulation accorded to their leader shone on them as well, and so, in other ways than financial, they all loved their work.

Even in listening to a Waller recording, from this or any other period, a perfunctory analysis will show the extent of the full co-operation of the whole combination. On almost every record, a piano introduction and first chorus is followed by one of Fats' vocals, supported by an instrumental section, featuring either reeds or trumpet. The number is usually wound up with a vocal half-chorus against a jam background, or just an instrumental ensemble, complete with vocal encouragement from their leader. The piano can always be heard setting the pace, but it remains in its proper place in the ensembles, proving Fats' excellent ability as a band pianist. That it equals his stature as a soloist, which is formidable, amply proves what an outstanding musician Fats was in every way. This quality can best be illustrated by listening to a record by the band and trying to imagine how the ensemble passages would sound were the piano absent. With this valuable solid foundation gone, the lift and ride that characterize Waller's band recordings would suffer immensely. This is not meant to detract from the fine contribution of the Waller drummers, but it is just that one has come to expect such a wealth of rhythm from his records that the absence of the powerful Fats piano would leave things very thin by comparison.

Fats' own asides, remarks, gags, and ad-libs do provide some basis for the argument that there was always an 'unseen instrument' present. But, besides being good showmanship, they make their own valuable contribution to the set-up of the whole band. They often provide a sort of bridge between sections of music and fill in where a pause developed, while also contributing the spur which drives the little band to such frantic effort. In the three-minute record, universal in those days, there was usually scant time in which to work up a really swinging jam session, but Fats Waller and his Rhythm could turn it on and off at will. In their version of *Sweet Sue*, one can hear a sort of duet between Fats' second vocal chorus and Herman Autrey's trumpet chorus, whilst in the final jumping chorus of *There Goes My Attraction* Fats pushes Autrey along to a tremendous climax.

While on the subject of the records, it must be added that it is useless to try and pick the best of their tremendous output, though certain records will always remain intensely satisfying and are so good that they promise to stay that way for ever. One such is *Christopher Columbus*, which, although subtitled *A Rhythm Cocktail*, is more like straight corn likker for strength. Fats has the early part of the record to himself with his piano and vocal, but nothing can dim the virtuosity of Sedric's solo, probably the best he ever recorded. An inspired trumpet follows Fats' own fast piano break, which would have left many lesser musicians without a note to their names; and, indeed, it seems that from all the Waller sidemen, Autrey was possibly the most strongly influenced by the drive of their leader. It is easy to see why these men reached their greatest heights within the framework of the Waller band; and, away from it, never quite maintained that same peak.

13

And so life went on. Out on the road, home for recordings and a little relaxation, and the occasional appearance at the 125th Street Apollo and the Harlem Opera House, more generally known as the 'Uproar House'.

On 24 March 1937, the RCA recording studio was the scene of a 'Jam Session at Victor' – possibly one of the most quickly assembled recording dates ever. Eli Oberstein, recording director at that time, hearing that Fats, Tommy Dorsey, Bunny Berigan, George Wettling, and Dick McDonough were all in town at the same time, arranged a recording session for them. George Wettling, the noted Dixieland drummer, says:

'It was supposed to be a four side date, with little planned, just the instrumentation. Tommy and Bunny were not on speaking terms at this time, they'd had a row over something or other, but that didn't stop them talking to each other with their horns. Bunny and I came along to the studio together, the others by themselves. Everybody was feeling fairly high, as I remember. Berigan had a pint in each pocket, and doubtless Fats, as usual, had his. We just went in there, and cut loose. We never did get more than two numbers finished. On one of the takes, we just went on and on. Nobody wanted to stop. It was too long to use, though. When it was all over, we all took off on our separate ways. Just like that.'

This really was a session. There is some beautiful solo work by everybody on the blues side, and the ensemble work on *Honeysuckle Rose* is, even considering the state of the participants, quite remarkable. It is to be regretted that more of the music made that day has never been released.

*   *   *

Early in the year, Arnold 'Scrippy' Bolden's death resulted in the signing on of 'Slick' Jones, a talented drummer with a flair for showmanship. Bolden's passing was a blow to the others, as he was held in high regard by the band. A favourite expression of his was 'No tilt', from the jargon of the pinball-machine crowd, a catch phrase he used on all kinds of occasions. Once, at a New Hampshire lake resort, the whole band, with Fats and Anita, were hanging around in bathing suits, getting up nerve to tackle the chilly water. Fats suddenly spied a seaplane taxi-ing along the lake. 'C'mon,' he shouted, 'let's take a ride.' Nobody made a move, so he grabbed the person nearest to him, who happened to be Scrippy. The pilot agreed to take them for a flight around the lake and countryside, and Fats and the unwilling drummer clambered aboard. The plane began to move slowly, but once aloft, the ride proceeded smoothly. Suddenly the small craft hit an air-pocket and lurched alarmingly. 'No tilt!' yelled Scrippy, and again 'No tilt!!' and then, as an after-thought, he added, 'please!'

Minutes later they were down on the surface again and had joined the others in the water.

Bobby Driver, Fats' valet and chauffeur, recounts that the day finished in ludicrous fashion. Fats had borrowed a pair of water-wings which he insisted on wearing back to front. A well-dressed gentleman, watching from the pier, was so keenly amazed at the proportions of the 'lady' he saw floating on the placid water that he took one step forward too many, for a closer look, and finished up in the sea.

Charlie Turner, after many years on the road, decided he wanted a change, and so he invested his savings in a chicken and turkey farm in upstate New York. He also opened a restaurant and saloon on St Nicholas Avenue in the West Side of Harlem, which he called 'The Fat Man on Sugar Hill'. Naturally enough, the upstate venture became known as 'The Fat Man on The Farm' – both were eminently successful, and justifiably so, for Turner was a good business man.

In this year Anita's cousin, 'Buster' Shepherd, joined the band as Fats' right-hand man. Fats now had need of someone who could help him through his 'saltier' moments, and Buster filled the bill completely. He was always standing by, ready to do anything from picking up some of Fats' 'liquid ham and eggs' to arranging reservations at the next stop. A tall, good-looking young fellow, his steadying influence on Fats often got things done when every-body else had given up trying.

1937

In October, the band was booked into a Boston theatre for a week and was then due back in New York for a recording session immediately thereafter. In order to get some new material to-gether, Fats asked Andy Razaf and J. C. Johnson to accompany him on the train, and during the few hours that it took them to get to Boston, a lot of work was accomplished. Several songs were written, the most famous being *The Joint Is Jumpin'*, a product of all three men.

Directly they arrived in Boston they headed for a chop suey joint, where the traditional Chinese dish was ordered, to be followed by steaks. The chop suey eaten, Andy and J. C. leaned back replete. They shook their heads sadly at the sight of the huge steaks which now appeared and pushed them away. 'Well, look there!' said Fats. 'What a shame to waste them pretty things!' So saying, he stuck his fork into the two steaks, added them to his own, and proceeded to demolish the lot. He even chided the waiter for being slow with the almond cookies, and finished off the meal with a large cut of pie!

Back in New York the following week, the number they wrote on the train, *The Joint Is Jumpin'*, was recorded. The idea was to convey the feel of a genuine Harlem house party, and so Andy and J. C., together with a couple of girls and several studio employees, provided the squealing and shouting background voices which serve as the rugged setting for Fats' amazing commentary. After a fairly conventional verse and first chorus, Fats goes into his patter, full of ad-libbed lines, 'Let it beat! Don't you hit dat chick! Dat's my broad – where'd you get dat stuff at? Why, I'll knock you to your knees!... What?... Put this cat outta here... What?... Get rid of it... Yeah – dat's what I'm talkin' 'bout... Hah, hah – Oh man, it's really ready... No baby, not now – I can't come over there right now...' At the height of things, a whistle blows and Fats sounds the alarm, 'I got bail if we go to jail, I said, The Joint is Jumpin'.... Don't give your right name, oh no, no, no!' – a noisy brawl of a recording but, when all is said and done, it is one of those things by which Fats was to be remembered the most. Others are the merciless shredding of Andy's lyrics to *S'posin'*, and

It's A Sin To Tell A Lie, where Fats abandons the three-quarter tempo of the original and substitutes for the mellow line, 'If you break my heart, I'll die', his rather more trenchant line, 'If you break my heart, I'll break your jaw and den I'll die.'

On nearly every record he made he added the little remark at the end – the dessert which he offered to round off the delightful musical repast.

*   *   *

Phil Ponce, the man who had handled Waller through all this period, now began to fail in health, and he was looking about for someone to take over the reins. The job he was offering was no easy one. It was one that would take a man's every waking moment. The Waller band wasn't one you could just send out on tour and then sit back and expect everything to run according to plan. No one road manager could keep up with the ebullient leader, and it took a personal manager's constant attendance and supervision to guarantee a tour free from jumped dates and complaints that Waller had threatened to pack up and return to New York before his contract was fulfilled. This was, in fact, one of the most provoking problems that Ponce had had to face. Directly a tour drew to its closing stages, the promoters of the final dance were like as not to be left without a band leader. Fats had the habit of striding up to Bobby Driver, his aptly-named chauffeur, and hollering, bag in hand, 'Holland Tunnel'. And off he'd go for his native city, leaving the rest of the band to fend for themselves. On one occasion, he even took with him Don Donaldson, the band's second piano man and arranger, leaving the band with no pianist at all. Myra Johnson and the road manager worked frantically that night filling out the show, to avoid a possible suit for damages.

Thus it was that the hot potato was dropped into the lap of one Wallace T. 'Ed' Kirkeby, a veteran of the band and recording business, and a man who had all the proper qualifications. Ponce gave him his blessing and Ed moved in, slowly at first, feeling his way, though with knowledge of the problems he would have to encounter. Fats Waller was not quite unknown to him.

Kirkeby had been in the New York musical scene since 1916,

when he joined the Columbia Record Company. The following year he advanced to the assistant managership of the recording laboratory. After a subsequent flyer in music publishing with the noted recording artist, Henry Burr, he came across a young group named the California Ramblers, and took over their management. A short time afterwards a smash opening at the Palace Theatre assured the band of a secure financial place in the entertainment world. At about the same time Kirkeby also landed a recording contract for the Memphis Five, supervising their many recordings including the tune that made them famous, *I Wish I Could Shimmy Like My Sister Kate*. While securing a Columbia exclusive recording contract for the Ramblers, he managed to record them on many competitive labels, using no less than seventeen pseudonyms.

He added Jimmy Dorsey, Tommy Dorsey and Red Nichols, who with Adrian Rollini on bass saxophone formed the backbone of the great white swing band of the Roaring Twenties. Their impact, style, precision and arrangements were the foundation of the swing era of the late Thirties. Throughout the Twenties Ed was in and around New York, building business at the swank Westchester roadhouses around his California Ramblers and even organizing a second California Ramblers for a tremendously successful Florida winter season. He opened a club on 53rd Street, Manhattan, which was so far ahead of its time that it folded soon after because of the trials of operating under Mr Volstead's Act. His band participated in the opening of vaudeville at the New York Hippodrome and did early commercial broadcasts from the new Columbia Radio Station, New York. Among his many accomplishments was the introduction of novelty instruments, amongst them the 'goofus'. This instrument, designed and played by Adrian Rollini, was renamed by Ed who thought Couesnaphone – Rollini's name for it – was hardly a name calculated to fit in with such slang terms as 'licorice stick', 'slush-pump', or 'skins', which were then currently in vogue.

Later years, in the depression era, saw Ed fronting a band which he formed, 'Ted Wallace and His Campus Boys', who had a highly successful radio, recording and personal appearance career. Bringing the Pickens Sisters from obscurity to national fame via radio and films was his next important achievement. In 1936, little more than a year after Fats began to record so prolifically for Victor, Kirkeby became Artists and Repertoire Manager for the popular catalogue of the RCA Victor Company. In this capacity he was able to closely observe the big fellow at work, and he knew well just the kind of records that Fats did best. So it was with considerable confidence that Kirkeby assumed control of the managerial duties that Ponce now gradually relinquished.

But a rude awakening was in store for him – he had never managed a Negro band or artist before, and he quickly found that there was a difference. The whole temperament of his new charges was quite unlike the more staid artists and groups he had handled before, and the circuits they travelled throughout the States were often in the most out-of-the-way places imaginable. The Negro theatres and one-nighter dance halls were not often to be found on Main Street. More often than not the touring musicians found themselves on a bumpy dirt road, unloading in a glade in some forest, or even having to haul their instruments upstairs over some garage or saloon to reach the place they were to play in.

But it was the complete unorthodoxy of the man whose band he now managed that became the biggest source of Kirkeby's new education. Fats began his association with his new pilot with enthusiastic co-operation as Ed set about enlarging the band for some new theatre dates. The job of getting together suitable musicians for this purpose fell on the shoulders of Don Donaldson, the second pianist and arranger. He and Fats searched the Harlem spots, and they didn't have to look far. In Small's Paradise, they listened to several bandsmen and hired them all: Cedric Wallace, bassist; Jimmy Powell, Alfred Skerritt, saxophonists; Jimmy Haughton, trombone; and Johnny 'Bugs' Hamilton, trumpeter.

In short order, this augmented Waller outfit rehearsed in a 54th Street rehearsal hall, in another room of which, incidentally, a young trombonist named Glenn Miller was also rehearsing a new band – a group destined to achieve some considerable fame.

From here on, Ed Kirkeby tells the story in the first person

187

14

I first met Fats Waller, when I was Artists and Repertoire Manager with RCA Victor – he was indeed the very first artist whom I took charge of for a session. What a man to pick for a new A. & R. man! Before the session commenced I had been told by all and sundry that Fats was difficult to control in the studio – that he drank too much on sessions, was impossible to advise and that he generally behaved like a real hellion in the recording studio. Happily, the stories about him were grossly exaggerated. True, he was happiest when what he called his libations were in plentiful supply, and was also at his best if a glamorous chick was on hand as well to spur him on by leaning on the piano by his elbow, but otherwise he was always ready to accept advice, and would work himself into the ground for anyone he liked.

The first time I actually met Fats was in June 1935. Record dates were nothing new to me, I had been supervising them with top artists for twenty years, but somehow I felt that the session I was on my way to supervise was going to be something a little different.

The session was to take place in the Camden church studio of the Victor Company, and by the time I walked in through the door the place was already jumping! Fats was standing in front of the little band, and a bottle of Old Grandad was being passed from hand to hand. 'Hi, Fats. Mornin', fellas. I'm Ed Kirkeby.'

'Mawnin', Mister Kirkeby.' Fats stepped forward with a huge smile and my right hand disappeared into his enormous paw. 'Hey, you cats, meet Mr Kirkeby. He's the man who set up them California Ramblers and made all them good records with Tommy Dorsey, Jimmy, Red Nichols and Adrian Rollini. That band jumped. What you got in mind for us to do today, Mr K.?'

'How about getting in the mood with that old gal friend of yours, Dinah?' I asked.

'Well, a-a-a-ll right then, Dinah, here I come.' Fats strode over to the piano. 'Now watch it, you cats; get on your feet and earn your bread. Send me, send me,' exhorted Fats, and the session was on.

From the control window I watched as that human volcano of energy urged on his band, and the studio rocked with the impetus of the greatest left hand in all pianodom. The great round brown face smiled across at me, and I knew that, without the slightest doubt in the world, here was a man I would love to the end of my days.

At many of his sessions throughout the years, we had a gag we used to pull that put him in good spirits and always got a laugh from the studio technicians and staff. Just as soon as I got in the control box, I'd look out at Fats, who was usually seated at the piano, with a bottle of his 'Old Grandad' 100 per cent proof bourbon whisky – lined up.

'Let's get started,' I'd yell through the control panel. 'Is that your last drink?'

'No, Mr Kirkeby,' would come the answer. 'This is my first bottle.'

I made many records with Fats to satisfy the growing demand in the jazz field and happily there were very few bad ones.

Phil Ponce, formerly with the National Broadcasting Company – Artist Division – had set up in business for himself and was handling Fats at this time. In 1938 I had left Victor and joined NBC in the set-up of their Band Booking Department. Shortly after, Ponce asked me to join him and so I moved over to Madison Avenue – and the panic was on! Phil was very ill – in fact a broken man – and I soon found that things were in a critical state. Fats owed Ponce a packet of dough for unpaid commissions and cash advances; he was way behind with his first wife's alimony payments, payments on his Lincoln car, and in trouble with the US Tax department. In addition he had had fines levied by the Musicians' Union, plus judgments secured by dance promoters hanging over his head. If that wasn't enough, his outsize thirst for liquor and 'leading the life I love' was costing him a fortune.

However, I felt that with an effort I could straighten Fats out, and so I turned to the one-nighter dance field for immediate work. I organized a new band and sent Fats south to earn some 'eating money'. I soon found, however, that his reputation on the road had suffered badly on his former tours by his heavy drinking, his disregard for contracts, and his jumping dates as he pleased. The public had marked Fats as unreliable and the tour was a flop; but there was more to come. I went south and quickly found the cause of the trouble. The promoter of the tour, a shrewd operator, had bought the band's time for a series of bookings for dance dates in the South and he was taking a cut from every night's show, much to the resentment of the local promoters who felt he was pulling too much gravy from the whole system. Sadly for him, however, the crowds were under par, and usually failed to provide a gate big enough to cover the advance guarantee. This bad business forced me to cancel the series after playing Columbia, South Carolina. Back on the road, heading north, I having returned to New York, Fats jumped a date in Durham with the result that when the band hit the Earle Theatre, Philadelphia, the box-office was attached for $850.00. Finally, just as the tour drew to a shaky close, Fats called the office from Newark, and told my secretary that he was tired, didn't care about playing Newark, and that he was coming on in. The girl luckily located me in town and relayed the bad news. Without delay I got the homesick Fats on the phone, and pleading with him like a Dutch uncle – after threatening to hold up his money – finally talked him into doing just this one last booking. It was the first in a long procession of such occurrences.

Fats now had a little money put aside and he could afford to relax at home, which after this he did for nearly a month. But eventually the financial pinch came, and so he had to take the band out again, this time to play the Capitol Theatre in Scranton, Pennsylvania. They wound up on Saturday night, and on Sunday morning the bus rolled into New York full of tired musicians. But over at the Criterion Theatre on Times Square, the weekly swing session, a regular feature of radio station WNEW, presided over by Martin Block, the famous disc jockey, was in full swing. This show had become great listening fare for the jazz enthusiast of those days – it was a gigantic affair, with celebrated musicians from all the bands in town in attendance. Fats of course was on his way there as soon as he heard of the proceedings, with Myra Johnson and a couple of the bandmen in tow.

On the stage, among the many jazzmen of note, were Louis Armstrong, Big Sid Catlett, Jack Teagarden, Bud Freeman and Cozy Cole. They had been whooping it up when Fats arrived, and a louder whoop than ever greeted his entrance. At a moment's notice, he, Louis and Jack teamed up in a three-way blues, *In The Crack*. The verses, improvised on the spur of the moment, run as follows:

(Fats) My, my, my, my, they've got me in the crack;
     My, my, my, my, they've got me in the crack;
     If Louis or Jack don't take the next one, I'm
        gonna break my back!

(Louis) I'm gonna snatch me a picket off somebody's fence;
     (Fats says, 'Oh, look out now.')
     I'm gonna snatch me a picket off somebody's fence;
     An' I'm gonna whip you over your big head until
        you learn some sense—

     (Fats and Louis roar with laughter and Fats says,
     'That's a killer!' amid laughs.)

(Jack) Oh, momma, momma, momma, where did you stay
        last night?—
     Oh, momma, momma, momma, where did you stay
        last night?
     'Cause when you came home your hair didn't look
        just right. . . .

Then follows a series of low-down blues choruses with excellent solos by all three. This marked the first time Fats and Louis had appeared together on a New York stage in nine years – since the run of 'Hot Chocolates'. When Louis formed his All Stars, many years later, this same number became a successful vocal feature for him and Jack Teagarden.

Another noteworthy occasion, during a benefit also run by Martin Block, had Fats and Lionel Hampton playing a duet on a single piano.

Two days after the Criterion session, a group of tunes was recorded at the Victor studios by Fats Waller, his Rhythm and his Orchestra. The first was a new arrangement of the familiar *In The*

Gloaming. A Don Donaldson arrangement, it remains, I think, one of the most pleasant sides the Waller band ever made. Unusual, because of the arrangement, which features a long and beautiful trombone solo by Jimmy Haughton. But it is a solo that calls forth sad memories for the Waller band. The number was featured as a showpiece in their theatre dates in this spring of 1938, with Haughton taking his solo out front. Tragically, just before the curtain rose on one evening's performance, he was handed a wire notifying him of the death of his mother. No one there that night will ever forget the poignancy of the moment as he stood there, tears streaming down his cheeks, playing his beautiful version of the tune.

*   *   *

In May another Southern tour came up. Another promoter bought a bunch of Waller bookings, and sold them to local dance promoters, but this skimming off of the cream of the profits by turning over the bookings for sizeable profits turned sour on him, too, as the local men gave him much opposition and little co-operation. The takings started to fall off, and the band had to take the box-office receipts in lieu of their guarantee, which soon added up to a lot of red ink in the Kirkeby–Waller office. Once more I had to rush off south and personally steer the affairs of the band into calmer waters.

Accommodation in the South wasn't usually too good in those days, particularly in the smaller towns, and, as Fats told me, strange things happened. Musicians and show people generally stayed at special boarding or rooming houses – one such place the band came across was run by a lady with an eye for extra money. The band had all retired for the night, when Don Donaldson and Gene Sedric, who were sharing a room, heard some mysterious noises coming up from the hall below. Hastily putting on some clothes, they peered into the darkness below. A murmur of voices excited their curiosity and they stole down the corridor, to see a line of people advancing one by one to a doorway. The landlady was selling the privilege of a look at that 'sleeping mountain' – Fats Waller in repose! The rate was twenty-five cents per head!

Actually, as I found to my cost, Fats hated sleeping alone, and would often stay up till dawn to avoid an empty hotel bedroom. If I wasn't available, then Buster Shepherd, his current valet, often kept him company, and could usually count on being kept up half the night by Fats' drinking and talking.

But Fats didn't always spend his nights talking, or even sleeping, as is borne out by this story from Billy Kyle. When Kyle was on tour with the John Kirby Band, they stopped off one night at a place called Flint, Michigan. Billy got a room with a Mrs Handy who kept a lodging house for professionals. After a good night's sleep, Billy, taking a pre-breakfast stroll on to the veranda and seeing under his bedroom window some fifty-odd empty bottles, asked Mrs Handy if she had been host to an Elks' convention. The good lady shook her head. 'No,' she replied, 'Fats Waller had your room last week.'

Another memorable evening, hardly of a pleasant variety for the Waller band, happened in a little rural district of Mississippi. Booked to play a Negro dance in the country, the band were amazed to find the hall perched on stilts in the centre of a wood. The night air was oppressively humid and even before they arrived, they were exhausted. One can imagine Fats' exasperation when, climbing on to the stand, he found no piano. The promoter blandly asserted that he didn't think they'd have to have one! Fortunately, a local parishioner owned an instrument, which was manhandled through the wood by a crew of volunteers, dragged to the rudimentary shack and installed. But meanwhile, the lamps had attracted so many bugs and mosquitoes that the lights were all but obliterated. This necessitated the installation of fans which, when switched on at once, blew away all the sheet music. Fortunately, sheet music was not of great importance to the Waller band.

At another stop on this same trip, a customer kept calling out for *Big Chief De Sota*. Annoyed by Fats' failure to play his request, he finally came down to the front of the stand, and with his feet planted firmly apart, yelled over the din, 'I've saved a penny a day for one hundred and twenty-five days to come to this show, and I ain't gonna leave till you play *Big Chief De Sota*.' Fats complied.

Taking the band out of the South, I finally got the remainder of the band's bookings picked up by GAC from Chicago. About mid-June they hit Rochester, Indiana, one afternoon for a dance date that evening. The lake resort was quiet and, tired of travelling and wishing he were back in Gotham, Fats began to take on board a large quantity of his 'liquid ham and eggs'. As the drinks went down, his mood grew more and more melancholy – what he wanted was his old Hammond organ. Strangely enough, I heard that a lady who lived nearby had just what Waller was wanting. I went to see her, got her permission, and secretly, and with the co-operation of a couple of members of the band, the instrument was dismantled, shipped over by truck, and set up in the little dance pavilion. Fats had wandered out to the lake-front, taken off his shoes and socks, and was fitfully swishing his toes in the placid Indiana water. His blues and frustration were such that he paid no need to the calls of his friends on shore. But the sound of an organ quickly got him to his feet and, from then on, every move was lightning. There was a lot of music played that night.

A stop in Kansas City, I remember, was the occasion of a fine reunion between Fats and his old friend, Count Basie. Basie hadn't hit the big time yet, but his little Reno Club combo were really jumping and Fats was all for taking them along with him. Fats and the Count tried to borrow a phonograph to play some of Fats' latest sides, but failing to find one, Waller walked into a store. Here he bought a combination record player and radio, which he presented to his friend on leaving town. For many years it was one of Basie's most treasured possessions.

Following this tour, I was heartily discouraged – completely fed up with one-nighters. I couldn't get Fats to stay on the job consistently, and we had exhausted the theatre circuit for the present. What to do? I realized that Fats was a 'tough sale' and that what was needed was new territory and a completely fresh start.

With this in mind I turned to Europe. Knowing the phenomenal interest in jazz in Britain and the Continent and how Fats' Victor record sales were booming there, I telephoned Tommy Rockwell of GAC, who had the Mills Brothers currently playing the Moss Empire Theatres in the United Kingdom, and asked him to cable for me to find out if they would be interested in Fats Waller for a ten-week tour as a single.

'How much?' Tommy asked.

'Twenty-five hundred dollars a week,' I replied.

'You're crazy,' gasped Tommy, 'they don't pay that kind of money over there.'

'Tommy,' I said, 'just send that cable.'

Later that afternoon he rang me to say he didn't really believe it but that it was okay – ten weeks at twenty-five hundred when Fats was available.

I called Fats at once.

'That's a Killer Diller from Manilla,' said Fats. 'Let's go.'

And so, in July 1938, with a somewhat diffident Waller in tow, we set off on our first European tour.

15

To keep the wolf from the door and at the same time to supply some new titles for issue while he was on tour, Fats and the Rhythm hustled to the Victor studio for a rush date. A coast-to-coast broadcast over NBC informed America that Fats was leaving to spread the gospel of American jazz abroad for the next ten weeks, with personal appearances in Scotland, England and Scandinavia. As always, nothing went smoothly, but after a last-minute visa hassle I finally got Fats and his wife Anita aboard the S.S. *Transylvania*, bound for Glasgow. As the Big Apple skyline receded I wondered what the future held for me and the Harmful Little Armful.

As you can imagine, it took no time at all for a young Scottish steward to latch on to Fats and show him the ropes. An introduction to the ship's orchestra led Fats to the piano and soon he was in his element. 'Keep a song in your soul' had always been Fats' credo and spurred on by the ship's luscious, loaded table and plenty of that fine Scotch whiskey, Fats soon coined the phrase, 'Don't be vague – gimme some of that fine John Haig.' The orchestra boys had the toughest work-out they ever had, for Fats kept them at it till four o'clock in the morning, but they enjoyed themselves and received a wonderful jazz grounding free, gratis and for nothing. Fats gave himself a treat by staying in bed until noon each day and the lack of exercise plus the fine Scottish food put five extra pounds on him during the voyage.

As the ship turned into the mouth of the Clyde a glorious day welcomed us to Bonnie Scotland. It was to prove an eventful day. At Greenock the ship hove to, the boys of the Scottish press scrambled aboard, and there followed a party which shook the ship from stem to stern all the way from Greenock to Glasgow. Those Scots were really two-fisted drinkers and Fats had a ball toasting a wee doch-an-doris. The Scottish press did a wonderful job, showing what a great honour they thought it was for Scotland to have his premier appearance. The strains of *Honeysuckle Rose*, played by Billy Mason and his band, greeted us as we walked down the gangplank. 'Hi,' said Fats with a happy smile. 'Man, that's a Gasser from Manassa.'

All that remained was the public's reaction to the 'Cheerful Little Earful' the following night at the Empire. Sunday was a day of rest, and Fats, Anita and I visited *with* Billy Mason for a tour of beautiful Loch Lomond. Fats happily absorbed the peaceful scene; signed an autograph for a cyclist who spotted him; and mused on the wonder of being recognized in the wilds of Scotland – thousands of miles from home. The chance meeting gave Fats a feeling of warm, friendly confidence.

At Monday's rehearsal Fats, cutting down much of the accompanying orchestration, got a good enough beat from the orchestra on the ride outs (last eight bars) which was all that mattered. We then settled – as calmly as possible – to wait for the 6.30 show. We need not have worried – let the Press chronicle Fats' fantastic success.

Evening News ('Round the Theatres'):

Swing musician in Victorian setting

Backcloths of old gold and rose . . . a mellow piano overlaid with old-fashioned carving and gilt stencilling . . . a swivel stool that came right out of the Nineties – into that Victorian setting at the Empire Theatre last night stepped no prim little Miss of a vanished century but the dynamic 285-pound King of Swing. The contrast between the mature staging and the ultra modern performance may have been accidental but it did not need any soft lights to make Waller's programme sweet music. His playing was nothing if not soothing, and even if there may be many of us who lay no claim to an understanding of 'swing', the last charge that anyone could lay at Waller's door is that of being noisy or raucous. Fats, in the words of his own composition, was not misbehavin'. He was, in fact, on his very best behaviour, even to the extent of refusing, pos-it-ively to swing 'Loch Lomond'.

Spotlight on Glasgow Shows continues:

'NO SWING,' says Fats Waller . . .

'No swing posi-tive-ly,' said Fats Waller – donning a tartan Glengarry and sitting down at the Empire's piano to play 'Loch

Lomond'. One chorus he played through and played it 'straight' as the jazz fans call it. Twenty stone – immobile save for eyebrows wagging fantastically in rhythm, his lips muttering private jokes to the keyboard, those chubby fingers caressed out the daintiest tinkling phrases. 'Ah, but you can't hold me down!' he chuckled, and slid into the melody of one or two typically 'Fats' phrases until he was mildly swinging the old ballad though not in the tuneless way that has made some Americans infamous. The audience loved it as they loved the rest of his act; Irving Berlin's 'Marie', his own 'Honeysuckle Rose', 'Handful Of Keys' and 'Ain't Misbehavin'' . . . and two big favourites . . . 'St Louis Blues' and 'I'm Gonna Sit Right Down And Write Myself A Letter'.

Fats had misty eyes as, after ten curtain calls, they eventually closed the tabs at the Empire that Saturday night.

With a start like this, Fats could really relax, for after conquering Glasgow, he had no doubt that England would follow suit. But he had one other engagement north of the border, Edinburgh, the Scottish capital city, dominated by the splendid castle which towers above the city like an eagle. It was here, on Princes Street, that I nearly died from shock. Finding that night life in Edinburgh consisted of one dance hall open until 1 a.m., we hailed a taxi and began the chugging uphill journey along Princes Street. The cab seemed to be on the point of giving out under the strain, but just as I thought we were coming to a halt a shift in gears would send the old taxi lurching ahead again. On one particularly sharp curve, the driver changed down into low gear, but as we surged ahead the rear door flew open, and out rolled Fats. Frantically, I stopped the driver and leaped from the car, expecting to see Fats unconscious in the street behind us. But there was Waller sitting on the kerb: 'Latch on, Mr Kirkeby,' he said with a reassuring grin, 'let's go. No need to worry, I broke that fall like I learned when I was a kid – an' you know I've got plenty to fall on, right here!'

'Clairty, Clairty – Nae Bother at All,' Fats chuckled to himself as he boarded the sleeper to London next day. 'Well a-a-a-all right, then. Let's go,' and we were off down south.

Waiting at the station to meet us in London was Fats' old friend Spencer Williams. Spencer, who with Fats composed *Squeeze Me*,

Fats' first success, hustled us off to his home at Sunbury-on-Thames where Spencer had cooked a tremendous meal of Southern fried chicken. Fats said it tasted just like Mama Rutherford's cookin', the acme of superlatives for him! In a mellow mood Fats sat down at the piano and tinkled off one of his oldies – a waltz, believe it or not. But it was sweet music, for that was his mood. A light rain pattering on the roof – inspiration for a song – and Fats was already fingering a melody. I suggested a title, Spencer joined us at the piano and in no time at all *A Cottage In The Rain* was born. Fats, happy with memories of his success in Scotland, played on for hours, but tomorrow's band call at the Palladium was for 11 a.m. so we downed one for the road and made our way back to London and a rented flat in Duke Street.

Arriving at the Palladium next morning, Fats viewed the front of the world-famous theatre with a happy smile, for there, topping the great electric sign was 'FATS WALLER – World's Greatest Rhythm Pianist' and, below his name, two of Britain's Variety stars – Florence Desmond and Max Miller.

Backstage, Fats was welcomed by Jack Brock, the stage manager, and shown to his dressing-room. Costumes were hung, orchestra books laid out, light cues given to stage and booth electricians, Fats' set dropped, the piano correctly positioned, and the rehearsal was on. Co-operating with Cliff Greenwood, Director of Music, and profiting from the Glasgow experience, a good deal of the orchestration was cut and the band did a fine job.

No problems developed and Fats was all set for the first show. Included in the Palladium programme under, 'FATS WALLER . . . The World's Greatest Rhythm Pianist', was a quote from Walter Winchell from the New York *Daily Mirror*:

The present controversy between Benny Goodman and Louis Armstrong over the title King of Swing is belittled by musicians . . . they contend that neither of them plays an instrument of rhythm . . . FATS WALLER however 'toys' with a piano and if we were a committee of one to decide matters, Fats would certainly get the title.

Londoners that night apparently agreed with Winchell, for Fats performed to thunderous applause and had to take curtain after curtain. As I listened to the wildly applauding audience, I knew then that I had an act for all Europe, and, I hoped, for all time.

The Press reviews were fabulous and during the weeks that followed, Fats was on the stage at night . . . and on the town till dawn; doubling the suburban theatres for Moss Empires with wild rides between theatres to make time schedules; four shows each night and, for relaxation, 'The Nest', a bottle club in Kingly Street, where Edmundo Ros drummed for a living. This was the rendez-vous where Fats, together with Django Reinhardt, Adelaide Hall, Spencer Williams, Reginald Forsythe, Ben Edwards and many other stars of the show world, gathered nightly to be entertained and entertain until dawn filmed the sky. In between, Fats found time to enable the *Daily Herald* in its column 'On the Air with Spike Hughes' to headline 'BBC CRY "SCOOP": Next Monday, the vast cheerful Negro pianist and singer will be guest artist with Jay Wilbur in the "Melody Out of the Sky" programme.' And the *Melody Maker* chronicled 'Fats Waller Records with British Band: Exciting news, for his thousands of record fans who have been hoping for some permanent souvenir of his visit to this country, is the announcement that "Fats" Waller has made a session here for HMV, the first coupling of which will be made available shortly.'

Another night spot that Fats enjoyed immensely was the Palm Beach Club, a bottle-party club where Ike Hatch was Master of Ceremonies, and a real staunch pal of the thirsty. During the whole of our European trip, we worked through Leslie Macdonnell of MPM Entertainments, one of the really great men of all time in show business. Leslie knew Fats by this time almost as well as I did, but he was rather more than shaken when he was aroused from his bed one memorable morning to hear Waller's voice on the telephone. Fats was at the Palm Beach Club and nothing was wrong, except that it was dawn and he was feeling lonesome and yearning for some home cooking. Fats was sorry, he told Leslie, but it was no good, he would have to find a substitute for him at the Palladium, as he had heard the *Queen Mary* sailed within a few hours, and Mr Waller was homeward bound.

Macdonnell, thoroughly awake by this time, said he was sorry too, but that Fats couldn't possibly leave without having a farewell drink with him; surely that would only be common courtesy. Quickly ringing off, Macdonnell then got through without delay to Ike Hatch and gave him instructions to entertain Fats until he got there. Ike promised to do his best. Leslie threw on some clothes, dug me out of bed at the Regent Palace and together we dashed with all haste to the Palm Beach. We needn't have worried, Ike Hatch had done his job only too well. John Haig and Mother Nature had, in that order, taken the Harmful Little Armful under their wing – Fats was fast asleep under the piano. But Fats was on stage as usual that night, tearing up his audience with his tongue in cheek, offering *Ain't Misbehavin'* – *Saving All My Love For You*.

Owing to the liquor he had downed the night before he was still a little hazy as to his whereabouts as he seated himself at the piano. He spread his arms until his hands grasped the extreme outside edges of the piano, then he lowered himself a little, stopping just short of the stool. Feeling about under his rump for the ridiculous little seat, he gave it a spin, and waited for the spiralling top to reach his behind. With a deep sigh of relief he sank down on the stool, but looking around behind him, asked solicitously, 'Is you all on there, Fatsy Watsy? Yes, I sees you is.' He prodded his posterior with a huge finger – the audience howled!

Realizing the possibilities of making some records commemorating Fats' first European tour, I had been talking to HMV about a session but was rather dubious about getting together a suitable group of jazz men to play with him. However Leonard Feather convinced us he could round up some fine men and we could add a couple of boys from The Nest who played with Fats nightly. I set up a date for Sunday which seemed the only time for all concerned. The *Melody Maker* reported that an amazing rush would be needed to round up the musicians for the recording session. David Wilkins, featured trumpet man from Ken Johnson's band, came down specially from Glasgow and hurried off immediately afterwards for Liverpool. George Chisholm, probably the first musician to interrupt a honeymoon for a recording session, flew back to his bride the following morning!

The rest of the personnel included Alfie Kahn, tenor sax and clarinet; Ian Sheppard, a Scottish boy from The Nest, tenor and violin; another Scot, Alan Ferguson, on guitar; Len Harrison on bass; and Edmundo Ros on drums. Titles recorded first were *Flat Foot Floogie*; Spencer Williams' *Pent Up In A Penthouse*; the current No. 1 song hit in America *Music, Maestro, Please*; and Ella Fitzgerald's *A Tisket, A Tasket*. In addition Fats, taking up the *Melody Maker* challenge that not even the great Fats could swing an organ, recorded Feather's *Don't Try Your Jive On Me* and *Ain't Misbehavin'* on the Compton Grand Organ. He was at the top of his form throughout the session – expressing the greatest praise for the British boys and wishing he could take them all on stage with him. The records were released as by 'Fats Waller and His Continental Rhythm'.

It is also reported – August 1938, to be exact – that Fats made four 'unofficial' sides in company with drummer Joe Daniels for the Parlophone label. The titles were *Mood Indigo, Narcissus, Whispering* and *Limehouse Blues*. In addition to Joe Daniels, the others present were Ted Bissett, guitar, Joe Nussbaum, bass, and Reggie Dare, from The Nest, on tenor. It must be admitted that the piano heard on these sides, excepting for one Wallerish break, does not sound like Fats at all, but both Daniels and Bissett insist he was present – so, as Fats himself might have put it, 'one never knows, do one?'

The following Sunday Fats again visited the HMV studios where he made six more solo organ sides. It was a lovely Sunday morning and six wonderful spirituals were recorded in an inspired session. *I Feel Like A Motherless Child* had been suggested, but the memory of his mother's recent death was too much for Fats and in the middle of the recording he broke down and wept. He refused to try again but insisted that Adelaide Hall, who had accompanied him to the studio, joined him in two numbers for old times' sake. The titles were *I Can't Give You Anything But Love, Baby* and *That Old Feeling*.

Keeping up the night and day pace, Fats shortly after this made a personal appearance at the Gramophone Shop in Sloane Street to sign autographs. He was made very welcome and imbibed so many Martinis that he fell sound asleep in the taxi on the way to the theatre. I let him sleep until the five-minute call when, using herculean measures, we pushed him on to the stage, just in time for curtain up. Fats was actually asleep on his feet leaving the wings but the thunderous welcome galvanized him into action.

The following week Fats doubled two of London's most important theatres, the Holborn Empire and the Finsbury Park Empire. He also, with Adelaide Hall, did a BBC radio programme, 'Broadcast to America', at midday on Friday. So by the time he bade farewell to London it was a tired but happy Fats who prepared to take off for Scandinavia.

Fats, in order to make the first concert date in Copenhagen on time, would have to travel from Vlissingen, Holland, to Hamburg, Germany, on the crack German train Mitropa, but when he heard the journey would take him through Hitler territory, he wanted no part of that. 'No, man . . . Ugh, that rascal Hitler don't like my kinda music,' Fats said, and it was not until arrangements were made for him to lock his stateroom door and be undisturbed until he changed on to the Danish train in Hamburg, that he agreed to go at all. Having some knowledge of German, I assured him that I could easily handle the German immigration and custom officials without him being present.

So Sunday, 11 September, we sailed from Harwich, England, arriving at Vlissingen, Holland, next day, then by train through Holland to Hamburg, arriving the following morning. The trip was serene and Fats got plenty of sleep which he badly needed. We made our way up the platform towards the restaurant to get some breakfast but had just turned the corner when we ran slap-bang into some of Hitler's legions as they goose-stepped through the station to be loaded aboard the troop trains. Fats turned tail. 'Man!' he said, 'I may have to be gettin' outta here fast, and out of here is the best place I know of!' However, I grabbed his arm and we boarded the Copenhagen train without further incident. The first concert was at 7.15 p.m. so we got to the hotel fast, unpacked, and made our way to the Oddfellow Palaeet. Otto Lington and his Swing Ensemble were backing Fats, the hall was packed, and as he stepped on to the stage to such a roar of applause, we knew we had another winner. The Danish Press: 'A World Attraction . . . Fats Waller . . . All Time Greatest Jazz-Pianist'. 'Swing-Pianist Fats Waller . . . A Fantastic Success'. Fats, with a wide grin, raised a glass – 'Skol!' he said. But after two weeks of concerts, backed by Sven Asmussen, through Norway and Sweden, the threat of war became so strong that the Scandinavian tour was cut short and we decided we'd better get heading for Home, Sweet Home. Three dance hall appearances, then back to Britain for Fats' first ever TV programme for BBC, from Alexandra Palace, with three more dance hall appearances while waiting for our ship.

The trip back to America on the *Ile de France* turned out to be one of trials and tribulations for most of the passengers aboard – mountainous seas put seventy per cent of them out of action, but Fats combated sea-sickness with double Martinis, and he and I roamed the decks and had almost exclusive use of the dining-room.

And so ended the first trip to Europe where Fats 'captured Scotland, England and Scandinavia, and received the greatest reception of his career'. Arriving in New York, and after a few days' rest, Fats and his Rhythm opened at the Yacht Club on 52nd Street for a long and successful run.

This engagement turned out to be the longest stand that Fats ever made at any one place with a band – they consisted of Waller, Autrey, Sedric, Casey, Wallace and Jones. Business was very good, and it was an enjoyable run for them all, as they were able to return home each night after work.

But all runs must end sometime, and this one, owing to some disagreement with the club managers, ended even before it had to, during mid-January. I pulled the band out in mid-week but luckily got them bookings at the Apollo Theatre in Harlem and, following that, at the Howard in Washington. The former being close to home, it was decided to take the Hammond organ from Fats' place in St Albans, across the Triborough Bridge to the 125th Street Theatre. But nothing happens easily in the band business, and hardly had Buster Shepherd got under way with the instrument when he was given a ticket for a traffic violation. Not knowing what had happened to him, everyone at the theatre was in a lather until he at last showed up with the precious organ just before the curtain was due to go up.

While in New York, Fats, whenever time allowed, was a constant visitor to the Onyx Club, where he was fascinated by the little group led by John Kirby. On his initial visit he met for the first time Kirby's pianist, Billy Kyle. He was delighted with his playing and told Billy that when he was in England he had actually had played to him, by some ardent collector, the Kirby record of *Rehearsal For A Nervous Breakdown*. 'That modulation you play from A flat to F was simply terrific!' said Fats, smacking Billy on the back. 'Where did you get that one from, man?'

'Took it off a record of yours,' replied the slightly nervous Billy Kyle.

The Wallers' new home on Long Island had been bought very quickly, once Fats decided he wanted to move, and they were one of the first Negro families to occupy a house in that section of St Albans, a thriving district of Queens Borough. This started what proved to be a sizeable influx of families from Manhattan and the Wallers were the forerunners of many famous show business names listed among the residents in that neighbourhood – Mercer Ellington, Lena Horne, Cootie Williams, Count Basie, Earl Bostic, Lester Young, Billie Holiday, and the two Brooklyn baseball idols, Jackie Robinson and Roy Campanella.

But Britain wanted him back and so we set sail again, this time on the *Queen Mary* on 10 March 1939. Fats, of course, had the usual ball encouraging the boys in the ship's orchestra to play jazz.

On arriving in London we found that Les Macdonnell had teamed us up with the famous Mills Brothers, co-starring at the Holborn Empire. Ted Ray, one of Britain's outstanding comedians, was also on the bill and we played to a sell-out throughout that week. The following Sunday the musicians' benefit – known as 'Jazz Jamboree 1939' – was held at the Gaumont State Theatre, Kilburn. All the great-name bands appeared including Ambrose, Carroll Gibbons, Nat Gonella and his Georgians, Jack Jackson, Sydney Lipton, Joe Loss and Lew Stone. Fats bought a fistful of tickets and invited many friends to meet him at the stage door. Unfortunately he failed to show up at curtain time and I had a hell of a job getting our friends in. Fats was remorseful next day and said he'd been visiting Una Mae Carlisle, who was sick in hospital, and he had forgotten all about the time. For the next few weeks, in company with the Mills Brothers, we toured the provinces doing wonderful business everywhere and, as Fats had it, 'living high on the hog'.

Fats did some composing on this trip. One of his most charming songs was written in Sheffield, the famous steel city of England. As was his habit, Fats had headed for an eatery after the theatre show and then went in search of any night life that was available in the town. But generally speaking, musical entertainment was non-existent after nine o'clock, and Fats just had to have an early night, like it or not. At about 5 a.m. the following morning, I was awakened by an insistent ringing of my phone, and on lifting the receiver, was not surprised to hear a familiar voice.

'What're you doin', Mr Kirkeby – you up?' Fats wanted to know.

'Am I up? Of course I'm up!' I said, slightly irritated. 'Can't you hear me eating my breakfast here in bed?'

'Don't get mad at me, Mister Kirkeby. I just wrote a song for you to hear – this is a killer.' He started to sing it to me over the wire. 'Slip on your robe and come on down, this song needs a lyric.'

I had hardly closed the door of Fats' room behind me when he began his story. It seemed that, after a long and fruitless search for some night life, Fats had gone to bed, wakened early, and had taken a walk in the park. It was dawn, the birds had surprised him with their sweet melodies. So he had hurried back to the hotel to set it to music before he forgot. Like a conjurer, Fats now produced a couple of bottles of sherry, and over these we duly finished out the remainder of the song, not calling it a day until ten o'clock when Fats retired peacefully to sleep – not to arise until show time. We called the song _Honey Hush._

But the most productive afternoon was probably some time later in London. On the boat, Fats and I had talked about a possible musical suite to be based on the various aspects of London. Nothing more had been done about it until one day when Fats was scheduled to do some work at a private recording studio. He had been up early, and had consumed two man-sized portions of his 'liquid ham and eggs' while shaving. Usually Fats could take anything, at any time, but this morning his stomach turned sour on him, and by the time he reached the studio, he was in no fit state either to play or compose.

Not wishing to waste the day entirely, I suggested that now was the time to work on the London Suite as we had visualized it. Fats was fighting a desire for sleep induced by his early drinks on an empty stomach, but he listened intently as I described to him some of the fascinating sections that make up the great metropolis. I soon caught his attention, and the place-names I mentioned suddenly translated themselves in his musical mind into harmonic patterns and themes. One by one we worked them into melodic sounds and finally we had musical pictures of brassy Piccadilly, sedate Chelsea, cosmopolitan Soho, mysterious Limehouse, depressing Whitechapel, and seductive Bond Street. Just as soon as these themes had become established, I insisted that they were instantly recorded, and, inside of an hour's time, Fats had composed and recorded his London Suite. These were only acetate recordings so I set up an immediate HMV session for Fats to record the Suite again under proper conditions. A few test pressings were taken from the HMV recordings shortly after they were made and the master was then returned to store. The war which followed in this year called a halt to the E.M.I.'s plans for releasing this Suite, and when finally, after the cessation of hostilities, the Gramophone Company looked for the masters, a search revealed that they had been destroyed in the blitz. They at once instituted a quest for the duplicates which had been made from the originals and, eventually, a complete set was discovered in London, in the offices of a music publishing company. So, only then, twelve years after, were the records made available to the public. In actuality, the Suite had been issued before as recorded by Ted Heath and his Orchestra on London Records – the scores were highly-arranged, but were nevertheless elaborations of Fats' own piano conceptions. But it was rather a case of putting the cart before the horse, as Fats' original version of the Suite had never been released at the time the Heath version was made. The latter version, however, is an exciting set and a splendid tribute to Fats Waller.

But the war clouds began to build up again – this time more ominously than before. President Roosevelt had stepped in and asked Hitler and Mussolini for a non-aggression pact, but we thought we'd better get home and so sailed for New York on 14 June on the *Ile de France*. I for one was very relieved to see the Big Apple skyline again – believe me.

16

After a short rest Fats was off again. A recording session for Victor, a week at the Apollo, an appearance at the World's Fair, and a recording date for Muzak while playing Loew's State theatre.

The Apollo had long since taken over the mantle of vaudeville in Harlem, and the Lafayette lost its trade steadily to the more crowded 125th Street theatres, and finally closed its doors later the same year. The Harlem Opera ('Uproar') House these days only occasionally played live shows, relying mainly on movies for its bill of fare.

Fats was always a great favourite at the Apollo, and was equally beloved by the stage hands, chorus line, and everyone who appeared at the theatre. During a run there, his visitors backstage looked like an edition of Who's Who of the Jazz World. If he happened to spy Earl Hines standing in the wings while he was near a microphone, he would say, 'Wait right there for me, Jug Brother, I'll be off soon, and we'll have a nip of the Grandad.' After the show, the two would get out of the theatre and head for a favourite spot where there was a piano. Entirely outclassed by Fats' formidable drinking, Earl would sometimes purposely stumble on the sidewalk and break a bottle of whisky – just to keep it from disappearing down Fats' throat. On one such occasion, Fats berated Earl severely for being so careless: 'Now you know what we're liable to do? We run into some chick an' if I ain't got no "lush" on board, I ain't got no nerve.' Later on that evening, as they arose from what had been an enormous meal, Fats looked at Earl, then, patting his full stomach, produced a prodigious belch. 'Man, just you look at that stomach – that's what makes me jovial!' – he passed out into the street with a roar of laughter.

The theatre cast and crew could always count on a big stage party when Waller was on the bill. He spent a great deal of money on these affairs, some of which would cost him as much as a thousand dollars. One such shindig in Philadelphia, however, on one afternoon before the show, caused disaster. The chorus line, all stoned to their eyebrows at curtain up, lost one of its members into the orchestra pit during a dance routine down front stage. 'Man overboard!' yelled Fats from the wings, but the management failed to see the funny side of the affair and threatened to fire the whole troupe on the spot. Even some fast talking by Fats only managed to stave off the mass discharge – the following week the theatre had a new line of girls.

But despite all this dissipation, Fats did have his more spiritual moments. Outstanding in the memories of his bandsmen are countless times when, in the dressing-room between shows, Fats would read to them from the Bible. A confirmed student of the Good Book, which he had read since childhood, he could quote long passages and was adept at translating the Old Testament meanings into everyday terms. Fats had many foibles and his way-wardness was a byword, but his bandsmen knew him for a man of deep feeling, a fair man, whose sympathy and honour were never to be questioned. The imprint of his Christian upbringing never left him, and rather than using it to cloak his more worldly habits, the reverse is probably nearer the truth. Fats always insisted that his children went to Sunday School and, when asked why he didn't go himself, he said simply that he didn't think the life he led in the entertainment world qualified him for proper church attendance. One may question the validity of this claim, but certainly not the sincerity of his belief.

These dates gave us a breather in New York in preparation for the long series of one-nighters which loomed ahead: Washington, D.C., Atlantic City, and the famous coloured resort in Millsboro, Delaware; back to New York for another Victor date and off to Chicago with the Rhythm for a four-week engagement at the College Inn; from there into Salt Lake theatre and the Regal, then back to New York and the Adams theatre in Newark, New Jersey, just across the Hudson; the Southland night club in Boston for two weeks, a one-nighter in New Haven, then into the Famous Door on New York's famous jazz street 52nd Street – Maxine Sullivan was second head-liner here and Fats insisted on accompanying her. A return engagement at the Panther Room in the Sherman Hotel, Chicago, lasted six weeks, and it was during this time that Fats wrote and I titled the now famous *Jitterbug Waltz*. Ashton Stevens, Chicago's celebrated music critic, acclaimed this composition, and he it was who wrote of Fats that 'the piano was the instrument of Fats Waller's stomach and the organ that of his heart' – Fats loved and nursed that Hammond organ of his, so the statement was exactly right.

This particular Christmas, Chicago was jumping, for, in addition to Fats' group, the bands led by Duke Ellington, Earl Hines and John Kirby were all in town. The cats all stayed at the Ritz Hotel which according to Billy Kyle was more shaky than ritzy. Up on the third floor Fats had installed his portable organ, and the vibration was such that when he played with all the stops out the windows fell open on the floors below. On Christmas Eve, after the show was over, Fats sat at his organ in his bedroom playing away with might and main. Soon the door opened and in came Earl, Duke, Billy Kyle and other odd band members. The bottles rotated from hand to hand and everybody got to laughing and telling their own particular favourite jokes. Other Christmas Eves were remembered – nearer home. Fats drifted into a more sombre mood and suddenly commenced playing some Christmas Carols. That music was just too much for that room full of homesick musicians! Duke blew his nose violently, Earl had trouble finding his handkerchief and in next to no time it was – as Billy Kyle described it – 'a roomful of the weepingest cats you ever did see.'

From Chicago to Detroit, where Fats broke all box office records at the Colonial Theatre – they stood in long lines in a raging snowstorm waiting to get in – the Colonial had never before seen such business, nor probably since. On to Canada to play Toronto's Sheas Theatre with a stop at Worccster, Mass., on the way back to New York. Believe me, anyone who thinks a top musician's life is just 'pork chops and gravy' has another think coming, for the going can be really tough and the hard road dims the glory plenty at times. Only the young in heart and the physically fit make the grade. The stairway to fame and fortune is tough to climb and the 60-dollar question is, 'Is it worth it?' The trick if you do get up there, in what they call the glory stable, is to remain there without blowing your top. Incessant road travel can do strange things to people.

210

After a month's rest in New York we took off again, this time for the great trek to Florida and a tour which was to take Fats and the big band for a series of one-nighters for the first time in that territory. We had high hopes. I had made arrangements for a private Pullman car to carry the band from Jacksonville to Miami and back, in the hope of avoiding the onerous conditions so often meted out to coloured artists working in Dixie, but at Jacksonville a bland railway official informed me that no facilities were available. Fats was furious and really 'pitched a bitch' and it was only with great difficulty he was persuaded to go on. When I remember the insults and the inconveniences Fats had to put up with on that trip, I still see red. At the time I swore I'd never ask him to do it again. I remember the many indignities such as the refusal of rest rooms, and even the refusal to sell gasoline to our bus driver who was, incidentally, white. Hotel accommodation was quite out of the question, and the band had to stay in private homes overnight, while I usually managed to arrange for Fats to be taken in by the local minister. In Fort Lauderdale, a two-gun sheriff came up to me while I was supervising the set-up of the band before the dance, and actually told me to get back in the bus, saying that he would take care of the business as no whites were allowed in the dance hall. I was thankful we had booked a short tour and that another five days would see us on our way back to New York.

During the ten-day rest in New York we did a record session for Victor, turning out eight good sides. But now started a coast-to-coast hop which was to be a corker. Our first date was at Danville, Virginia, and from there we travelled through North and South Carolina, Virginia, West Virginia, Ohio and Michigan by bus, grinding out one-nighter after one-nighter. After each show we fell into the bus exhausted and went roaring off to the next stop, sometimes an overnight journey of more than 500 miles.

From Gull Lake, Michigan, to St Louis by railroad, on to Jackson and Greenville, Mississippi, and the principal cities in Texas and Oklahoma and New Mexico. Next stop Phoenix, Arizona, where it was so hot that one could, and did, fry eggs on the sidewalk. The dance that night I remember was a 'flopperoo' and the promoter lost a fistful. We piled into a chartered bus to make a 400-mile hop across the desert in time for an opening at the Paramount Theatre where Fats co-headlined with Jack Benny's Rochester for two weeks. I shan't forget this Paramount Theatre for it was here that Fats, introducing the singer Kitty Murray, who was built like a brick house, gazed at her retreating posterior goggle-eyed and came up with the classic remark, 'My, my, my, all that meat and no potatoes!' I later wrote a lyric using that title – Fats added the music, and the result became quite a hit. Our next destination was Oakland, about 400 miles north, straight up the Pacific Coastline. Just outside San Francisco, this lovely town lay just across the Golden Gate bridge, and we made it our headquarters while we played one-nighters in the surrounding territory and two local dances at Sweet's Ballroom. But this easy living soon came to an end and we went off again, this time a night hop to Salt Lake City; this was a trip to write home about, especially in a 'puller-type' bus. But we made it and survived, buoyed by the knowledge that we were at last headed eastward and home.

Next stop Denver, Colorado, for a dance date – a healthy five hundred and twenty-one road miles, over and through the Rocky Mountains. Luckily the weather was good and we made it. What held us up physically I don't know, but we travelled on with the comforting thought that we were headed towards the Hudson Tunnel and New York. The following day we again piled aboard Old Methuselah (our bus), and headed south-east for a gruelling six hundred and forty-three miles' trip to Kansas City, Missouri. It was a heartbreaker, and doubly so when we found upon arrival that our booking was cancelled. Fats, physically, mentally and spiritually exhausted, and remarking that this business would 'turn the stomach of a goat', headed off to see Count Basie who was in town. Leaving them sharing a jug, I caught a cab to the Musicians' Union local to lodge my complaint about the cancellation, but when I got back to Count Basie's place, I found that Fats had taken off for the railroad station. He'd had enough and home was calling. I caught up with him just as he was boarding the train, and implored him to stand by until I had straightened matters out with Petrillo, the boss of A. F. of M. I had to talk fast as Fats was already tired to death of irresponsible promoters who failed to meet their obligations. As our next dates at St Louis, Cincinnati and Indianapolis had been booked by the same promoter and he had paid no deposits, I knew we were in the clear, so Fats went to Chicago and on to New York, while I and the band rolled on the last 729-mile run home to a much needed rest.

Our travels recommenced in August, and from then on until the end of September, the small band, plus Fats' Hammond organ, played another series of one-nighters. In October we found ourselves in Manitowoc in upper Wisconsin – man, was it cold! We had to stay in unheated cabins outside the town for the night as no hotel accommodation was available, and during that freezing night I wondered how the Indians, who named the town, had had the fortitude to withstand that fearful winter climate.

After a few days in New York for a Victor recording date and a knockout show at the Apollo Theatre, Harlem, our next big job was at the College Inn, Sherman Hotel, Chicago. A seven-week engagement, and the rest was a godsend. A wild New Year's Eve celebration, a recording date in the Victor Chicago studios, a week in State Lake Theatre, and back home to rehearse the big band for an opening at RKO Strand Theatre in Syracuse. But the pace was too telling and Fats just couldn't take it – a bad cold and we had to cancel the booking. Looking back over the years, I wonder how he took it as well as he did – it was a hectic life!

But after a few days' rest, the resilient Fats bounced back like a rubber ball. With the aid of the odd case or two of Scotch, Fats started rehearsing the big band, and in February we took off on 1941 another of those nightmares, a six-week tour of the South. Solidly booked one-nighters that started in Maryland, through Washington, D.C., Virginia, North Carolina, South Carolina, Georgia, and as far south as Fort Lauderdale, Florida. Before we left New York, Fats had a thorough medical check, and was warned that if he did not lay off the liquor and other frivolities, his doctor wouldn't be responsible for the consequences. Fats, somewhat strangely, took heed of the warning, and for a time drank only soda pop – but by the case load – and laid off, as opposed to on, those other 'frivolities'. But the season of temperance didn't last too long, for we shortly had a return date at the Blatz Palm Garden in Milwaukee for a guy named Joe Schweitzer. Milwaukee is famous for its wonderful beer, and Fats had no intention of insulting his hosts. In addition, Old Grandad bourbon whiskey became his favourite libation. One night after hours, I saw Fats and the band polish off two bottles of this 100-proof liquid lightning, washing down each drink with copious pints of champagne. Full of good cheer, off to a Chinese restaurant for a gargantuan meal to help 'put out the fire'. Fats' energy certainly needed repairing, for like the true artist and showman he gave his all with every performance. Three weeks in Milwaukee, three theatre dates, and three days' rest in New York took Fats to the Howard in Washington, D.C., for a week which was to be the last date for Fats in the East for quite a time. For after a week's rest in New York another coast-to-coast twelve-weeker was on the agenda.

This trip was very much on the same lines as the 1940 tour, but to break it up we did have a week's run at the Tunetown Ballroom in St Louis and two weeks in Los Angeles, which included the Paramount Theatre and a Victor Record date, which also helped. Nevertheless, the going was tough, and the wide open spaces rolled up the bus mileage to an enormous figure. The biggest hops on this tour were Idaho Falls to Denver (559 miles) and Denver, Colorado to St Louis, Missouri (898 miles) – a total of 1,457 in two days. But, with no illness and no accidents, I gave thanks to providence upon the tour's successful conclusion.

A month's vacation and we were off again to Grandview, Virginia, on another one-nighter razzle-dazzler. South to Maryland, north to Massachusetts and Maine, then a series of theatre dates including the Apollo, Howard, Royal and RKO, Syracuse; the Colonial in Detroit; the Grand, Evansville; the Regal in Chicago; and then back to New York for more radio, and Fats' Carnegie Hall Concert of 14 January 1942.

This was the very first time a solo jazz artist had played Carnegie Hall, and Fats really came into his own. The reviews of the concert were terrific, and Fats got a tremendous ovation from the capacity crowd of 2,800 enthusiasts who jammed the hall.

Our next stop was the Down Beat Room, Chicago. It was unfortunate that the Sherman Hotel impresario was very displeased at Fats playing a competitive spot in that city, but Fats not only put the room on the map, but did terrific business there during his four-week stay. Joe Sherman, the owner, was delighted with the nightly crowds, but I nearly lost my voice arguing with him about the validity of Fats' bar bills. Sure, Fats drank a lot and entertained plenty, but of course the house milked him for all they could. Fats paid up, smiled and just kept rollin' along. One night whilst at the Down Beat, Jack Robbins, one of the big New York music publishers, actually wept as Fats, spotting him in the audience, did an *ad lib* résumé of his career. Jack had made his way up from the bottom, and the story, set to Fats' inspired piano background, was the talk of Chicago's Tin Pan Alley for many a day. It was at the Down Beat Room that Fats launched a young blues singer, Dinah Washington, upon her career. He it was who first introduced her, accompanied her on the piano, and generally inspired her first performance.

After four weeks, we took off for Flint, Michigan, where the town's mayor was the guiding genius. As it happened, the rest of the city fathers believed that conviviality begins at home so the club did a roaring business. One night, after much over-wining and dining, Fats and I, feeling no pain, had just got back to our hotel when suddenly Fats complained he didn't feel well. Frankly, I wasn't surprised, but it was then four o'clock in the morning, and for a full hour I tried to get an ambulance, a doctor, a nurse, anything to take care of Fats' complaint, for I really believed that he was ill.

My room was across the hall from his and I did the telephoning from there, moving back and forth from room to room, leaving both doors open for easy access. It must have been while I was across the hall that a sneak thief entered my room through the open door and snatched a hundred bucks from my wallet. When I told Fats what had happened, he made a most miraculous recovery. In no time at all he was out of bed, phoning his brother-in-law in Detroit to come and get him. His brother-in-law was a sergeant detective on the Detroit police force and as soon as he arrived I told him about the robbery. He looked at Fats, shook his head and said very little could be done about the matter. The combination of Fats' sudden recovery and the loss of my wallet really got my goat, so I blew my top and gave Fats such hell that he and the detective beat a hasty, undignified retreat. When Fats got high, there was no telling what would happen . . . and it usually did.

215

Fats had become such a sensational success all through the midwest that Minneapolis, three hundred and fifty miles north, beckoned with an engagement at the 'Happy Hour' a favourite rendezvous of the Army boys from Fort Snelling, an important base just out of the city. Here it was that Fats had a thrill he had not anticipated, through meeting a contemporary whom he greatly admired. It happened this way:

While at the Blatz Palm Gardens in Milwaukee the year before, knowing Fats' devotion to classical music, I had taken him between sets to the concert hall which was just across the street. There Dimitri Mitropoulos was conducting the Minneapolis Symphony Orchestra in Prokofiev's Third Piano Concerto. Fats was enthralled as Mitropoulos brilliantly played the piano and conducted the huge orchestra. I actually had to drag him away in order to get him back on his own job. 'A solid sender,' said Fats as he vowed he would see more of the dynamic Mitropoulos if ever the opportunity occurred. And now it was to come about.

Cedric Adams, celebrated columnist on the *Minneapolis Star Journal* was organizing a huge benefit to raise funds for the production of special sports motion pictures for the Minneapolis Service men. Would Fats aid the cause by making an appearance at the Swing Parade Concert on Sunday? The Casa Loma band would be there with many other local bands and celebrities and . . . Dimitri Mitropoulos was to lead the complete cast of 122 swing musicians and Navy Chorus of Forty in the finale. 'Fine, wonderful, perfect,' said Fats, 'I'll be there!' And, Cedric continued, 'How about setting up an appointment for Fats to meet Mitropoulos in his home?' 'Fine, wonderful, perfect,' said Fats again . . . and so the two got together.

Fats and Mitropoulos had a ball. They played piano for each other, and swapped stories of early piano lessons – Fats at 5 years of age, Mitropoulos at 7. They talked jazz and the classics, Broadway and Carnegie Hall, the road with its concerts and one-nighters. Two famous musicians, two similar souls. The press said of one, 'Fats Waller, He lived for Music' . . . and of the other, 'Dimitri Mitropoulos, Whose life was Music'.

The Benefit at the Niccolet was a sell-out, and Fats got the kick of his lifetime as he jubilantly played the piano as Mitropoulos conducted *Anchors Aweigh* and the *Star-Spangled Banner* to close the show. Fats had invited Mitropoulos to the 'Happy Hour' for the late show there, so the get-together continued as Fats entertained with a special set for his special guest.

It was indeed a great evening for all, and it was with regret that we said good night to the Mitropoulos party. Later that same evening we were joined by Fats' buddy of the 'Connie's Inn' days, Cab Calloway, who had arrived in town with his band for a theatre date. After the show we adjourned to a nearby Chinese restaurant for some much needed food. The talk was about the gifted Mitropoulos and the great Minneapolis Symphony Orchestra and its 100 musicians, when Cab suddenly burst out with tremendous enthusiasm: 'You know what?' he said. 'Some day I'm goin' to get up there in front of a hundred men, and I'll lead them through one of those big symphonies!'

Fats, engrossed with a forkful of chow mein, looked up, and in a confidential tone said, 'When you do that, Cab, and when you get to Beethoven's Fifth, you goin' to give it an upbeat or a downbeat? Tell me that!'

All through 1942 a series of one-nighters, theatres, radio, recordings and night clubs provided the necessary 'eating' money to continue the battle to get Fats out of the red. Wherever the work was, North, South, East, or West, that's where we went. Playing for the armed forces wherever he could, Fats did the Army Bases, Canteens, Hospitals, and never missed a Bond Drive on the Radio for Uncle Sam. And that meant from coast to coast! Anytime . . . anywhere.

Fats had been playing with the small band and the big band, but we had finally disbanded the latter in Chicago and sent them back to New York with the rest of the cast, which included the Deep River Boys who had also been with our show. Fats and I travelled on to California, where we arrived on 20 January 1943. The reason for the trip was the film 'Stormy Weather' to be made on the 20th Century lot in Hollywood.

Needless to say, Fats was in his element in Hollywood. It was his first big film break, and 'Stormy Weather' was to be a picture of major importance with an all-coloured star cast. The first rehearsal was called at the Fox Studios, and Irving Mills, the associate producer, had recruited a great band for the occasion, with Benny Carter on trumpet; Zutty Singleton on drums; Gene Porter, clarinet and tenor sax; Alton Moore, trombone; and Slam Stewart, bass. Fats' tune *Ain't Misbehavin'* was to be included and I suggested that he and Benny Carter should get together and try to write an original number for the picture, to make some additional bucks. Fats hit upon a catchy riff and in no time at all he developed a melody which Benny transcribed and I entitled *Moppin' And Boppin'*. I wrote a lyric for the song, and a few days later Irving Mills gave us a couple of hundred dollars advance.

Fats enjoyed every minute on the 'Stormy Weather' set. He and Bojangles Robinson, the greatest Negro dancer of all time, pulled off some unscheduled inspirational entertainment which had the studio directors and technicians applauding loud and long. Whenever Fats and Bojangles got together, everything stopped dead on the set until they had finished. The high spot for these two was undoubtedly the last day. They had been ordered to report to the lot early in the morning, and Fats, dressed in white tie and tails, kept his valet primping, brushing and powdering for hours while he waited for his scene with Bill Bojangles Robinson to be shot. The scene called for Fats to open a door to disclose the prostrate body of the villain whom Bojangles had knocked out with a punch to the chin. The script read, 'show surprise, facially and vocally'. Fats really rose to the occasion and actually stole the scene. With a fearful leer he glanced at the body, and in a high-pitched voice came out with the classic, 'One Never Knows, Do One?'

Before the film was completed, another big break came along for Fats. For months I had been discussing with Dick Kollmar the use of Fats in a Broadway musical he was planning to produce, and it was while we were in Hollywood finishing up 'Stormy Weather' that he wired me that he was ready to go ahead. Waller was to have a featured part in the show, both playing and singing, and could we come to New York as quickly as possible for a get-together? So directly we finished the picture we dashed off to New York and a conference with Kollmar. The part was a good one for Fats, and everything was set, male and female lead, director, choreographer, vocal coach, set designer, orchestra, director and music arranger. The book and lyrics were by Hollywood's George Marion, Jr, but no composer for the score had been found as yet. Here was a golden opportunity, and I talked fast. Surely, one who could write such hits as *Ain't Misbehavin'*, *Honeysuckle Rose*, *I've Got A Feelin' I'm Fallin'*, *My Fate Is In Your Hands* and over four hundred other songs – plus five musical shows including 'Keep Shufflin'' and 'Hot Chocolates', both Broadway hits, could easily write another score. Within minutes, I had Kollmar convinced that Fats was his man. A hurried phone call to George Marion, Jr for his consent, and the deal was closed for Fats to write the music for the show, as well as play a feature role. And Fats got a thousand bucks advance on the spot.

The show was to be called 'Early To Bed', and Fats leisurely turned out the melodies one by one as Marion submitted the lyrics. Towards the end of the month all of the songs excepting two were finished, but so was Fats' supply of cash. So I booked him into the Apollo Theatre in Harlem for a week to replenish his 'eatin' money'. Fats was always a softy for a touch, besides which he entertained lavishly, and was extremely generous with gifts for his family – money lasted with him no time at all, and we were soon on the hunt for more gold. One night, higher than a kite, he called me on the telephone and informed me that he had just spoken with Dick Kollmar and offered to sell him his entire interest in the score of the show for a mere thousand dollars. Dick called me in a panic, for Fats had still two more songs to write to complete the score. I told him to forget it. Fats hadn't meant to leave the show, it was just one of the tantrums brought on by an over-indulgence in Old Grandad. So I made a date with George Marion for the following morning, and phoned Fats with the promise of some cash. Finally the songs were all on schedule, but it was at this point that it was mutually agreed to release the rollicking Fats from his stage role in the show.

'Early To Bed' opened at the Shubert Theatre in Boston on 24 May, and Fats, Anita and I travelled there for the opening.

Here again I bumped smack into another colour incident that burned me to a crisp. And in Boston, of all places!

I had made reservations by long-distance telephone for rooms for the Wallers and myself at a leading hotel, and upon arrival went to the desk to pick them up. But the clerk, seeing Fats and Anita standing in the lobby and observing their colour, coldly disclaimed having any such reservations. I called for the manager – same thing. I was shaking with indignation as I sent Fats and Anita over to the theatre, and as I scouted for other accommodations I choked, 'America, America; the land of the free and the home of the brave; when will you wake up?' The show was a terrific hit and was held over.

But Fats, restless as usual, travelled to Philadelphia where he played the Cove Club while waiting for the show to open in New York at the Broadhurst Theatre. June 17 was the date, and Fats gave thanks for the show's success by playing a Red Cross benefit aboard the U.S.S. *New Jersey* in the Brooklyn Navy Yard. If anyone had a heart as big as his body, it was surely Thomas Fats Waller.

Seeing the show successfully launched in New York, we travelled to Boston and opened at the Tic Toc Club. After a few days, summer came in with a terrific heat-wave. Owing to war-time black-out requirements, the club had little or no ventilation. Fats became ill and we had to cancel the engagement.

Meanwhile, in spite of the tremendous heat, 'Early To Bed' was doing excellent box-office business. Fats wasn't needed in New York, so we decided to extend the rest period and at the same time earn some money while enjoying the lakeside cool of Canada's famous Brant Inn. So Fats, Anita, and his two boys, Maurice and Ronald, travelled to Canada to spend two weeks regaling the customers with Fats playing his own music from 'Early To Bed'. The climate was glorious, and we were given the use of impresario Murray Anderson's speedboat, his penthouse overlooking Lake Ontario, and his Cadillac car. Good food and liquid libations were in plentiful supply, and Fats, as he called it, 'lived high on the hog'.

But Fats had to get back to New York for a guest appearance on the radio show 'Lower Basin Street', an appearance which gave him an opportunity to plug the show 'Early To Bed', which, despite the midsummer heat, was doing very well indeed. Mindful of Fats' suffering in hot weather, I declared a holiday until late August when, with the nights getting cooler, Fats booked in for a two-week engagement in Philadelphia at Palumbo's, a well-known Italian restaurant in that city. It being only a two-hour run from New York, we were able to return for a guest appearance on the

Million Dollar Band show on NBC on Saturday, getting back to Palumbo's to finish out the engagement.

All this time, War Bond Drives, Hospital Shows, both on radio and in person, and Canteen appearances really kept us on the go. One thing at this time we sadly missed doing were our record dates for Victor. The Musicians' Union row with the record companies was still going strong, and to make matters worse, Fats couldn't record his 'Early To Bed' tunes on commercial records. Fats opened a three-week engagement at the Greenwich Village Inn in September. It was a sensational run, and coincided with 'Early To Bed' enjoying top box-office business in uptown New York at the Broadhurst Theatre. Fats was riding high!

In September, Steve Sholes, who was in charge of the unit for making V-Discs for the Armed Forces, had Fats down to the Victor studios where he recorded some of the tunes from 'Early To Bed'. He made a total of thirteen sides, vocals with piano and Hammond organ. Fats said the date was a killer-diller, and so it was, for it was the first session in the Victor studios since July 1942, when Fats had made his last date with his Rhythm on the 13th, and on the 30th sung a vocal refrain for a special record made by The Victor First Nighter Orchestra. The song *That's What The Well Dressed Man In Harlem Will Wear* was from the All-Soldier Show 'This Is The Army' by Irving Berlin.

Fats had a return date at the Tic Toc Club in Boston to replace the one cancelled by the previous June heat-wave. So, the weather now being cool, and a Steinway Grand provided, Fats was assured of a pleasant engagement playing to packed houses. Here the great success of 'Early To Bed' was repeated by Fats playing solo, and the 'joint was jumping' every night.

Back to New York for a day's rest before another trip to Hollywood. This time I broke the transcontinental jump with two weeks at the Beachcomber in Omaha, Nebraska. Fats was due to open on the Saturday, 23 October, but we put the date forward as Fats felt he needed the extra rest. This was the opportunity I had been waiting for – I had been after Fats to sign his Will which had been drawn up by his attorney at my urgent insistence some time before, but with the vast and hectic amount of travel we had been doing, the chance had never presented itself. Stressing the fact that he must do something for the protection of his family, I finally got him down to his lawyer's office, and he finally signed his Will.

The day following we set off on what turned out tragically to be Fats' 'last go round'!

17

Travelling all night and the following day, Fats arrived just in time for the first show at the Beachcomber. Omaha was a big Army town, and as we had plenty of customers from the base, an enthusiastic audience was assured. A clause in the contract called for rooms at a first-rate hotel for Fats and myself, to ensure our comfort. This was a usual procedure, but it is worth mentioning that, while the rooms had been booked for us, we were denied the use of both the dining-room and room service! Here we were, well up north, and prejudice was again rearing its ugly head. I could hardly believe it, for here was an internationally acclaimed artist whose music on records, radio, stage, screen and night clubs had given joy and entertainment to millions throughout the world. You can add to this the really big hunk of unstinted time and energy Fats had given to the war effort, and this an Army Base town. What, I wondered, had happened to the commandment about brotherly love?

But, smilingly and cheerfully, Fats continued to do his bit for democracy. During the second week in Omaha he performed at a dinner for the U.S. Army officers at the Chamber of Commerce; did a benefit performance for the Air Corps Cadets at Creighton University; entertained the Army lads at Fort Crook, ten miles out from the city; and even did a second benefit show for the Air Corps cadets. Fats certainly did his bit, and when I look back on those war efforts of his, I think it can truthfully be said that Fats was indeed giving his life for his country.

To get from Omaha to Hollywood the following day in time for the first show at the Florentine Gardens, we somehow had to flag the Los Angeles Streamliner, a train which passed through Omaha daily but didn't stop. Here was a major problem, for all transportation facilities were loaded with U.S. Armed Forces personnel and all schedules were rigorously enforced. However, one hand washes the other, as they say, and this time it was the Army who came through for Fats. A signal was received that the Streamliner would stop and pick us up and we were briefed to be ready and waiting. So we wrapped up the last show at the Beachcomber, dashed back to the hotel to pick up our bags, and away to a station locked tight and dark as the night itself. We had some minutes to wait, and with the air damp and a cutting wind whistling round our legs, I shivered as the minutes seemed like hours until the headlights of the Streamliner broke through the mist and bore down on us. As the train slowed down, we spotted a pullman porter waving to us from the steps of a sleeper. We threw our luggage aboard, the conductor in charge of operations gave the signal, and we were off. Bundled into the smoking compartment we were told that no sleeping accommodation was available, but something might turn up at Salt Lake City – a thousand miles away. I groaned, but Fats hunched himself into his overcoat, turned up his coat collar, had himself a couple of snorts of Old Grandad, and proceeded to get some sleep.

Fortunately the trip was uneventful. At Salt Lake City some sleepers became available and we pulled into Los Angeles on Monday morning as per schedule. It was a lovely, balmy day, and the sun felt good after the windy cold of Omaha. Fats headed for the Clarke Hotel and the Annex accommodation there that he liked, and I for the Knickerbocker Hotel in Hollywood, just around the corner from the Florentine Gardens. Built like an igloo it could dine and dance a thousand guests. Nils T. Granlund was there with a big floor show in which Fats was to appear. He then finished out the evening in the Zanzibar Room doing a solo spot. As Fats' contracts always called for the provision of a Steinway grand piano perfectly tuned to 440 pitch, I had arranged with him to meet me at the Gardens after checking in at his hotel. I arrived a little early, met the owner, and asked to see the piano. He explained, as we walked towards the Zanzibar Room, that he had just had the piano tuned, and that while it wasn't a grand piano, nevertheless he thought it a good one which Fats would like. Here was a situation with a time bomb attached, for I saw Fats coming in the door that moment, and from past experience knew what was about to happen. But before Fats had seen what lay in wait for him, I quickly told the owner that the contract meant exactly what it said. No Steinway grand as specified – no Fats Waller on that stand tonight! He winced, but calmly replied, 'I will get a Steinway. Just have Fats pick out the one he wants, and I will buy it and have it delivered in readiness for tonight.' Fats, meanwhile, had walked over to the piano, sat down, and run his fingers over the keyboard.

'Mister Kirkeby, let's go home!' he said shortly.

'That's not for you, Fats,' I said. 'Our good friend, Mr Bruni here, has arranged for you to go over to the Steinway agent in Los Angeles and pick out the piano of your own choice.' That night a happy Fats laid it on for the enchanted customers who packed the Zanzibar Room to capacity.

During the first week, in addition to the Zanzibar, Fats did a great show on the RCA Victor 'What's New' programme for the National Broadcasting Company. I took this on because it sweetened up the kitty plenty, and was great publicity for Fats' Victor Records sales. But wanting Fats to rest up as much as possible, I turned down the many requests for Armed Forces Canteen appearances.

1943

The Zanzibar Room was air-conditioned, but unknown to me there were ventilators both above and to the back of the piano, ventilators which poured a steady blast of refrigerated air down on Fats' head and shoulders as he sat at the piano. Any artist who is worth a damn gives everything he's got all the time and Fats would come off the stand dripping with perspiration. That's where the handkerchief on the head came from. Fats would mop his brow with an ever-ready 'kerchief, then put it over his head and go into the *Sheik Of Araby*. But while that air conditioner cooled Fats, it also fooled him, and on Wednesday of the second week, Fats went down with a severe case of 'flu.

He would not hear of being removed to a hospital as I suggested, so I had two doctors in constant attention on him at his hotel. I saw that he had everything he needed, brought him special food and personally spent several hours a day with him. Ten days in bed – then a clean bill of health from his doctors, and back went Fats to the Florentine to finish his contract. The doctors warned Fats to take it easy, but he really just didn't know how. As soon as he was back on his feet, and even though still weak, he insisted on appearing at a postponed benefit for 'Coloured U.S.A.' the following day. The next day came with a Command Performance on CBS with Dinah Shore, and Abbott and Costello, followed by the Charlie McCarthy–Edgar Bergen Show on NBC; and yet another on NBC called 'News From Home'. To round off that week, he insisted on doing another 'Hollywood Canteen' show for the Armed Forces. A whole last week of extras and Fats had only three days more to go at the Zanzibar Room.

Fats' return to the Zanzibar brought back capacity crowds, and each night the 'joint was really jumpin'.' Came Saturday night and a very happy boss paid Fats for the week and as a bonus gave him a case of Scotch whisky plus a half-dozen bottles of champagne. I tried to talk Fats into taking the stuff back to New York for the Christmas holidays, but finally ended up with only some of it, while Fats went off to a party at Benny Carter's home with the rest to help cover the needs of the thirsty. That shindig went on until the dawn and well into the morning. I know that, for Fats called me on the telephone every hour on the hour, for many hours, to remind me not to forget the Press party to be held in his honour that day. In response to each phone call I said, 'Okay, I'll be there. Go get some sleep!'

By the time I arrived at the Press party Fats was already there, and I could see from the way he looked that he had been up all night. He was playing the piano, but was fighting hard to keep his eyes open. When I asked him what happened to his promise to get some sleep, he playfully took a pillow from a divan and said, 'I'm gonna get some now!' and without further ado he lay down on the floor and proceeded to go fast asleep. What the guests thought I don't know, but I cornered our hostess, reminded her that Fats was only just out of a sick bed and also had performances at the Florentine Gardens that night, and that he should be taken to the Clarke Hotel and put to bed without delay. I stayed for the Press, a worried manager, for I wondered whether Fats would be fit enough to do his last night's show. Wanting him to get as much sleep as possible, I left him in bed until the last minute and only picked him up a full half-hour past the time his set at the Zanzibar was due to start. I later found out that the owner notified the police that Fats hadn't shown up, and wasn't to be found.

Fats did his solo spot and returned to our table bleary-eyed. I got him some coffee, a drink he very seldom drank, and dashed back to my hotel to pack. By the time I got back to the Zanzibar, Fats had done another set and was back at the same table – sitting disconsolately in front of his untouched coffee. The place was beginning to jump, but Fats for once showed little interest. Suddenly through the swing doors came a beautiful babe, high brown complexion, perfect teeth fronting a wondrous smile. Spying Fats, she walked straight over to his table. 'Hello, Fatsy Watsy. Remember me from Cleveland?' she cooed.

The effect on Fats was galvanic. Rising and cupping her hand in both of his, Fats looked her straight in the eye. 'Why sure, honey, of course I remember.'

'Mr Kirkeby,' he beamed a gigantic smile in my direction, 'order the lady a bottle of champagne. I'll be back in a few minutes, honey, you stay right there!' No longer tired and depressed, Thomas Waller was a new man from there on.

Getting Fats out of the Zanzibar that night presented plenty of problems, for I was determined to try and dodge the groups of steamed-up well-wishers who were waiting in the lobby to wish Fats good night and *bon voyage*. Finally I got him out through the kitchen and into a taxi. I charged the driver to take Fats direct to the Clarke Hotel and to see that he got to bed without further ado. I then rang the hotel to see that Fats' bedroom telephone was cut off. Sleep was the essence now, for I was to pick Fats up at 10 a.m. to catch the Santa Fé Chief out at 12 noon for Home Sweet Home. Fats was looking forward to spending the Christmas holidays at home with his family – and so was I !

Next morning we got away from the hotel on time and headed for the Santa Fé railroad station. There Fats was met by a few friends, including his tailor with a tidy bill for six suits of Hollywood clothes that Fats had ordered.

As the train eventually pulled out, Fats collapsed with a groan: 'Oh man, I can't take this much longer!'

'You'll never have to do one-nighters again,' I said. 'You'll have enough now from record royalties, incomes from shows, concerts and your Ascap payments – no more one-nighters for you, that's for sure!'

Later that day we walked along to the club car, where Fats was greeted, it seemed to me, by people from all over the world. 'Hey

Fats, glad to see ya,' and the party was on again! Eventually we took some people up forward to our room, but near on midnight, I started taking off my coat and said I was going to bed. It was the only way to break things up.

At eleven o'clock the next morning, I woke and asked Fats how he felt.

'Man, I'm sure gonna get some more shut-eye!' he said, and turned over with his face to the wall.

'Good idea,' I said. 'I'll meander down to the diner and get some breakfast. If you want anything, just ring for the porter and I'll tell the dining-car steward to be on the alert.'

Fats slept all that day – not really unusual, for at times he used to hibernate the same way at home. From time to time I checked the porter and the room, content that Fats was at last really getting the rest he needed so badly. Meanwhile, I passed the time with our friends of the night before, and kept them from disturbing Fats.

About two that morning I opened the door to the sleeper and was hit by a blast of cold air.

'Jesus, it's cold in here!' I said, as I saw Fats was awake.

'Yeah, Hawkins is sure blowin' out there tonight,' Fats replied.

The train was roaring through the Kansas plains in a howling blizzard, which reminded Fats of the blustery sax playing of his friend Coleman Hawkins.

'Are you warm enough?' I asked.

'You'll be okay when you get into bed,' he replied.

So I washed quickly and piled into bed.

It was about five o'clock in the morning when I woke and heard a choking sound coming from Fats' bed. Quickly I switched on the light and saw Fats over there in bed, trembling all over. I jumped out of bed, and shaking him by the shoulder, called him to wake up. It seemed he was having a bad dream, but I couldn't wake him. Frantically I rang for the porter. The train, as it happened, had stopped in Kansas City Station, but no porter was on hand. I ran back quickly to the club car, found the bar steward and we both rushed back to Fats. By the time we got back to the sleeper, our porter and several others were there gazing at Fats' motionless figure.

'Get a doctor quickly,' I called, 'and don't move this train until we do.'

A doctor appeared very quickly, for he had been called to attend another passenger. In absolute silence, while we watched, the doctor moved his stethoscope about, tested for pulse, breathing and eyelids, and, after what seemed to me ages, looked up and quietly said, 'This man is dead!'

I was stunned. For, until that very moment, I believed Fats was in some kind of a coma.

'Dead!' I said. 'From what?'

The doctor asked if Fats had been ill lately, and I told him about his bout of influenza. He said it could well be a relapse, but that an autopsy would have to be made, and the body removed for the coroner's investigation.

By this time the police had arrived, and I was escorted, still in a dazed condition, to the Muehlbach Hotel, actually under technical arrest.

Fats had died of unknown causes, and therefore an autopsy was necessary.

The Muehlbach Hotel hadn't a single vacant room, but the manager, a good friend, realizing my trouble, was kind enough to turn over to me his own personal quarters to await developments.

They came in a rush. No sooner had I entered his sitting-room than the telephone began to ring. Call after call from the United Press, the Associated Press, the Negro Press, in fact all the Press – all wanting details of Fats' death. As I repeated the story, the tragic event was brought home to me even more strongly – even more deeply. Why, why, I kept asking myself? I had no answer.

At six o'clock the coroner's autopsy report came through. Fats had died of influenzal bronchial pneumonia! He had evidently had this condition for some days, and I grieved that his great heart and consideration for others, especially me in this instance, had not allowed him to complain – he certainly had made no complaint to me. Fats' work was done and his hands now lay peacefully crossed in rest – the hands that had played and created such beautiful melodies and thundered out the world's most famous rhythm. Fats Waller, the greatest Swingmaster of them all.

By a strange coincidence, at the very time that Fats died, another train was in a siding waiting for ours to go through. On board was the one and only Louis Armstrong, who, on being told the news by a railroad porter, cried all night.

A few hours later, I was back at the railroad station. I was informed that the casket had arrived, but that my train to Chicago was five hours late. 'Hawkins', as Fats had named the blizzard, was still out there and blowing up a storm that had crippled all train schedules. A long, sad and lonely vigil lay ahead of me, and as I waited I began to worry about how I was going to make train connections out of Chicago. I figured that with luck I could just make it, but I had to get Fats' body from the Santa Fe terminal on the west side of Chicago over to the New York Central on the east side. To cut a long story short, I just made the Advance Commodore out of Chicago with the lavish use of Uncle Sam's folding money, and sank down into my seat exhausted, as the train pulled out on its overnight trek to New York.

It was my last go round with the lovable Fats – and the saddest journey I ever remember.

"Fats" plays last date to packed house. Famous composer-pianist funeralized at Abyssinia Baptist Church on Monday', were the headlines for the story carried by the New York *Amsterdam News*, a story which continued: 'Thomas Wright Waller played to a packed house Monday morning, December 20, at the Abyssinia Baptist Church. It was his final show after a life of thirty-nine years of creative joy and merriment for millions in America. Though a grand piano sat not ten feet away from him and an organ sat on the balcony just above his head, he was not demonstrating his genius at either. For "Fats", as he was known by the world, was making his last appearance, at his own funeral. In a dull grey casket; resting peacefully in the midst of a bank of about 100 floral pieces above which the Reverend A. Clayton Powell, Jr, pastor of the church, the Reverend Ben Richardson, assistant pastor, and others paid the pianist-organist-composer and comedian a final tribute. "We are gathered here this morning to mourn the passing of a simple soul," the Reverend Mr Powell began, "a soul touched with the genius of music which brought relief from our cares and woes. Thomas Waller and his songs shall live again. His sweetest songs are yet to be heard – in glory." '

The words from the minister swept, like the music from the great church organ, out over the thousands of mourners packed in the pews, the vestibule, the steps, and even downstairs and out into the street. Nobody knows how many, but they must have exceeded ten thousand people.

The Waller family sat quietly in their pew, but Waller's legion of admirers, who had gathered hours before the service began, remembered their 'happy-go-lucky-bundle-of-joy' for all the happiness he had brought them, and demonstrated their love for him by their tears. His spirit and songs belonged to the people, for no single individual had a monopoly on the artist; a fact that was evidenced by the people who packed every seat in the church – celebrities and contemporaries, black and white, all come to bid farewell to the man they loved.

The crowd in the street and on the rooftops stretched from Seventh to Lenox Avenues. Traffic was brought to a standstill within three blocks of the church. 'We've got to send our hero off just right,' remarked someone in the crowd – a remark which must have been taken as a signal for an extraordinary demonstration of affection for the deceased. Suddenly, and without warning, many of the women in the crowd began quietly taking flowers from the enormous number of floral tributes which were carried by three cars. They took them to treasure – floral remembrance of their idol. The enormous crowd streamed down the street following the funeral procession as it headed towards Long Island where the remains were cremated at the Fresh Pond Crematory.

The pallbearers included Don Redman, Claude Hopkins and Andy Kirk, orchestra leaders; Andy Razaf and J. C. Johnson, authors who collaborated with Fats on many song hits; Clarence Williams, composer and publisher, who published Fats' first song, *Squeeze Me*; Donald Heywood, writer; and James P. Johnson, Fats' early mentor and lifelong friend.

Thomas 'Fats' Waller was indeed a colourful character and a lovable genius, with gifts which will surely place him in the Valhalla of Musical Greats.

★　　★　　★

Fats was many things to many men – you will have heard much of this man and his music. To you he will be perhaps a gravelly voice on a record; a patron saint of a whole school of pianists; the composer of your favourite song; a buffoon who led a jumping group of jazzmen in monstrous sessions; or he may even be to you, by chance, a giant among jazz men, whose recordings with his little band can lift you to the heights of ecstasy. Or maybe your position will lie somewhere in between all these? But whatever your position, it is surely not a negative one. No one has ever said, 'I can take Waller or leave him.'

The Music of Thomas "Fats" Waller

A selective discography compiled by the "Storyville Team"

ABBREVIATIONS

AE	Spanish H.M.V.	Fwy	Folkways	NE	Indian H.M.V.
AFCDJ	Association Française	G	Australian Regal-	OdF	French Odeon
	Collectionneurs de		Zonophone	OdG	German Odeon
	Disqe de Jazz	Ge	Gennett	OFC	Only for Collectors
AV	Italian H.M.V.	7GF	Electrola	OK	Okeh
	(Voce del Padrone)		(German H.M.V.)	Or	Oriole
B	English H.M.V.	GW	Italian H.M.V.	PaAu	Australian Parlophone
Ba	Banner		(Voce del Padrone)	PaE	English Parlophone
BA	Blue Ace	GY	Spanish H.M.V.	PaIt	Italian Parlophone
BB	Bluebird	Ha	Harmony	PaS	Swiss Parlophone
BD	English H.M.V.	HE	Swiss H.M.V.	PC	Palm Club
Bilt	Biltmore	Hg	Harmograph	Pe	Perfect
BrE	English Brunswick	HJCA	Hot Jazz Club of	Ph	Philips
BrF	French Brunswick		America	Pir	Pirate
BrG	German Brunswick	HMV	His Masters Voice	Pm	Paramount
BRS	British Rhythm Society	HN	Italian H.M.V.	R	Italian H.M.V.
	(U.S.A.)		(Voce del Padrone)		(Voce del Padrone)
Bu	Buddy	IM	Irish H.M.V.	RCA	Radio Corporation of
C	English H.M.V.	ImpCz	Czech Imperial		America
Cam	Camden	ImpG	German Imperial	RD	Reader's Digest
Cap	Capitol	IP	Irish H.M.V.	Ri	Ristic
Cen	Century	IW	Spanish H.M.V.	Riv	Riverside
Ci	Circle	JC	Jazz Collector	Ro	Romeo
CLP	English H.M.V.	JF	English H.M.V.	SG	Electrola
Co	American Columbia	JG	Jazz Guild		(German H.M.V.)
CoAu	Australian Columbia	JK	Swiss H.M.V.	SH	Electrola
CoE	English Columbia	JO	English H.M.V.		(German H.M.V.)
CoF	French Columbia	JP	Jazz Panorama	Swg	Swaggie
CoG	German Columbia	JR	Jolly Roger	33 SX	English Columbia
COLL	Collector	JS	Jazz Society (French)	TCF	20th Century Fox
Com	Commodore	Jtn	Jazztone	Tempo	Tempo
CRC	Columbia Record Club	K	French H.M.V. (V.S.M.)	UHCA	United Hot Clubs of
De	Decca	L	French H.M.V. (V.S.M.)		America
DLP	English H.M.V.	Lib	Liberty	VD	V-Disc
EA	Australian H.M.V.	LoE	English London	Vi	Victor (U.S.A., Canada,
EB	Australian H.M.V.	Me	Melotone		South America)
7EG	English H.M.V.	MFP	Music for Pleasure	ViJ	Japanese Victor
ENC	Encore	MH	English H.M.V.	Vo	American Vocalion
Epc	Epic	Ms	Mainstream	VoE	English Vocalion
FDLP	French H.M.V. (V.S.M.)	MW	Montgomery-Ward	WRC	World Record Club
FKX	Swiss H.M.V.	N	Indian H.M.V.	X	English H.M.V.

as	alto sax	ce	celeste	ds	drums	org	organ	tp	trumpet	vn	violin
bj	banjo	cl	clarinet	g	guitar	p	piano	ts	tenor sax	vo	vocal
bs	bass	co	cornet	nv	no vocal	tb	trombone	tu	tuba		

Piano Rolls

The following is believed to be a fairly complete list of "Fats" Waller's piano rolls — much of the original information having been supplied by Ed Kirkeby.

2149 Gotta cool my doggies now. Riv RLP.12–103
2213 Laughin' Cryin' Blues. LOE. L.808, De BM31059, Riv RLP.12–103
2245 Your time now. LOE. AL.3507 RLP.1010. RLP.12–103
2256 Snake Hips. LOE. AL.3507 RLP.1010 Para 14024
2270 'Tain't nobody's biz-ness if I do. LOE. AL.3507 RLP.1010 RLP.12–103, GP105
2286 Papa, better watch your step. LOE. AL.3057 RLP.1010 RLP.12–103
2304 The Haitian Blues.
2322 Mama's got the Blues. LOE. AL.3507 RLP.1010 RLP.12–115 GP105 SPD11
2331 Midnight Blues. RI.8 Les Amis de Fats (unnumbered)
2363 Last go round Blues.
2444 Last Man Blues. LOE. AL.3507 CEN.4025 RLP.1010 RLP.12–103 GP105
2666 Clearing House Blues.
2670 Jail House Blues.
2708 Do it, Mr. So-and-so.
2711 Don't try to take my man away Riv.12–103
3352 Squeeze Me. LOE. AL.3507 RLP.1010
3377 18th Street Strut (*issued on a record*).LOE. AL.3507 RLP.1010 CEN.4001 JCL45
3818 If I could be with you (*duet with James P. Johnson*).
3997 Nobody but my baby (is getting my love).

233

THOMAS WALLER. (Piano): October, 1922.
S-70948-D	Muscle Shoals Blues	OK 4757, Bilt 1005, JS AA503
S-70949-D	Birmingham Blues	OK 4757, Bilt 1005, JS AA503

SARA MARTIN. (Vo. acc. Fats p.): Late 1922.
S-71068-C	'Tain't nobody's business if I do	OK 8043
S-71069-B	You got everything a Sweet Mama needs but me	OK 8043
S-71105-B	Mama's got the Blues	OK 8045
S-71106-B	Last go round Blues	OK 8045

SARA MARTIN and CLARENCE WILLIAMS. (Vo. duet, acc. Fats p.):
S-71984-B	I'm certainly gonna see 'bout that	OK 8108
S-71985-B	Squabblin' Blues	OK 8108
	Monkey Man Blues	OK
O-477	18th Street Strut	

JAMAICAN JAZZERS. (Clarence Williams, Clarence Todd, kazoos; Justin Ring, wood block; Fats, p): New York Early 1924.
S-72514-A	You don't know my mind blues	OK 40117
S-72515-A	West Indies blues	OK 40117

ALBERTA HUNTER. (Vo. acc. Fats p.): 1925.
	Stingaree Blues	Pm 12049

ANNA JONES. (Vo. acc. Fats p.): 1925.
1468-1	Sister Kate	Pm 12052, Hg 859
1469-1	You can't do what my last man did	Pm 12043
1473-1	Trixie Blues	Pm 12052
1473-2	Trixie Blues	Hg 859

HAZEL MEYERS. (Vo. acc. Fats p.): 1925.
13467-2	Maybe Someday	Vo 14861
13469-3	When your troubles are just like mine	Vo 14861

CAROLINE JOHNSON. (Vo. acc. Fats p.): 1926.
	Mama's losing a mighty good chance	Ge 3307, Bu 8033
	Ain't got nobody to grind my coffee	Ge 3307, Bu 8034

ALTA BROWN and BERTHA POWELL. (Vo., duet, acc. Fats p.): 1926.
	Nobody knows the trouble I see	Ge 3318
1010-2	I've got the Joogie Blues	Ba 6043
1009-2	Black Snake Blues	Ba 6043

MAUDE MILLS. (Vo., acc Fats p.): 1926.
953-1	Anything that happens	Ba 6019
954-1	My Old Daddy	Ba 6019
1009-1	Black Snake Blues	Ba 6043
1010-1	I've got the Joogie Blues	Ba 6043

✓ **FLETCHER HENDERSON AND HIS ORCHESTRA.** (Tommy Ladnier, Russel Smith, Joe Smith, tpts; Charlie Green, tb; Buster Bailey, cl; Don Redman, as; Coleman Hawkins, ts; Fletcher Henderson, dir; Charlie Dixon, bj; June Cole, bs; Kaiser Marshall, ds; Fats p on 1st title, org on 2nd): 3rd November, 1926.
W-142902-2	The Henderson Stomp	Co 817-D, CoE 4421, DB5030 CBS, BPG 62001
W-142903-1	The Chant	Co 817-D, CBS BPG 62001

THOMAS WALLER. (Pipe-organ): Camden, N.J. 17th November, 1926.
A-36773-1	St. Louis Blues	Vi 20357, HMV B8501, JR 5037, RCA RD 7599
A-36774-4	Lenox Avenue Blues	Vi 20357, HMV B8501, JR 5037, RCA RD 7599

14th January, 1927.
A-37357	Soothin' Syrup Stomp	Vi 20470, RCA RD 7599
A-37358	Sloppy Water Blues	Vi 20472
A-37359-3	Loveless Love	Vi 20470, 23260
A-37361	Messin' around with the Blues	Vi 20655, RCA RD 7599
A-37362	The Rusty Pail	Vi 20472

16th February, 1927.
A-37819	Stompin' the bug	Vi 20655, RCA RD 7599
A-37820	Hog Maw Stomp	Vi 21525
37822 (piano)	Blue Black Bottom	Unissued
A-38160	Shufflin' Sadie	Unissued

✓ **FLETCHER HENDERSON AND HIS ORCHESTRA.** As before, but Jimmy Harrison, tb, added, and Bob Escudero, bs, replaces June Cole): 11th May, 1927.
W-144132-1	Whiteman Stomp	Co 1059-D, CoE 4561, CoF LF227, DF3081, BF 409, BPG 62001
W-144133-3	I'm coming Virginia	Co 1059-D, CoE 4561, PaE R2540, CoF LF227, DF3081, BF 409, BPG 62001

THOMAS WALLER. (Pipe-organ). Vo. on titles indicated by Alberta Hunter: 20th May, 1927.
A-38044	Sugar (nv)	Vi 21525, 23331, BB 5093, MW 4904
A-38045	Sugar (vo)	Vi 20771, Bilt 1020
A-38046	Beale Street Blues (vo)	Vi 20771, Bilt 1020
A-38047	Beale Street Blues (nv)	Vi 20890
A-38048	I'm goin' to see my Ma (vo)	Vi 21539
A-38049	I'm goin' to see my Ma (nv)	Unissued

THOMAS WALLER with MORRIS' HOT BABIES. (Thomas Morris, co; Charlie Irvis, tb; Fats, org and p; unknown g; and Eddie King ds):

20th May, 1927

A-38050	Fats Waller Stomp	Vi 20890, HMV B10472, RCA RD 7599
A-38051	Savannah Blues	Vi 20776, HMV B5417, RCA RD 7599
A-38052	Won't you take me home?	Vi 20776, HMV B5417, RCA RD 7599

JUANITA STINETTE CHAPPELLE (Vo., acc. Fats org):

14th November, 1927.

A-40077	Florence	Vi 21062

THOMAS WALLER. (Pipe-organ Solos):

14th November, 1927.

A-40078	Memories of Florence Mills	Unissued
A-40079	(Unknown title)	Unissued

BERT HOWELL. (Vo., acc. Fats org):

14th November, 1927.

A-40080	Bye, bye, Florence	Vi 21062

THOMAS WALLER with MORRIS' HOT BABIES. (Tom Morris, co; James Archey, tb; Waller, p; Bobbie Leecan, g; Eddie King?, d. *Pipe organ solos. ‡Vocal by Waller and Morris):

1st December, 1927

A-40093-2	He's gone away	Vi 2120, HMV EG7892, RCA RD 7599
A-40094-2	*I ain't got nobody	Vi 21127, BB 5093, BB 10133 MW M4904, Vi 23331, RD 7599
A-40095-2	‡Red Hot Dan	Vi 21127, HMV B10472, RD 7599
A-40096-1	*The Digah's Stomp	Vi 21358, HMV EG7892, RD 7599
A-40097-1	Geechee	HMV EG7882, RD 7599
A-40097-2	Geechee	Vi 21358
A-40098-2	Please take me out of Jail	Vi 21202, HMV EG7882, RD 7599

JOHNNY THOMPSON. (Vo., acc. Fats, p; Howard Nelson, vn; David Martin, co):

New York City   17th January, 1928.

W-145534-3	Nobody knows how much I love you	Co 14285-D

THE LOUISIANA SUGAR BABES. (Fats, org; Joe Smith, or Jabbo Smith, tp; Garvin Bushnell, cl, as. and bassoon; James P. Johnson, p):

27th March, 1928.

A-42566-1	Willow Tree	Vi 21348
A-42567-1	'Sippi	Vi 21348
A-42567-2	'Sippi	BB 10260
A-42568-1	Thou Swell	BB 10260
A-42568-2	Thou Swell	Vi 21346
A-42569-1	Persian Rug	Vi 21346, HMV EA397

"FATS" WALLER AND HIS BUDDIES. (Fats, p; Charlie Gains, tp; Charlie Irvis, tb; Arville Harris, cl and as; Eddie Condon, bj):

New York City   1st March, 1929.

49759 and 49762 are piano solos

A-49759-1	Handful of Keys	Vi V-38508, 27768, HMV B4347, B4902, N4480, X4480, X6292, RCA RD 27185
A-49760-2	The Minor Drag	Vi V-38050, 20-1583, BB 10185, HMV EA3265, FDLP 1005, HE 2367, JF1, K8196, X6252, DLP 1008
A-49761-2	Harlem Fuss	Vi V-38050, BB 10185, HMV EA 3713, HE2367, K8196, X6252, CDN 131
A-49762-2	Numb Fumblin'	Vi V-38508, 25338, HMV B4347, B4917, HE2381, X6292, DLP 1111

THOMAS WALLER. (Piano):

Camden, N.J. 2nd August, 1929.

A-49492-3	Ain't Misbehavin'	Vi 22108, 20-1581, HMV B3243, Vi 68-0073, EA641, FDLP 1005, Vi 22092, DLP 1008
A-49493-2	Sweet Savannah Sue	Vi 22108, BB 10264, HMV EA641, DLP 1111
A-49494-2	I've got a feeling I'm falling	Vi 22092, 22108, HMV B3243, EA622, DLP 1111
A-49495-3	Love me or leave me	Vi 22092, BB 10263, DLP 1111
A-49496-1	Gladyse	Vi V-38554, HMV HE2366, JF4
A-49497-2	Valentine Stomp	Vi V-38554, BB 10263, DLP 1111 HMV HE2366, JF4

THOMAS WALLER. (Pipe-organ):

24th August, 1929.

A-56067-1	Waitin' at the end of the road	Unissued
A-56068-1	Baby, Oh where can you be?	Unissued
A-56068-2	Baby, Oh where can you be?	Unissued
A-56068-3	Baby, Oh where can you be?	Unissued
A-56069-1	Tanglefoot	Unissued
A-56069-2	Tanglefoot	Unissued
A-56070-1	That's all	Unissued
A-56070-2	That's all	Vi 23260

THOMAS WALLER. (Piano Solos):

29th August, 1929.

A-55375-1	Waitin' at the end of the road	BB 10264

A-55376-1	Baby, Oh where can you be?	Unissued
A-55376-2	Baby, Oh where can you be?	HMV DLP 1111

(As before): New York City   4th September, 1929.

A-56125-1	Goin' about	Unissued
A-56125-2	Goin' about	HMV DLP 1111
A-56126-1	My feelin's are hurt	Vi V-38613, 25338, DLP 1111

THE LITTLE CHOCOLATE DANDIES. (Rex Stewart, tp; Claude Jones, tb; Don Redman, saxes; Benny Carter, as; Coleman Hawkins, ts; Fats, p; unknown tuba, bj and ds.):

12th September, 1929.

W-402965-C	That's how I feel today	OK 8728, PaE R542
W-402966-D	Six or seven times	OK 8728, PaE R542, R2550, PaAu A7483, PaS PZ11127

THOMAS WALLER. (Piano): New York.

24th September, 1929.

A-56710-2	Smashing Thirds	Vi V-38613, 25338, HMV B4902, B8546, DLP 1111

"FATS" WALLER AND HIS BUDDIES. (Fats, p; Charlie Gains, tp; Jack Teagarden, tb; Otto Hardwick, as; Albert Nicholas, as; Larry Binyon, ts; Al Morgan, bs; Gene Krupa, ds; *The Wanderers*, vo):

30th September, 1929.

A-56727	Lookin' good but feelin' bad	Vi V-38086
A-56728	I need someone like you	Vi V-38086

McKINNEY'S COTTON PICKERS. (Joe Smith, Sidney DeParis, Len Davis, tp; Claude Jones, tb; Don Redman, as & vo; Benny Carter, as; Coleman Hawkins, Ted McCord, ts; Fats, p; Dave Wilborn, bj; Bill Taylor, bs; Kaiser Marshall, ds): New York

5th November, 1929.

A-57064-2	Plain Dirt (nv)	Vi V-38097, Vi 40-0115, BB 11590, Vi 62-0083, HMV B4990, K6950, RCA 430272, LEJ8
A-57065-1	Gee, ain't I good to you? (vo)	Vi V-38097, BB 5205, 10249, 11590, HMV JK2155, HMV B4967, K6950, RD 7561, RCA 430272

6th November, 1929.

(As before):

A-57066-2	I'd love it (nv)	Vi V-38133, BB 10706, HMV B4967, JK2474, RD 7561, RCA 430272
A-57067-2	The Way I feel today (vo)	Vi V-38102, BB 10232, HMV B6204, B4901, JK2166, RD 7561, RCA 430272, Vi 760-001
A-57068-2	Miss Hannah (vo)	Vi V-38102, BB 10232, HMV B4901, B6215, JK2166, RD 7561, RCA 430272, Vi 760-001

(As before):   14th November, 1929.

A-57139-1	Peggy (nv)	Vi V-38133, BB 10706, RD 7561, RCA 430272, Vi 62-0069
A-57140-2	Wherever there's a will (vo)	Vi 22736, BB 10259, HMV BD135, JK 2155, RD 7561, RCA 430272

GENE AUSTIN. (Vocal, acc. Fats, p., and Orchestra. Remainder of personnel unknown):

25th November, 1929.

A-57170-1	My fate is in your hands	Vi 22223, HMV B3297, JSoc LP12-1

JIMMY JOHNSON AND HIS ORCHESTRA. (King Oliver, Dave Nelson, tp; Jimmy Archey, tb; Charlie Frazier, sax; Teddy Bunn *or* Bernard Addison, bj; Harry Hall, bs; James P. Johnson and Fats, p; Eva Taylor and the *Keep Shufflin'* Trio, vo):

28th November, 1929.

A-57701-2	You've got to be modernistic	Vi V-38099, HMV R14398, 7EG 8164
A-57702-2	You don't understand	Vi V-38099, HMV R14398, 7EG 8164

THOMAS WALLER. (Piano):

4th December, 1929.

A-57170-1	My fate is in your hands	Vi V-38568, Pirate MPC 506
A-57191	Turn on the heat	Vi V-38568, DLP 1111, RCA 'X' LVA 3035, 130247

"FATS" WALLER AND HIS BUDDIES. New York City
This session seems to be a get-together for the boys. The following are known to be present: Henry Allen, Len Davis, tpts; Jack Teagarden, J. C. Higginbotham, poss Charlie Green, tb; Albert Nicholas, Otto Hardwicke, Larry Binyon, poss; Charlie Holmes, Happy Cauldwell, reeds; Fats Waller, pno; Bernard Addison, Will Johnson, gtr/bjo; Pops Foster, Al Morgan, bs; Kaiser Marshall, ds.

18th December, 1929.

A-57926-2	When I'm alone (vo)	Vi V-38110
A-57927-3	Ridin' but Walkin' (nv)	Vi V-38119, HMV B4971, B6390, EA3265, SG431, Vi IAC-0135
A-57928-1	Won't you get off it, please? (nv)	Vi V-38119, HMV B4971, B6549, EA3713, SG464, Vi IAC-0135, COLL COL12-7
A-57929-1	Lookin' for another Sweetie (vo)	Vi V-38110

THOMAS WALLER and BENNIE PAINE. (piano duet): New York City

21st March, 1930,

A-59720-1	St. Louis Blues	Vi 22371, HMV B8496, GW1341, Vi 68-0830
A-59721-1	After you've gone	Vi 22371, HMV B8496, GW1341, Vi 68-0830

Part of 59720 was used on HMV C2885 *"Jazz Histories"* (Jack Hylton).

TED LEWIS AND HIS BAND. (Muggsy Spanier, co; Dave Klein, tp; George Brunies, tb; Benny Goodman, cl; Ted Lewis, cl. & vo. (on 151395 & 151397); Don Murray, sax; Bud Freeman, ts;

Sam Shapiro, Sol Klein, vns; Fats p. & vo. on 151396, 151397, 151398; Tony Gerardi, g; Harry Barth, bs; John Lucas, ds; unknown accordion):

5th March, 1931.

W-151395-2	Egyptian Ella	Co 2428-D, CRC D77
W-151396-2	I'm crazy about my baby	Co 2428-D, CRC D77

(As before):

6th March, 1931.

W-151397-3   Dallas Blues   Co 2527-D, Co CL6127, CoE CB446, FB2820, CoF DF765,

(17065-1)   Ph BBE 12106, 429194 BE, CoG DW4053-11, Co 4-38841, 38841 (Co 35684, CoAu DO2756, PE 16109. Me M 13379, Ba 33412, Or 3132, BRS 1009, Ro 2506)

W-151398-2   Royal Garden Blues   Co 2527-D, Co CL6127, CoE CB446, FB2820, CoF DF765, Ph BBE 12106, 429194BE CoG DW4053-11, Co 4-38840, 38840

(17064-1)   (Co 35684, CoAU DO 2756, OK 41579, BRS 1009)

Matrix and issue numbers in brackets are re-recordings. Co35684, CoAu DO 2756 were labelled *Ted Lewis and his Orchestra;* BRS 1009 was labelled *Spanier-Brunies Dixielanders.*

THOMAS "FATS" WALLER. (Vo, p)   **13th March, 1931.**

W-151417-3   I'm crazy 'bout my baby   Co 14593, Vo 3016, PaE R1197, Palt B71078, PaS PZ11241, OdF 279746, OdG 31817, 33SX 1506

W-151418-2   Draggin' my heart around   Co 14593, Vo 3016, PaE R1197, Palt B71078, PaS PZ11241, OdF 279746, OdG 31817

JACK TEAGARDEN AND HIS ORCHESTRA. (Charlie Teagarden, Sterling Bose, tp; Jack Teagarden, tb & vo; Tommy Dorsey, tb; Artie Shaw *or* Pee Wee Russell, cl & as; Bud Freeman, ts; Fats, p; Dick McDonough, g; Artie Bernstein, bs; Stan King, ds; Max Farley, baritone sax):

14th October, 1931.

W-151839   You rascal you (vo)   Co 2558-D, CoE CB424, HJCA 611, 335X 1545

W-151840   That's what I like about you (vo)   Co 2558-D, HJCA 611, DO 667, Epic Sn6044, JPan1807, 33SX 1545

W-151841   Chances are (vo)   OK 41551, Ha 1403H

W-151842   I got the Ritz from you (vo)   Unissued

THE RHYTHMAKERS. (Henry Allen, tp; Jimmy Lord, cl; Pee Wee Russell, ts; Fats, p; Eddie Condon, bj; Jack Bland, g; Pops Foster, bs; Zutty Singleton, ds; Billy Banks, vo): New York City.   **26th July, 1932.**

B-12119   I would do anything for you   BrF 500316 Ba 32530, Or 2534, Me M 12457, Pe 15651, BrE 02508, UHCA 105, OFC 14, JP LP 1808, JRog 5025, Swg JCS 33764

B-12120   Mean Old Bed Bug Blues   Ba32502, Or 2554, Me M 12457, Pe 15669, VoE S20, V1021, BrF 500315, UHCA 105, ImpCz 6003, JRog 5025 ImpG18012, JP LP 1808, Swg JCS33764 Co 35882 OFC 14

B-12121   Yellow Dog Blues   Co 35882, Ba 32502, Or 2554, Me M 12481, Pe 15669, VoE S20, V1021, BrF 500315, PaE R2810, Pal DPE 9, PaAu A7399, UHCA 107, OFC 14, PaS PZ11148, ImpG 18012, ImpCz 6003, JP LP 1808, Swg JCS 33764

B-12122   Yes Suh!   Ba 32530, Or 2534, Me M 12481, Pe 15651, BrE 02078, PaE R2810. BrG A9940, PaS PZ11148, Pal DPE 9, PaAu A7399, UHCA 107, JP LP 1808, Swg JCS 33764, OFC 14

Ba, Me, Or, BrE, PaE, PaAu, Pal, PaS issued as *"The Rhythmakers".*
VoE, UHCA, JP issued as *"Billy Bank's Rhythmakers".*
Pe issued as *"Jack Bland and his Rhythmakers".*
ImpCz, ImpG issued as *"Billy Bank's Chicago Rhythm Kings".*
BrF issued as *"The Chicago Rhythm Kings".*
BrG issued as *"Eddie Condon and his Rhythmakers".*

"FATS" WALLER AND HIS RHYTHM. (Fats, p. vo; Herman Autrey, tp; Ben Whittet, cl & as; Al Casey, g; Bill Taylor, bs; Harry Dial, ds & vibes):   **16th May, 1934.**

82526   A Porter's Love-song to a Chambermaid   Vi 24648, BB 10016, HMV EA2279, DLP 1118, LPM 1503

82527-1   I wish I were twins   Vi 24641, HMV EA1508, EG3703, JF1, DLP 1118, RCA 130278

82528   Armful of Sweetness   Vi 24641, BB 10149, G24194, HMV HE2358, JF7, DLP 1118, RCA 130278

82529   Do me a favor   Vi 24648, HE2358, JF7, RCA RD 27185, LPM 1503

237

(As before, but Gene Sedric, cl & ts, replaces Whittet):		17th August, 1934.
83699	Georgia May	Vi 24714, BB 10078, G24308, HMV JF12, DLP 1118, RCA 130278
84106	Then I'll be tired of you	Vi 24708, HMV JF13, DLP 1118, LPM 1503
84107	Don't let it bother you	Vi 24714, HMV JF12, RCA 130278, LPV 516
84108	Have a little dream on me	Vi 24708, HMV JF13, DLP 1118, LPM 1503

(As before, but Floyd O'Brien, tb added, and Milton "Mezz" Mezzrow, cl & as, replaces Sedric.)
New York City.   28th September, 1934.

84417	Serenade for a Wealthy Widow	Vi 24742, BB 10262, HMV GW1318, HE2619, JF8, K7863, DLP 1118
84418	How can you face me?	Vi 24737, BB 10143, HMV HN727, JF14, K7863, RCA RD 27185, LMP 1502
84419	Sweetie Pie	Vi 24737, BB 10143, HMV GW1318, HE2619, JF8, K7861, DLP 1118
84420	Mandy	Vi 24738, HMV GY281, JF11, DLP 1118
84421	Let's pretend there's a moon	Vi 24742, HMV EA1510, JF14, DLP 1118
84422	You're not the only oyster in the stew	Vi24742, 20-2218, BB 10261, LPT 1001, HMV BD298, GY281, HE2344, HMV X4464, HN727, JF11, K7861, K8526, DLP 1017

(Fats, p & vo; Bill Coleman, tp; Gene Sedric, cl & ts; Al Casey, g; Bill Taylor, bs; Harry Dial, ds):
7th November, 1934.

84921	Honeysuckle Rose	Vi 24826
84922	Believe it, Beloved	Vi 24808, HMV BD 134, EA 1509, EG3703, JF15, X4430, DLP 1056, RCA 430571
84923-2	Dream Man	Vi 24801, BB 10261, HMV BD117, LPM1502, RCA RD 27185, EA1457, HE2344, K7454, K8526, BA 1048
84924	I'm growing fonder of you	Vi 24801, HMV BD117, EA1510, K7454, BA 1048, RCA 430521
84925	If it isn't love	Vi 24808, HMV JF15, RCA 430521, LPV 516
84926	Breakin' the ice	Vi 24826, HMV EA1457, RCA 430521, LPV 516

THOMAS "FATS" WALLER. (Piano Solos):   16th November, 1934.

86208	African Ripples	Vi 24830, BB10115, HMV B8546, EA1458, HE2289, JF11
86209	Clothes Line Ballet	Vi 25015, BB 10098, HMV EA1524, JF35
86210	Alligator Crawl	Vi 24830, BB 10098, ViJ A1337, HMV B8784, EA1458, HN2632, IP370, IW89, JF11, K8176, X4490, X4507
86211	Viper's Drag	Vi 25015, 27768, BB 10133, HMV B8784, EA1524, HN2632, IP370, IW89, JF35, K8176, N4480, X4480

"FATS" WALLER AND HIS RHYTHM. (As before, but Charles Turner, bs, replaces Bill Taylor):
Camden, N.J.   5th January, 1935.

87082-1	I'm a hundred-per-cent for you (vo)	Vi 24863, RD 27047
87082-3	I'm a hundred-per-cent for you (nv)	Vi 24867, HMV IW96, JO 179, K7508, RCA 430521
87083-1	Baby Brown (vo)	Vi 24846, BB 10109, RCA 430521
87033-3	Baby Brown (nv)	Vi 24867, HMV GY361, HE2361, JF45, K7508, SG464, X4454
87084	Night Wind (org)	Vi 24853, HMV EA1482, GY361, RD 27047
87085	Because of once upon a time	Vi 24863, HMV BD134, RCA 430571
87086	I believe in miracles (org)	Vi 24853, HMV EA1482, JK2796, LPT 3040, CDN 131, CAL 473
87087	You fit into the picture	Vi 24863, HMV ED5333 EA1509, EG6369, JO179

(Fats, p, ce, vo; Herman Autrey, tp; Rudy Powell, cl & as; Al Casey, g; Charles Turner, bs; Harry
Dial, ds): New York City   6th March, 1935.

88776-1	Louisiana Fairy-Tale (vo)	Vi 24898
88776-2	Louisiana Fairy-Tale (vo)	HMV HE3083
88777	I ain't got nobody (vo)	Vi 24888, DLP 1138, LPV 516
88778	I ain't got nobody (nv)	Vi 25026, HMV AE4565, JF32, RCA 430571
88779	Whose honey are you? (vo)	Vi 24892, HMV EA1500, LPV 516

88780	Whose honey are you? (nv)	Vi 25027, HMV EG3398, GY362, HE2361, JF45, SG431, RCA 430571
88781	Rosetta (vo, ce)	Vi 24892
88782	Rosetta (nv, ce)	Vi 25026, ViJ A1241, BB10156
88783	Pardon my love (vo)	Vi 24889, HMV B5278, GW1103
88784	What's the reason? (vo)	Vi 24889, Vi 20-2643, HMV BD156, EA1500, GW1103, RCA RD 27185
88785	What's the reason? (nv), (ce)	Vi 25027, HMV AE4565, EG3398, JF32, RCA 430571
88786	Cinders (vo, ce)	Vi 24898
88787	Dust off that old pianna (vo)	Vi 24888, HMV BD156, EA1508, GY362, IW101, RCA 430571, LPV516

THOMAS "FATS" WALLER. Piano and vocal), Rudy Powell (clt.): New York.
11th March, 1935.

Baby Brown; Vipers Drag; How Can You Face Me; Down Home Blues; Dinah; Handful of Keys; Solitude; I'm Crazy 'Bout My Baby; Believe It, Beloved. (Vic LPT 6001, RD 7552, 430208, CLP 1035.)
Tea For Two. (Vic LPT 6001, RD 7552, 430208, CLP 1035, Vic LPM1246, EPC 1246-3.)
Sweet Sue; Somebody Stole My Gal; Honeysuckle Rose; Where Were You On June 3rd; Clothes Line Ballet; Don't Let It Bother You. (Vic LPT 6001, RD 7552, 430209, CLP 1035.)
E Flat Blues; Alligator Crawl; Zonky. (Vic LPT 6001, RD 7553, 430209, CLP 1042.)
Hallelujah; Do Me A Favour; California Here I Come; I've Got A Feelin' I'm Fallin'; My Fate Is In Your Hands, Ain't Misbehavin'. (Vic LPT 6001, RD 7553, 430208, CLP1042.)
You're The Top; Blue Turning Grey; Russian Fantasy. (CLP 1042, RD 7553.)
"FATS" WALLER AND HIS RHYTHM. As 6-3-35; Fats sings on all titles): New York City.
8th May, 1935.

89760	Lulu's Back in Town	Vi 25063, HMV AE4571, EA1563, HE2631, JF47, RCA RD 27185
89761	Sweet and Slow	Vi 25063, HMV AE4571, EA1563, HE2631, JF47, RCA RD 27185, LPM 1502
89762	You're been taking lessons in love	Vi 25044, DLP 1056, LPV 516, 7M208
89763	You're the cutest one	Vi 25039, BB 10129, GW1214
89764	I'm gonna sit right down and write myself a letter	Vi 25044, ViJ A1241, HMV BD5031, B9935, EG3602, GW1238, HE2362, 7EG 8255, SG304, Bilt 1099, RCA RCX 1053, DLP 1017
89765	Hate to talk about myself	Vi 25039, HMV GW1214, DLP 1138

(Fats, p, vo; Herman Autrey, tp; Gene Sedric, cl, ts; James Smith, g; Charles Turner, bs; Arnold Bolden, ds): Camden, N.J. **24th June, 1935.**

88989	Dinah	Vi 25471, HMV AE4555, BD5040, EA2083, EG3683, HE2356, JF46, 45 RCA 1189
88990	Take it easy	HN2996, SG383 Vi 25078, HMV BD5199, EG3643
88991	You're the picture	Vi 25075, HMV HE3083, DLP 1138
88992	My very good friend—the Milkman	Vi 25075, HMV BD1218, BD5376, 7EG 8255, HN 2584, 7M128, RCA RD 27185, DLP 1056
88993	Blue because of you	BB 10322, LPV 516
88994	There's going to be the devil to pay	Vi 25078
88995	12th Street Rag	Vi 25087, ViJ JA585, A1114, HMV BD262, GW1236, GW1900, GY886, K7601, SG174, LPV 516
88996	There'll be some changes made	BB 10322, Vi 20-2216, RCA RD 27185, DLP 1082, LPM 1502
88997	Somebody stole my gal	Vi 25194, ViJ JA691, HMV EA1630, JF46, Bilt 1099, LPV 516
88998	Sweet Sue	Vi 25087, ViJ JA585, A1114, HMV AE4555, BD298, DLP 1056

(As before, but Rudy Powell, cl & as, replaces Sedric; & Harry Dial, d, vbs replaces Bolden: New York City. **2nd August, 1935.**

92915	Truckin'	Vi 25116, HMV BD262, GW1236, GY886, K7601, SG174
92916-1	Sugar Blues	Vi 25194, ViJ JA691, HMV EA 1630, DLP 1082
92917-1	Just as long as the world goes 'round and around	HMV HE3018, JO 291, SG492
92918	Georgie Rockin' Chair	Vi 25175, BB10288, ViJ A1261, HMV AE4606
92919	Brother seek and ye shall find	Vi 25175, ViJ A1261
92920	The girl I left behind me	Vi 25116, HMV B10439, EA1605, 7M 157

New York City. **20th August, 1935.**

92992	You're so darn charming (ce)	Vi 25120

92993	Woe! is me	Vi 25140, HMV BD5031, EA1590, EG3602, GW1238, HE2362
92994	Rhythm and Romance (ce)	Vi 25131, HMV BD5199, EA1587, RD 27047
92995	Loafin' Time	Vi 25140, HMV EA1590, DLP 1082
92996	A sweet beginning like this (ce)	Vi 25131, HMV EA1587, DLP 1082, BA 1048
92997	Got a bran' new suit	Vi 25123, HMV BD5012, EG3702, HE2896, JO 196, N14065
92998	I'm on a See-Saw	Vi 25120, HMV EA1605, EG3660, HE3018, JO 291, SG492, RD 27047
94100	Thief in the night	Vi 25123

"FATS" WALLER. (Piano and vocal with unknown group. Titles taken from sound track of 20th Century-Fox film *King of Burlesque:*

October/November, 1935.

	I've Got My Fingers Crossed!	Unissued
	Shootin' High	Unissued
	Oh, Susanna	Unissued
	Too Good To Be True	Unissued

"FATS" WALLER AND HIS RHYTHM. Fats. p & vo; Herman Autrey, tp; Gene Sedric, cl & ts; James Smith, g; Charles Turner, bs; Yank Porter, ds): New York City.

29th November, 1935.

98171	Sweet Thing	Vi 25196, HMV AE4606, EA1631, 7EG 8078
98172	When somebody thinks you're wonderful	Vi 25222, HMV BD5040, EG3683, 7EG 8255, HE2356, HN2996 SG383, 45 RCA 1189
98173	I've got my fingers crossed	Vi 25211, HMV BD5052, EA1637, IM122, NE286
98174	Spreadin' Rhythm Around	Vi 25211, HMV EA1637, EG3702, NE286, DLP 1138
98175	A little bit independent (ce)	Vi 25196, HMV BD5012, EA1631
98176	You stayed away too long	Vi 25222, 20-2216, BA 1049

"FATS" WALLER, HIS RHYTHM AND HIS ORCHESTRA. (Fats, Hank Duncan, p & vo; Herman Autrey, Sidney de Paris, tp; Benny Morton, tb; Edward Inge, cl; Rudy Powell, cl & as; Don Redman, as; Gene Sedric, Bob Carroll, ts; James Smith, gtr; Charles Turner, bs; Yank Porter, ds): New York City.

4th December, 1935.

98196-1	Fat and Greasy (vocal chorus by rest of Orchestra) (ce)	Unissued
98196-2	Fat and Greasy (vocal chorus by rest of Orchestra((ce)	Unissued
98197-1	Functionizin' (nv)	HMV SG315, HE2902
98198-1	I got Rhythm (vo)	HMV SG315, HE2902

"FATS" WALLER AND HIS RHYTHM. (Fats, p & vo; Herman Autrey, tp; Gene Sedric, cl & ts; James Smith, g; Charles Turner, bs; Yank Porter, ds); New York City.

1st February, 1936.

98894	The panic is on	Vi 25266
98895	Sugar Rose (ce)	Vi 25266, HMV BD5062, B9885, EG7622, GW1282, HE2813, HN2763, IM133, JO 133. N14052
98896	Oooh! Look-a there, ain't she pretty? (ce)	Vi 25255, 20-2218, HMV EA1722 DLP 1138, CDN 131, CAL473
98897	Moon Rose	Vi 25281, HMV EA1704, RD 27047, BA1049
98898	West Wind	Vi 25253, HMV BD5052, EA1677, IM122
98899	That never-to-be-forgotten night	Vi 25255, HMV BD5062, EA1722, GW1282, IM133
99035	Sing an old-fashioned song	Vi 25253, HMV BD5135, EA1677
99036	Garbo Green	Vi 25281, HMV EA1704, RD27047, BA1049

"FATS" WALLER AND HIS RHYTHM. (Fats, p & vo; Herman Autrey, tp; Gene Sedric, cl & ts; Al Casey, g; Charles Turner, bs; Arnold Bolden, ds; Elisabeth Handy & Fats vo on last title): New York City.

8th April, 1936.

101189	All my life	Vi 25296, HMV BD5077, EA1726, GY487, IM144
101190	Christopher Columbus	Vi 25295, HMV EA1744, EG3682, RD 27047
101191	Crosspatch	Vi 25315, HMV BD5098, EA1729, EG3690, GW1345
101192	It's no fun	Vi 25296, HMV BD5087, EA1726, EG3718
101193	Cabin in the sky (ce)	Vi 25315, HMV BD5077, EA1729, EG3690, GY487, IM144, GY897
101194	Us on a bus	Vi 25295, HMV EA1744, EG3682, JO 123, RD 27047, LPM 1502
101195	Stay (ce)	T-2408-1

(As before, but Yank Porter, ds, replaces Bolden):

5th June, 1936.

| 101667 | It's a sin to tell a lie | Vi 25342, 20-1595, ViJ A1230, Vi 27-0037, HMV BD5087, EA1773, EG3718, JO 205, VD 359, RCP REX1053, DLP 1017 |

101668	The more I know you	Vi 25348, HMV BD5159
101669	You're not the kind (ce)	Vi 25353, HMV BD5115, EA1779, EG3767, RCA 130208
101670	Why do I lie to myself about you?	Vi25353, HMV BD5150, EA1779, GW1390, HE2360, RCA 130206
101671	Let's sing again	Vi 25348, HMV BD5098, GW1345
101672	Big Chief de Sota	Vi 25342, ViJA1230, HMV EA1773, RCA 130208

(As before, but Arnold Bolden, ds, replaces Porter): New York City. **8th June, 1936.**

102016	Black Raspberry Jam	Vi 25359, HMV BD5376, RD 27047, LPM 1393
102017	Bach up to me	Vi 25536, HMV BD5225, GW1597, HE2368, 7EG 8242
102018	Fractious Fingering	Vi 25652, 25656, HMV X6014, RD 27047
102019	Paswonky	Vi 25359, HMV BD5354, EG6383, HE2345, K8227, SG92
102020	Lounging at the Waldorf	Vi 25430, HMV K8227, SG92
102021	Latch on	Vi 25471

                     1st August, 1936.

102400	I'm crazy 'bout my baby	Vi 25374, HMV BD5120, GW1343, LPM 1503
102401	I just made up with that old girl of mine	Vi 25394, HMV BD5159, RCA RD 27815, LPM 1502
102402	Until the real thing comes along	Vi 25374, 20-2640, HMV BD5115, EG3767, 7EG 8255, RCA 1010
102403	There goes my attraction	Vi 25388, HMV BD5120, GW1343, K7779
102404	The curse of an aching heart	Vi 25394, HMV BD5116, EA1791, Jazztone 1247
102405	Bye-bye, Baby	Vi 25388, HMV BD5116, EA1791, K7779

                   9th September, 1936.

OLA 0339	S'posin'	Vi 25415, 20-2220, BB 10156, HMV BD5135, RCA 130206
OLA 0340	Copper colored gal	Vi 25409, HMV BD5133
OLA 0341	I'm at the mercy of love	Vi 25409, HMV BD5133
OLA 0342	Floatin' down to Cotton Town	Vi 25415, DLP 1082, BA1048
OLA 0343	La-de-de, la-de-da	Vi25430, HMV BD5150, EA1580, GW1390, HE2360

Chicago: **29th November, 1936.**

1801	Hallelujah! Things look rosy now (vo)	Vi 25478, ViJ A1144, HMV BD5178
1802	Hallelujah! Things look rosy now (nv)	Vi 25489, HMV EG3895, K8228
1803	'Tain't good (vo)	Vi 25478, HM VBD 5178, EA1530, EG3880
1804	'Tain't good (nv)	Vi 25489, HMV EG3895, K8228, RD 27047
1805	Swingin' them Jingle Bells (vo)	Vi 25483, 20-1602, Vi LPT 1001, BB 10016, ViJ A1144, HMV BD1229, EA2302, HE2672, HN2426, JO 81, SG65, DLP 1017
1806	Swingin' them Jingle Bells (nv)	Vi 25490, HMV EG3893, HN2599
1807	A Thousand Dreams of You (vo)	Vi 25483, HMV BD5184, EA1868, HE2359
1808	A Thousand Dreams of You (nv)	Vi 25490, HMV EG3893
1809	A Rhyme for love (vo)	Vi 25491, HMV EA1856, DLP 1138
1810	I adore you (vo)	Vi 25491, HMV EA1856

                  24th December, 1936.

3840	Havin' a Ball	Vi 25515, BB 10100, ViJ A1246, DLP 1138, RCA 130208
3841	I'm sorry I made you cry	Vi 25515, ViJ A1246, DLP 1138, RCA 130208
3842	Who's afraid of love?	Vi 25499, HMV EA1851, RCA 130208
3843	Please keep me in your dreams	Vi 25498, HMV BD5184, HE2359, RCA 130208
3844	One in a million	Vi 25499, HMV EA1851, RCA 130208
3845	Nero	Vi 25498, HMV EA1868, DLP 1082

As before, but Slick Jones, d, replaces Bolden): **22nd February, 1937.**

4949	You're laughing at me (ce)	Vi 25530, HMV BD5215, RCA RD 27185
4950	I can't break the habit of you	Vi 25530, HMV EA1933, DLP 1082
4951	Did anyone ever tell you?	Vi 25537, DLP 1082, BA1048
4952	When love is young	Vi 25537, RCA 130208
4953	The meanest thing you ever did was kiss me	Vi 25536, 20-2219, HMV BD5431, EA1933, EG6676, RCA 130298

(As before):		18th March, 1937.
6413	Cryin' Mood	Vi 25551, HMV BD5278, EA1939. 7EG 8242
6414	Where is the Sun?	Vi 25550, ViJ JA1016, HMV BD5212, IM 292, K7936
6415	You've been reading my mail	Vi 25554, HMV B10191, EA1960, EG7719, HE2997, Jo 274, SG357
6416	To a sweet pretty thing	Vi 25551, HMV EA1939, DLP1138
6417	Old Plantation	Vi 25550, ViJ JA1016, HMV BD5212, IM 292, K7936
6418	Spring Cleaning	Vi 25554, DLP 1082, RCA 130206

JAM SESSION AT VICTOR. (Bunny Berigan, tp; Tommy Dorsey, tb; Fats, p; Dick McDonough, g; George Wettling, ds): New York City.   **24th March, 1937.**

√ 6581	Honeysuckle Rose	Vi 25559, HMV B8580, EG7551, GW1473, JK2296, K7921, RCA 75492
√ 6582	Blues	Vi 25559, HMV B8580, EG7551, GW1473, JK2296, K7921, RCA 75492

"FATS" WALLER AND HIS RHYTHM. (Fats, p & vo; Herman Autrey, tp; Gene Sedric, cl & ts; Al Casey, g; Charles Turner, bs; Slick Jones, ds, also vibes on 7755): New York City.   **9th April, 1937.**

7745	You showed me the way (vo)	Vi 25579
7746	You showed me the way (nv)	Vi 25565, RD 27047
7477	Boo-hoo (nv)	Vi 25563, HMV BD5229, EA1938, GY394, RCA 130206
7748	The love-bug'll bite you (nv)	Vi 25563, HMV BD5229, EA1938, GY 394, RCA 130206
7749	San Anton' (vo)	Vi 25579
7750	San Anton' (nv)	Vi 25565, BB 10109, HMV BD5215
7751	I've got a new lease on love (vo)	Vi 25580
7752	I've got a new lease on love (nv)	Vi 25571, HMV EA1960, K8262, SG95, DLP 1056, 7M 208
7753	Sweet heartache (vo)	Vi 25580, HMV BD5225, GW1597, HE2368, DLP 1056
7754	Sweet heartache (nv)	Vi 25571, HMV K8262, SG95
7755	Honeysuckle Rose (nv)	Vi 36206, Vi LPT 1001, ViJ NB6004, HMV C2937, EB114, 7EG 8148, FKX121, Vic 25779, DLP 1017

    9th June, 1937.

10647	Smarty	Vi 25608, HMV B10168, EA1976, HN 3043, SG410, RD 27047
10648	Don't you know or don't you care?	Vi 25604, 20-2642, HMV BD5258, EA2045
10649	Lost love	Vi 25604, HMV BD5258
10650	I'm gonna put you in your place	Vi 25608, BB 10008, HMV BD5493, EA2260, LPM 1503
10651	Blue turning grey over you (nv)	Vi 36206, Vi LPT 1001, ViJ NB6004, DLP 1017, HMV C2937, EB114, FKX121, Vi 25779

THOMAS "FATS" WALLER. (Piano):   **11th June, 1937.**

10652	Keepin' out of mischief now	Vi 25618, 27767, BB 10099, ViJ JA 1047, HMV B8625, EA2382, EG6757, HE2290, N4479, X4479
10653	Stardust	BB 10099, Vi 20-2638, HMV EA2382, EG6757, HE2290, JO 132, N14051, Jazztone 1247, LPM 2246
10654	Basin Street Blues	Vi 25631, 27767, BB 10115, ViJ A1263, HMV B8636, EA1985, HE2289, N4479, X4479
10655	Tea for two	Vi 25618, 27766, ViJ JA1047, HMV B8625, EA3685, N4478
1065	I ain't got nobody	Vi 25631, 27766, BB 10133, ViJ A1263, HMV B8636, EA1985, N4478, DLP 1138

"FATS" WALLER AND HIS RHYTHM. (As before): New York City.   **7th September, 1937.**

13344	You've got me under your thumb	Vi 25672, HMV BD5310
13345	Beat it out	Vi 25672, HMV BD5377, EG6445, K8174, SG91
13346	Our love was meant to be	Vi 25681, 20-2643, HMV BD5310, EA2033, R 27047, LPM 1502
13347	I'd rather call you baby	Vi 25681, EA2033, DLP 1082, BA 1048
13348	I'm always in the mood for you	Vi 25671, HMV BD5297
13449	She's tall, she's tan, she's terrific	Vi 25671, HMV BD5297, EA2045

242

| 13350 | You're my dish | Vi 25679, HMV EA1990 |
| 13351 | More power to you | Vi 25679, HMV BD5314, EA1990, EG6294, GW1621, GW1900 |

(As before): New York City. **7th October, 1937.**

14645	How can I?	Vi 25864, HMV EA2263
14646	The joint is jumping	Vi 25689, 20-1582, HMV BD1079, EPBT 3024, FDLP1005, RCA RCX1053, DLP 1008
14647	A hopeless love-affair	Vi 25689, HMV BD5314, EA2068, EG6294, GW1621
14648	What will I do in the morning?	Vi 25712
14649	How ya, baby?	Vi 25712, HMV BD5354, EA2128, EG6383, HE2345
14650	Jealous of me	Vi 25864, HMV BD1079
14651	Call me Darling (vocal: Dorothea Driver)	Unissued

(Fats, p & vo; Paul Campbell, tp; Caughey Roberts, cl & as; Ceele Burke, g & Hawaiian g on 9887, 9888; Al Morgan, bs; Lee Young, ds): Hollywood. **16th December, 1937.**

9884	Every day's a holiday	Vi 25749, HMV BD5333, EA2068
9885	Neglected	Vi 25749, HMV BD5342, EG6369
9886	My window faces the South	Vi 25762
9887	Am I in another world?	Vi 25753, HMV BD5360
9888	Why do Hawaiians sing Aloha?	Vi 25762, HMV BD5342
9889	My first impression of you	Vi 25753, HMV 7GF 160

(Waller, p & vo; ce in first and last title; Herman Autrey, tp; Gene Sedric, cl & ts; Al Casey, g; Cedric Wallace, bs; Slick Jones, ds): New York City. **11th March, 1938.**

21150	Something tells me (ce)	Vi 25817, HMV BD5387, EG6540, JO 92, N14038
21151	I love to whistle	Vi 25806, HMV BD5360, EA2083, EG7727, JO 273, NE699
21152	You went to my head	Vi25812, HMV EA2128, RC 24004,
21153	Florido Flo	Vi 25806, HMV FDLP1013, HE2702, JO 110, SG164
21154	Lost and Found	Vi 25812, HMV BD5377, EG6445, LPM 1503
21155	Don't try to cry your way back to me	Vi 25817
21156	If you're a viper (ce)	Unissued

"FATS" WALLER, HIS RHYTHM AND HIS ORCHESTRA. (Fats, p & vo; Herman Autrey, John Hamilton, Nathaniel Williams, tp; George Robinson, John Haughton, tb; Gene Sedric, Samuel Simmons, William Allsop, James Powell, Alfred Skerritt, saxes; Al Casey, g; Cedric Wallace, bs; Slick Jones, ds): **12th April, 1938.**

22429-2	In the gloaming (nv)	Vi 25847, HMV EA2167
22430	You had an evening to spare	Vi 25834, HMV EA2263, 7GF160, DLP 1056
22431	Let's break the good news	Vi 25830, HMV EA2155, HE2357
22432	Skrontch	Vi 25834, HMV BD5387, EG6540, FDLP1013, K8174, SG91
22433	I simply adore you	Vi 25830, HMV EA2155, HE2357
22434-2	The Sheik of Araby	Vi 25847, HMV EA2167, Jazztone 1247
22435-2	Hold my hand	Vi 26045, HMV EA2296, FDLP1013, JO 89, N14030, SG56 Vi 26045
22436-2	Inside	Vi 26045

"FATS" WALLER AND HIS RHYTHM. (Fats, p & vo; Herman Autrey, tp; Gene Sedric, cl & ts; Al Casey, g; Cedric Wallace, bs; Slick Jones, ds): New York City. **1st July, 1938.**

23760	There's honey on the moon tonight	Vi 25891, HMV B10297, EA2199, HN 3079, SG502, RC 24004, LPM 1503
23761	If I were you	Vi 26002, HMV BD5452, EA2223, FDLP1013, GW1696, K8281, SG96
23762	Wide open places	Vi 26002
23763	On the bumpy road to love	Vi 25898, HMV BD5431, EG6676
23764	Fair and Square	Vi 25891, HMV B10234, EA2199, RC 24004
23765	We, the people	Vi 25898, HMV EA2223

"FATS" WALLER AND HIS CONTINENTAL RHYTHM. (Fats, org & vo; Dave Wilkins, tp; George Chisholm, tb; Alfie Kahn, cl & ts; Ian Sheppard, ts & vn; Alan Ferguson, g; Len Harrison, bs; Harry Schneider & Edmundo Ros, ds): London. **21st August, 1938.**

| 6383-1 | Don't try your jive on me | HMV BD5415, EA2189, EG6389, 7EG8042, EG7584, IM1020, BB10100, 7EG8602, LPT3040, Cap T10258, FELP133, MFP 1062 |
| 6384-2 | Ain't Misbehavin' | HMV BD5415, EA2189, EG6389, Cap T10258, EG7584, IM1020, BB10288, 7EG 8602, FELP133, MFP 1062 |

THOMAS "FATS" WALLER (Compton organ.): London. **28th August, 1938.**

| 6385-3 | Swing low, sweet chariot | Cap T10258, FELP 133, HMV B8818, EG6647, Vi 27458, JR 5037, 7EG8304, MFP 1062 |

6386-3	All God's Chillun got wings	Cap T10258, FELP 133, HMV B8818, Vi 27460, JR 5037, 7EG 8304, MFP 1062
6387-3	Go Down, Moses	Cap T10258, FELP 133, HMV B8816, EG6647, K8214, Vi27458, JR 5037, 7EG 8304, MFP 1062
6388-3	Deep River	Cap T10258, FELP 133, HMV B8816, K8214, Vi 27459, JR 5037, 7EG 8304, MFP 1062
6389-2	Water Boy	Cap T10258, FELP 133, HMV B8845, Vi 27460, JR 5037, 7EG 8602, MFP 1062
6390-1	Lonesome Road	Cap T10258, FELP 133, HMV B8845, Vi 27459, JR 5037, 7EG 8602, MFP 1062

ADELAIDE HALL. (Vocal, acc Fats, Compton organ):

| 6391-1 | That old feeling | HMV B8849, Enc 181 |
| 6392-2 | I can't give you anything but love | HMV B8849, Enc 181 |

"FATS" WALLER AND HIS CONTINENTAL RHYTHM. (As before. Fats, p & vo. On 6703 Fats plays celeste and Chisholm does not play.) 21st August, 1938.

6701	Flat Foot Floogie	HMV BD5399, EG6557, 7EG 8341, ENC 181
6702	Pent up in a Penthouse	ENC 181, HMV BD5399, EA2245, EG6557, 7EG 8341
6703	Music, Maestro, Please	ENC 181, HMV BD5398, EA2245, EG6556, 7EG 8341
6704	A-tisket, a-tasket	HMV BD5389, EG6556, 7EG 8341, ENC 181

"FATS" WALLER AND HIS RHYTHM. (Fats, p & vo, Hammond Organ; Herman Autrey, tp; Gene Sedric, cl & ts; Al Casey, g; Cedric Wallace, bs; Slick Jones, ds): New York. 13th October, 1938.

27289	Two sleepy people	BB 10000, Vi 20-1583, HMV BD5452, FDLP 1005, GW 1696, K8281, SG96, DLP 1008
27290	Shame! Shame!	BB 7885, HMV EA2261, RC 24004
27291	I'll never forgive myself (p & org)	BB 10000, HMV EA2302
27292	You look good to me	BB 10008, HMV B10297, EA2260, HN 3079, SG502
27293	Tell me with your kisses	BB 7885, HMV EA2261, RC 24004
27294	Yacht Club Swing (org, nv)	BB 10035, HMV EA2279

7th December, 1938.

30363	Love, I'd give my life for you	BB 10070, G24244
30364	I wish I had you	BB 10078, G24308, DLP 1056
30365	I'll dance at your wedding	BB 10070, G24244, HMV HE2896, JO 196, N14065, RC 24004, LPM 1502
30366	Imagine my surprise	BB 10062, G24194, HMV BD1073
30367	I won't believe it	BB 10062, G24346, HMV B10168, HN3043, SG410
30368	The Spider and the Fly	BB 10205, HMV BD5486, GY394, BA 1049
30369	Patty cake, patty cake	BB 10149, HMV BD5476, K8328

MARTIN BLOCK PROGRAM (WNEW). Louis Armstrong, tp & vo (A); Fats, p & vo (F); Jack Teagarden, tb; Bud Freeman, ts; Al Casey? g; Zutty Singleton? ds: New York City. 12th December, 1938.

Honeysuckle Rose (nv) Palm Club 10
On the Sunny Side of the Street (A)
Tiger Rag (nv)
In the Crack (AF)
Jeepers Creepers (A)
I got Rhythm (nv)

"FATS" WALLER AND HIS RHYTHM. (As before): 19th January, 1939.

31530	A good man is hard to find	BB 10143, HMV B10439, 7M 157
31531	You out-smarted yourself	BB 10116, G24346
31532	Last night a miracle happened	BB 10136, G24563, HMV BD5469, B10050, GY474, HE2976, HN3042
31533	Good-for-nothing but love	BB 10129, HMV BD5476, K8328
31534	Hold tight	BB 10116, Vi 20-1581, HMV BD5469, FDLP 1005, GY474, DLP 1008, LPM 1246
31535	Kiss me with your eyes (p & org)	BB 10136, HMV EA2296, DLP 1138

(Fats plays Hammond Organ; Gene Austin, vo; unknown gtr): 27th February, 1939.

| 33993 | Sweet Sue | Unissued |
| 33994 | I can't give you anything but love | Unissued |

(As before): 9th March, 1939.

| 32942 | You asked for it—you got it | BB 10170, G24859, HMV BD1036 |

32943	Some rainy day	BB 10192
32944	'Taint' what you do	BB 10192, HMV BD 5486, GY541, BA 1049
32945	Got no time	BB 10170, G24938, HMV BD5493
32946	Step up and shake my hand	BB 10184
32947	Undecided	BB 10184
32948	Remember who you're promised to	BB 10205

"FATS" WALLER. (Piano & Vocal, acc John Marks ds):   **27th March/3rd April, 1939.**

MM 406	You can't have your cake and eat it	Tempo A76, Ci R3005, JS AA576
MM 406	Not there—right there	Tempo A76, Ci R3005, JS AA576
RM 13	Cottage in the rain	Ri 8
	Piccadilly	Unissued
	Chelsea	Unissued
	Soho	Unissued ("London Suite")
	Bond Street	Unissued
	Limehouse	Unissued
	Whitechapel	Unissued

The above Session took place in a private recording studio in London. Titles were made on acetate and are not of very high quality. Ed Kirkeby has these original acetates and says they are entirely different from the issued version.

✓ **"FATS" WALLER.** (Piano Solos, acc. Max Lewin, ds): London. ("London Suite").
    13th June, 1939.

OEA7878	Piccadilly	HMV B10059, EG7630, HE2721, ENC 181
7879	Chelsea	HMV B10059, EG7630, HE2721, ENC 181
7880	Soho	HMV B10060, EG7631, HE2722, ENC 181
7881	Bond Street	HMV B10060, EG7631, HE2722, ENC 181
7882	Limehouse	HMV B10061, EG7632, HE2723, ENC 181
7883	Whitechapel	HMV B10061, EG7632, HE2723, ENC 181
7885-2	Signing on at HMV	Unissued
7884-2	or Hallelujah	Unissued

"FATS" WALLER. (Organ & Vocal): London   **13th June, 1939.**

| 7982 | Smoke dreams of you | HMV B8967, MFP 1062 |
| 7983-1 | You can't have your cake and eat it | HMV B8967, MFP 1062 |

"FATS" WALLER AND HIS RHYTHM. (Fats, p & vo; Herman Autrey, tp; Chauncey Graham, ts; John Smith, g; Cedric Wallace, bs; Larry Hinton, ds): New York City.
    28th June, 1939.

38207	Honey Hush	BB 10346, G24220, HMV B10191, EG7719, FDLP1013, HE2997, JO 274, SG357, 7M
38208	I used to love you	BB 10369, Vi 20-2219, G24274, LPM 1502, HMV BD5533, K8469, RCA RD 27185
38209	Wait and see	BB 10405, HMV GY552
38210	You meet the nicest people in your dreams	BB 10346, G24220, LPM 1503, 7EG 8078
38211	Anita	BB 10369, G24938, HMV BD5533, K8469, 7EG 8242
38212	What a pretty Miss	BB10437, HMV B10050, HN3042, NE 810

✓ **"FATS" WALLER.** (Fats, p & vo; John Hamilton, tp; Gene Sedric, cl & t; John Smith, g; Cedric Wallace, bs; Slick Jones, d & vibes): New York City.   **2nd August, 1939.**

	The moon is low; Honeysuckle rose	LPT 6001, RD 7552, 430209, CLP 1035
	Sheik of Araby; B Flat blues	LPT 6001, RD 7552, 430209, CLP 1035, Camden CAL 473, CND 131, LCP 23
	Ain't Misbehavin'; Nagasaki	JS AA536
	Sweet Sue; Lonesome me	JS AA535
	Crazy 'bout my baby	LPT 6001, RD 7553, 430209, CAL 473, CDN 131, LCP 23, CLP 1042
	Spider and the fly; After you've gone	LPT 6001, RD 7553, 430209, CLP 1042

"FATS" WALLER. (Piano solos):

	Tea for two	LPT 6001, RD 7553, 430209, CLP 1042
	Poor Butterfly; St Louis blues	LPT 6001, RD 7553, 430208, CLP 1042
	Handful of keys	LPT 6001, 430209
	Hallelujah	Unissued

(As above):   **10th August, 1939.**

| 41528 | Squeeze me | BB 10405, Vi 20-2217, HMV GY552, FWY FJ2811, Vi LEJ 12, JO 132, N14051, CDN 131, CAL 328, CAL 473 |
| 41529 | Bless you | BB 10393, HMV MH52 |

41530	It's the tune that counts	BB 10393, HMV JO 89, N14030, SG56
41531	Abdullah	BB 10419, Vi 20-2639, G24166, HMV NE724, BA 1049
41532	Who'll take my place?	BB 10419, Vi 20-2642, G24166, BA 1049, HMV NE724, DLP 1056
41533	Bond Street (nv)	BB 10437, G24274, HMV NE810

(As before; Una Mae Carlisle, vo in last title): **3rd November, 1939.**

43346	It's you who taught it to me	BB 10527, HMV HE2731, JO 128
43347	Suitcase Susie	BB 10500, HMV HN2426, JO 81, NE790
43348	Your feet's too big	BB 10500, Vi 20-1580, VD 308, HMV B9582, FDLP 1005, HN2359, MH52, NE790, RCA RX 1053, DLP 1008
43349	You're lettin' the grass grow under your feet	BB 10527, HMV, EG 7727, JO 273,
43350	Darktown Strutters' Ball	BB 10573, Vi 20-2220, HMV FDLP 1013, JO 116, N14045, SG388, DLP 1017
43351	I can't give you anything but love	BB 10573, Vi 20-1582, HMV FDLP 1005, IW341, DLP 1008

LEE WILEY with MAX KAMINSKY'S ORCHESTRA. (Max Kaminsky, co; Pee Wee Russell, cl; Fats, p & ce; Eddie Condon, g; Artie Shapiro, bs; George Wettling, ds; Brad Gowans, arr; Lee Wiley, vo): New York City. **15th November, 1939.**

| WP26270A | I've got a crush on you | Lib L282, LMS 1004 |

LEE WILEY (Lee Wiley, vo. acc. Waller, organ):

| WP26271A | Someone to watch over me | Lib L282, LMS 1004 |

LEE WILEY with MAX KAMINSKY'S ORCHESTRA. (As before):

| WP26272A | How long has this been going on? | Lib. L281, LMS 1004 |
| WP26273A | But not for me | Lib 284, LMS 1004 |

"FATS" WALLER. (Hammond Organ): **20th November, 1939.**

| 43185 | Go down Moses; Swing low, Sweet Chariot; Hallelujah! I'm a bum; Hand me down my walkin' cane (*vocals on all* 4) | Riverside RLP 12-109, RLP 1021, World Record Club T 336, LOE AL3521 |
| 43186 | Frankie and Johnnie; She'll be comin round the mountain; Deep River; The Lord Delivered Daniel (*vocals on all* 4) | Riverside RLP 12-109, RLP 1021, World Record Club T336 LOE AL 3521 |

"FATS" WALLER ("Swinging with a Steinway."):

| 43187 | Ah! so pure; Then you'll remember me; Lucia di Lammermoor; My heart thy sweet voice (*no vocals*) | LOE AL 3522 |

"FATS" WALLER. (Piano solos):

| 43188 | Cavalleria Rusticana; When you and I were young, Maggie; Loch Lomond; Oh! Susanna (*vocals on all but first*) | Riverside RLP 12-109, LOE AL 3522 (except "Cavalleria"), World Record Club T 336, RLP 1022 |
| 43189 | The old oaken bucket; Oh! dem golden slippers; Waltz from *Faust*; Annie Laurie (*vocals on all but "Faust"*) | Riverside RLP 12-109, RLP 1022 World Record Club T 336, LOE AL 3522 |

"FATS" WALLER AND HIS RHYTHM. (As for 2nd August, 1939): Chicago. **12th January, 1940.**

44597	Swinga-Dilla Street (org; nv)	BB 10858, G24504, LPT 3040
44598	At twilight	BB 10803, HMV JO 96, N14033
44599	Oh Frenchy!	BB 10658, Vi 20-1595, VD 359, HMV HE2291, 7EG 8078
44600	Cheatin' on me	BB 10658, G24563, HMV HE2291
44601	Black Maria	BB 10624
44602	Mighty fine	BB10744, HMV GY447, IW339, 7EG 8054
44603	The moon is low (nv)	BB 10624, HMV EA2571
44604	The moon is low (Part 2; (nv)	Unissued

EDDIE CONDON AND HIS BAND. Marty Marsala, co; George Brunies, tb; Pee Wee Russell, cl; Fats, p; Eddie Condon, g; Artie Shapiro, bs; George Wettling, ds); New York City. **24th March, 1940.**

29054-1b	Georgia Grind	Com 536, Stateside SL 10010
29055-2	Oh Sister, ain't that hot?	Com 535, SL 10010
29056-1	Dancing fool	Com 536, SL 10010
29057-1	(You're some) Pretty doll	Com 535, COM CEP 43, SL 10010

"FATS" WALLER AND HIS RHYTHM. (As before): New York City. **11th April, 1940.**

| 48775 | Old Grand Dad | BB 10698, HMV B10262, GY547, HN3013 |

48776	Fat and Greasy	BB 10803, HMV JO 116, N14045
48777	Little curly hair in a high chair	BB 10698, HMV BD1235, EA2571, FDLP 1013, GY547, SG 363
48778	Square from Delaware	BB 10730, HMV GY553, IW341
48779	You run your mouth, I'll run my business	BB 10779, HMV GY512
48780	Too tired	BB 10779, HMV B10406, GY512
48781	"Send me" Jackson	BB 10730, HMV BD1228, FDLP 1013, GY 553, HE2672, HN2599, IW342, SG65
48782	Eep, Ipe, wanna piece of pie	BB 10744, HMV BD906, IW343

16th July, 1940.

51865	Stop Pretending	BB 10829 G24859, HMV B10406
51866	I'll never smile again	BB 10841, DLP 1056
51867	My Mommie sent me to the store	BB 10892, G24800, HMV HE2731, JO 128
51868-2	Dry Bones	BB 10892, G24813, HMV B9885, EG7622, HE2813, HN2763, JO 133, N14052
51869	"Fats" Waller's original E flat blues	BB 10858, G24504, HMV BD906, RCA RD 27185, LPM 1502
51870	Stayin' at home	BB 10841, HMV BD 1235, SG363
51871	Hey! stop kissin' my sister	BB 10829, G24813, HMV HE2702, JO 110, SG164

"FATS" WALLER AND HIS RHYTHM. (Fats, p & vo; also celeste on 57087; John Hamilton, tp; G ne Sedric, cl & ts; Al Casey, g; Cedric Wallace, bs; Slick Jones, ds; Catherine Perry, CP, vo on last title): New York City. 6th November, 1940.

57083	Everybody loves my baby	BB 10989, Vi 20-2217, G25009, HMV B9935, SG304
57084	I'm gonna salt away some sugar	BB 10943, HMV JO 92, N14038
57085	'Tain't nobody's Biz-ness if I do	BB 10967, HMV JO 96, N14033, SG388
57086	Abercrombie had a Zombie	BB 10967
57087	Blue Eyes (ce)	BB 10943, HMV JO 123
57088	Scram! (nv)	BB 10989, G25009
57089	My Melancholy Baby CP	Unissued

(As before: Myra Johnson & Fats vo on all titles): New York. 7th November, 1940.
Titles taken from the sound-tracks of four film shorts made for Official Films, New York (16mm.).

	Ain't Misbehavin'	Unissued
	Honeysuckle Rose	Unissued
	Your feet's too big	Unissued
	The joint is jumping	Unissued

"FATS" WALLER AND HIS RHYTHM. (Fats, p & vo; John Hamilton, tp; Gene Sedric, cl & ts; Al Casey, g; Cedric Wallace, bs; Slick Jones, ds.) Chicago. 2nd January, 1941.

53794	Mamacits (org, nv)	BB 11078, LPT 3040
53795	Liver Lip Jones	BB 11010, 7EG 8054
53796	Buckin' the dice	BB 11102, Vi 20-2640, G24853, DLP 1017
53797	Pantin' in the Panther Room (nv, p & org)	BB 11175, G24836, HMV B10262, HN 3013, 7EG 8042, LPT 3040
53798	Come down to earth, my Angel (p & org)	BB 11010, HMV JO 205, 7EG 8042
53799	Shortnin' Bread	BB 11078, HMV BD1218, HN2584
59100	I repent (org & p)	BB 11188, 7EG 8042, LPT 3040

(Fats, p & vo; John Hamilton, tp; Gene Sedric, cl & ts; Al Casey, g; Cedric Wallace, bs; Slick Jones, ds; vocal chorus by Rhythm on 62762): 20th March, 1941.

62761	Do you have to go?	BB 11222, HMV BD5787, NE699
62762	Pan-pan	BB 11383, HMV BD1011, HE2416, MH131
62763	I wanna hear Swing Songs	BB 11115, HMV BD1028, HE2346
62764	You're gonna be sorry	Vi 20-1602
62765	All that meat and no potatoes	BB 11102, VD 308, G24800, 7EG 8054
62766	Let's get away from it all	BB 11115, 7EG 8054, LPT 3040

"FATS" WALLER. (Piano Solos): 13th May, 1941.

63887	Georgia on my mind	Vi 27765, HMV HE2975, N4477, 7EG 8098
63888	Rockin' Chair	Vi 27765, HMV EA 3685, HE2975, N4477, 7EG 8098
63889-2	Carolina Shout	Vi 27563, HMV AV722, 7EG 8098, CDN 131
63890	Honeysuckle Rose	Vi 20-1580, HMV FDLP 1005, DLP 1008
63891	Ring dem Bells	Vi 27563, HMV AV722, RCA RD 27185

"FATS" WALLER AND HIS RHYTHM. (As before): 13th May, 1941.

63892	Twenty-four Robbers	BB 11222, G24853, HMV BD1011, JK2651, MH131
63893	I understand	BB 11175
63894	Sad Sap Sucker am I	BB 11296, G24895, HMV HE2428
63895	Headlines in the news	BB 11188, G24836

"FATS" WALLER, HIS RHYTHM AND HIS ORCHESTRA. (Fats, p & vo; John Hamilton,

Herman Autrey, Bob Williams, tp; Ray Hogan, George Wilson, tb; Jimmy Powell, Dave McRae, as; Gene Sedric, Bob Carroll, ts; Al Casey, g; Cedric Wallace, bs; Slick Jones, ds): Hollywood.
1st July, 1941.

61334	Chant of the groove (nv)	BB 11262, Vi 20-2638, G24895
61335	Come and get it (vo)	BB 11262, Vi 20-2448, RC24004
61336	Rump and Steak Serenade (vo)	BB 11296, HMV B9582, HN2359, JK2475
61337	Ain't nothing to it (nv)	Unissued

"FATS" WALLER AND HIS RHYTHM. Fats, p & vo; John Hamilton, tp; Gene Sedric, cl & ts; Al Casey, g; Cedric Wallace, bs; Slick Jones, ds: New York. **1st October, 1941.**

67946	Oh Baby, Sweet Baby	BB 11383, HMV BD1036, HE2416
67947	Buck Jumpin' (nv)	BB 11324, G25055, HMV HE2446
67948	That gets it, Mr. Joe	BB11425, G25055, HMV BD1028, HE2346
67949	The Bells of San Raquel	BB 11324, HMV HE2446
67950	Bessie, Bessie, Bessie	CAL 588
67951	Clarinet Marmalade	BB 11469, HMV AV750, HE2371, Jazztone 1247

(Fats, p & vo; Herman Autrey, tp; Gene Sedric, cl & ts; Al Casey, g; Charles Turner, bs; Arthur Trappier, ds): New York City. **26th December, 1941.**

68810	Winter Weather	BB 11469, HMV AV750, B10234, HE2371, RC 24004
68811	Cash for your trash	BB 11425, HMV HE2428, RC24004
68812	Don't give me that jive	BB 11539, G24989, HMV BD1077
68813	Your socks don't match	BB 30-0814, HMV BD 1073

"FATS" WALLER, HIS RHYTHM AND HIS ORCHESTRA. (Fats, p, org & vo; Herman Autrey, John Hamilton, Joe Thomas, Nathaniel Williams, tp; Herb Fleming, George Wilson, tb; George James, Lawrence Fields, as; Gene Sedric, cl & ts; Bob Carroll, ts; Al Casey, g; Cedric Wallace, bs; Arthur Trappier, ds): New York City. **16th March, 1942.**

73440	We need a little love (vo)	BB 11518
73441	You must be losing your mind (vo)	BB 11539, G24989, HMV BD1077
73443	The Jitterburg Waltz (nv org)	BB 11518, Vi 20-2639, Vi LPT 1001, HMV HE2976

"FATS" WALLER AND HIS RHYTHM. (Fats, p & vo; Deep River Boys, vo D; John Hamilton, tp; Gene Sedric, cl & ts; Al Casey, g; Cedric Wallace, bs; Arthur Trappier, ds): New York City. **13th July, 1942.**

75423	By the light of the silvery moon D	BB 11569, Vi 20-2448, HMV AV749, NE688, Jazztone J1247
75424	Swing out to Victory	BB 11569, HMV NE688
75425	Up jumped you with love	BB 30-0814, HMV BD 1045, LPM 1502
75426	Romance a la mode D	HMV BD1045, BB 30-0805

"FATS" WALLER AND HIS RHYTHM. (Fats, p & vo; Ada Brown, vo on last title B; Benny Carter, tp; Alton Moore, tb; Gene Porter, cl & ts; Irving Ashby, g; Slam Stewart, bs; Zutty Singleton, ds): Hollywood. **23rd January, 1943.**

6215	Moppin' and Boppin'	Vi 40-4003, HMV C3737, EB556, FKX192, SH1, 7EG 8148, TCF 202
6216	Ain't Misbehavin'	Vi 40-4003, HMV C3737, EB556, TCF 203, FKX192, SH1, CAL 473, 7EG 8148, CDN 131
VP471	That ain't right B	VD 165, TCF 201, Palm Club 10

"FATS" WALLER. (Piano and Vocal): New York City. **23rd September, 1943.**

VP154	Ain't Misbehavin'/Two Sleepy People	VD 32, 133 Palm Club 07
VP155	Slightly less than wonderful/ There's a gal in my life	VD32, 133, 7EG 8212, Palm Club 07, EPA 449
VP157	This is so nice it must be illegal/Martinique	VD 74, 145, 7EG 8212, EPA 449
VP181	Waller Jive/Hallelujah	VD 74, 145
	Reefer Song/That's what the bird said to me	JR 2002

"FATS" WALLER. (Hammond Organ Solos—with vocal comments): New York City. **23rd September, 1943.**

JDB10	Solitude	VD 658, 7EG 8212, EPA 449, Palm Club 07
JDB11	Bouncin' on a V-Disc	VD 630, Palm Club 07
JDB12	Sometimes I feel like a Motherless Child	VD 743, 145, 7EG 8212, Palm Club 07

THE CHARLIE McCARTHY SHOW. (Fats, p & vo; patter by Fats, Edgar Bergen and Ray Noble): This is a radio transcription. **Late 1943.**

	Ain't Misbehavin' (vo); Handful of Keys	Unissued

This is an abridged version of the most comprehensive listing of Waller's musical activities which is currently being serialized in Storyville magazine (28 Urswick Road, Dagenham, Essex) and which is to be published in booklet form

DATE DUE

NOV. 18.1980			
DEC. 22.1988			
MAR 16.1992			
GAYLORD			PRINTED IN U.S.A.